W9-DBH-158

Toward
HUMANIST SOCIOLOGY

Alfred McClung Lee

Library of Congress Cataloging in Publication Data

Lee, Alfred McClung
  Toward humanist sociology.

  Includes bibliographical references.
  1. Sociology.   I. Title.
HM51.L355   301   72-5858
ISBN   0-13-925776-4

H M
5 1
. L 355

© *1973 by* PRENTICE-HALL, INC., *Englewood Cliffs, New Jersey*

Printed in the United States of America

10   9   8   7   6   5   4   3   2   1

Prentice-Hall International, Inc., *London*
Prentice-Hall of Australia, Pty. Ltd., *Sydney*
Prentice-Hall of Canada, Ltd., *Toronto*
Prentice-Hall of India Private Limited, *New Delhi*
Prentice-Hall of Japan, Inc., *Tokyo*

To

My *Pieria:*
Dr. Elizabeth Briant Lee

Contents

PREFACE   *xi*

INTRODUCTION:
MAN IS NOT A TOOL;
SOCIETY IS NOT A SYSTEM   *1*

*Resistances to Dehumanization. Instrumental versus **Human** Values.
Undiminished Man. Where We Come From. Issues of **Human** Concern. Social Wisdom and Individual Potential.*

I HOW HUMANITY CAN THRIVE
       WITH SCIENCE AS ITS INSTRUMENT   *7*

*Science and Scientism. Five Tyrannies. Exploiting Ethnic Identities.
A Distorting Mirror. A Set of Blinders. Our Patchwork "Social System." Garbage In, Garbage Out. On Keeping Alive. To Use All
Human Resources.*

2 HOW SOCIOLOGY CAN MAGNIFY THE INDIVIDUAL 28

Rapping About Sociology. Sociology Through Studying Slices of Life. "Sociology" as an Escape. Enticements of the Laboratory. Uses of the Sociological Laboratory. How Intimate Must Sociological Learning Become? Sociological Writing as Autobiography. What Sociology Can Give to People. "Gutsy" versus Bland Sociology. "Sociology" as a Social Problem. Sociology's Debts to Literature. Sensitivity and Action. To Stimulate Social Change. Clinical Sociologists in American Conflicts. Who Co-opts Whom? Much More Than Just "Interesting."

3 SOCIAL "THERAPY" VERSUS THE SEARCH FOR KNOWLEDGE 53

The Retailers and Retellers. Contrasting Statements. "Alienation." "Marginality" Rather Than "Alienation." Privacy and Leisure. Mind Twisting. The American Home. The Information Explosion. American Violence. Summary.

4 COURTIERS OR PARTICIPANTS? 87

Elitism's Tempting Guises. Basic Issues in Social Control. The Manipulated and the Participant Society. Facilitation Rather Than Manipulation. Rewards in the Participant Society. The "Unstranding" of the Common Man. The Possibility of a Humane Society. No Static Blueprint for the Future. The Society We Can Now Have.

5 THE MANY FACES OF AUTONOMY 99

Questions Foreigners Ask. Democracy in American Practice. Democracy as Social Philosophy. A Paradigm for Senses of Autonomy. Autonomy on Different Status Ladders. The Biases of Sociologists. Comparative Utility of the Four Types of Aspiration and Autonomy. The Recognition of Sociology's Multivalence. Summary.

6 IDEOLOGIES IN SOCIAL STRUGGLES   *112*

Ideology's Premature Obituary. Avoiding Traps of Definition. To Understand Conflicting Viewpoints. Ingredients of Ideologies. To Typify Ideologies. Ideologies Change; Ideology Persists.

7 IDEOLOGIES WITHIN SOCIOLOGY   *122*

Normal Science as a Paradigm. Sociology's Three Rough Paradigms. Organization Man's Sociology. The Technician's Sociology. Sociology for People. The Crisis in Both Society and Sociology. Some Sociologists Struggle; Many Join Up. Revolts Against Dehumanized Social Science. A Push Toward a More Involved Sociology. The Revolts Continue. The Social Crisis Cannot Be Disguised.

8 DEFENSES AGAINST MANIPULATION   *139*

Ideology in Action. Society is the Actionist's Stockpile. To Exploit Individual Potentialities. To Control Social Structures. To Cast Nets of Symbols. To Gain Access to Audiences. To Find Compelling Appeals. To Utilize the Current Climate of Opinion. The Struggle Against Being Manipulated.

9 PERPLEXITIES OF SOCIAL PERCEPTION   *164*

The Investigator's Intimate Obstacle. Obstacles and Pathways to Perception. To "Tell Things Like They Are." To Be Upsetting, Way-Breaking. To Look Beyond Normality and Abnormality. To Probe the Criminal Stereotype. To Penetrate Popular Excuses for Pugnacity. To Avoid a Faustian "Cop-Out." To Understand What it Costs to "Belong." To Avoid a Limiting Context. To Empathize with the Culturally Different.

10 HOW SOCIOLOGISTS CAN SERVE MAN   *180*

Candor About "The Games We Play." Trivia. Technology for Management and Manipulation. Criticisms and Proposed Modifications of Public Policy. Sociology for Liberal Education. Sociology for Everyman.

II SOME THINGS PEOPLE NEED TO KNOW   *202*

*We Are All Hypocrites.   Value Conflicts Are Now More Obvious.   Why
a Revolt Now?   The Revolt Against Multivalence.   Current Challenges
to Social Scientists.*

INDEX   *211*

Preface

Sociologists and other social scientists are greatly divided over how they should fit their efforts into the changing twentieth-century situation. Can they and should they proceed with research under subsidies from those in power or should they only be investigators committed solely to their own humanist goals? Can they somehow do both? Can research be an independent sideline of another occupation, such as teaching? If so, can this preserve the researcher's autonomy? Must research really be just a private hobby in order to avoid being distorted by subsidizers? Or are the above questions simply naïve? Should the social scientist simply pick his cause and do work related to that cause, whether it be for a political party, corporation, social agency, or voluntary association?

For my own work, my answer to the above questions is to avoid commitment to any personal, ideological, or organizational loyalty that undesirably colors my work. My research and writing have been carried on chiefly as hobbies subsidized by my professorial employment. Both in my writing and teaching, I have tried to identify and to grasp opportunities for the magnification of the individual's potential in society. I have opposed the development of elitist theories and of other controls that would diminish human stature and dignity. I have contended that man need not be deformed into a mere tool of impersonal bureaucracies or of rash power-seekers, and I believe that he will not be.

Like Walt Whitman, I have attempted to penetrate "the inertness and fossilism making so large a part of human institutions." [1] Like that

[1] Walt Whitman "Democratic Vistas" (1870), in his *Complete Prose Works* (Philadelphia: David McKay, 1891), p. 221.

bard, but through a quite different and more modest medium, I have tried
to address "him or her within whose thought rages the battle, advancing,
retreating, between democracy's convictions, aspirations, and the people's
crudeness, vice, caprices." [2] My main preoccupation, in the words of
sociologist Herbert Blumer, has been "to lift the veils that cover . . .
group life. . . . The veils are not lifted by substituting, in whatever
degree, preformed images for firsthand knowledge. The veils are lifted
. . . by digging deep . . . through careful study," [3] especially through
participant observation. Thus I have sought to reveal social life a little
more accurately and understandably to its participants. I believe that with
clearer social knowledge, people will understand themselves better and
relate more humanely to one another.

By probing into the nature of freedom, autonomy, and slavery in
some of their confusingly varied forms, I have sought to help people to be
more autonomous and thus more free. I have tried to reflect the great
humanist tradition in the United States—not only the influence of Walt
Whitman and Herbert Blumer, but also that of Thomas Jefferson, Samuel
L. Clemens, the historians Andrew D. White, Charles A. Beard, and Harry
Elmer Barnes, the psychologists William James and Abraham H. Maslow,
the philosophers John Dewey and George Herbert Mead, and the sociologists William Graham Sumner, Charles Horton Cooley, Robert E. Park,
Ernest W. Burgess, Maurice Rea Davie, Willard Waller, and C. Wright
Mills, among others. [4]

In the present work, an "existential humanist" deals with sociology

[2] *Ibid.,* p. 204.
[3] Herbert Blumer, *Symbolic Interactionism* (Englewood Cliffs, N.J.: Prentice-
Hall, 1969), p. 39.
[4] Representative works of the writers to whom reference is made are the following: Thomas Jefferson, *Notes on the State of Virginia* (1782), ed. by William Peden
(Chapel Hill: University of North Carolina Press, 1955); S. L. Clemens [Mark
Twain], *Autobiography,* ed. by A. B. Paine (New York: Harper & Bros., 1924) and
ed. by Charles Neider (New York: Harper & Bros., 1959); A. D. White, *A History
of the Warfare of Science With Theology in Christendom* (1896; New York: George
Braziller, 1955); C. A. Beard, *The Rise of American Civilization* (New York: Mac-
millan, 1927–1942), 4 vols.; H. E. Barnes, *An Economic History of the Western
World* (New York: Harcourt, Brace, 1938); William James, *The Principles of Psychol-
ogy* (1890; New York: Dover Publications, 1950); A. H. Maslow, *Toward a Psy-
chology of Being* (Princeton: D. Van Nostrand, 1962); John Dewey, *Freedom and
Culture* (New York: G. P. Putnam's Sons, 1939); G. H. Mead, *Mind, Self, and
Society,* ed. by C. W. Morris (Chicago: University of Chicago Press, 1934); W. G.
Sumner, *Folkways* (1906; New York: New American Library, 1960); C. H. Cooley,
Life and the Student (New York: Alfred A. Knopf, 1927); R. E. Park, *Society,* ed.
by E. C. Hughes et al. (Glencoe, Ill.: Free Press, 1955); E. W. Burgess, *The Urban
Community* (Chicago: University of Chicago Press, 1926); M. R. Davie, *The Evolu-
tion of War* (New Haven: Yale University Press, 1929); Willard Waller, *The Sociol-
ogy of Teaching* (New York: John Wiley, 1932, 1965); and *The Family* (New York:
Cordon Co., 1938), rev. ed. by Reuben Hill (New York: Holt, Rinehart & Winston,
1951); C. W. Mills, *White Collar, The Power Elite,* and *The Sociological Imagination*
(New York: Oxford University Press, 1951, 1956, 1959).

and social science concerned with the current problems that impinge upon people's lives. In thus characterizing myself, I trust that I may be permitted to insist upon simple, nondoctrinaire, popular definitions of those words. I am not a follower of the "existentialist" Jean-Paul Sartre [5] nor of the "humanist" Karl Marx,[6] to mention but one each to whom those labels are commonly attached. Existentialism and humanism of those and other sorts [7] stir up intellectual and social controversies that are sometimes quite useful. At the same time, they represent a variety of contradictory viewpoints.

Among those called "existential" are the atheists Sartre and Martin Heidegger,[8] the Protestant theologians Søren Kierkegaard,[9] Karl Barth,[10] Paul Tillich,[11] and Reinhold Niebuhr,[12] the Roman Catholic Thomist Jacques Maritain,[13] the philosophers Karl Jaspers [14] and Gabriel Marcel,[15] and the literary figures Franz Kafka,[16] Simone de Beauvoir,[17] and Albert Camus.[18]

[5] Jean-Paul Sartre, *Existentialism*, trans. by Philip Mairet (London: Methuen, 1947).

[6] Karl Marx, *Capital*, trans. by Samuel Moore, Edward Aveling, and Ernest Untermann, ed. by Frederick Engels (4th German ed., 1890; Chicago: Charles H. Kerr & Co., 1906, 1907, 1909), 3 vols; *The German Ideology*, ed. by R. Pascal (London: Lawrence & Wishart, 1938).

[7] See Nicola Abbagnano, *Critical Existentialism*, trans. and ed. with an intro. by Nino Langiulli (Garden City, N.Y.: Anchor Books, 1969); Walter Odajnyk, *Marxism and Existentialism* (Garden City, N.Y.: Doubleday, 1965); Erich Fromm, ed., *Socialist Humanism: An International Symposium* (Garden City, N.Y.: Anchor Books, 1965). Close to my view of humanism is that of F. W. Matson, *The Broken Image* (New York: George Braziller, 1964), when he says (p. vii) that "our most pressing educational and cultural need is not for the indoctrination of men in the directives of science, but . . . for the enlistment of science in the cause of man."

[8] Martin Heidegger, *Existence and Being* (1927), trans. with an intro. by Werner Brock (Chicago: Henry Regnery, 1949).

[9] Søren Kierkegaard, *Either/Or*, I, trans. by D. F. and L. M. Swenson, II, trans. by Walter Lowrie, rev. with forewords by H. A. Johnson (1843; Garden City, N.Y.: Doubleday, 1959).

[10] Karl Barth, *Theological Existence Today* (1933; Naperville, Ill.: Alec R. Allenson, 1962).

[11] Paul Tillich, *Courage to Be* (New Haven: Yale University Press, 1952).

[12] Reinhold Niebuhr, *Moral Man and Immoral Society* and *Nature and Destiny of Man*, 2 vols. (New York: Charles Scribner's Sons, 1932, 1949).

[13] Jacques Maritain, *Existence and the Existent*, trans. by Louis Galantiere (New York: Random House, 1949).

[14] Karl Jaspers, *Philosophy of Existence*, trans. by Richard F. Grabau (Philadelphia: University of Pennsylvania Press, 1971).

[15] Gabriel Marcel, *Existential Background of Human Dignity* (Cambridge: Harvard University Press, 1963).

[16] R. D. Gray, ed., *Kafka: A Collection of Critical Essays* (Englewood Cliffs, New Jersey: Prentice-Hall, 1962).

[17] Simone de Beauvoir, *Second Sex*, trans. by H. M. Parshley (New York: Alfred A. Knopf, 1953); see also, Edith Kern, *Existential Thought and Fictional Technique* (New Haven: Yale University Press, 1970).

[18] Albert Camus, *The Stranger* and *The Plague*, trans. by Stuart Gilbert (New York: Random House, 1946, and Modern Library, 1948).

A galaxy of figures has been called "humanist." It includes Giovanni Boccaccio [19] and Francesco Petrarca (Petrarch) [20] of the fourteenth century, Lorenzo Valla,[21] Lorenzo (il Magnifico) de'Medici,[22] Desiderius Erasmus,[23] and Thomas More [24] of the next two centuries, and Karl Marx, F.C.S. Schiller,[25] Irving Babbitt,[26] and C. F. Potter [27] of the nineteenth and twentieth centuries. This list of "humanists" includes pagans, Protestants, a Roman Catholic saint, poets, essayists, rulers, business men, and academicians.

The "existentialism" or "humanism" of the people mentioned has many different meanings, and I do not wish to be bound by any one of them or by any others. My existentialism and humanism spring from roots or traditions more radical and earthy and less doctrinaire than most of those listed.

When I say that I am an existential humanist, I mean only that my intellectual focus is upon what exists and upon what is most relevant to man. I consider this to be the most tenable intellectual orientation for a person dedicated to the scientific study of human interrelationships. In such a view, first causes (or origins) and ultimate consequences, as well as absolutes and infinites, are irrelevant except as human artifacts to be considered as such. Methods and tenets useful in other sciences are to be treated as possibly helpful suggestions. Techniques of research and theories must serve human understanding of man's lot.

While working on another book, *Multivalent Man,*[28] one of the sociologists I asked to read the typescript said he was surprised at some of my views. For example, he could not understand why a nonelitist should be so concerned with individualism. And why is an admirer of individualism optimistic about the present and future possibilities of man in a

[19] Vittore Branca, *Boccaccio,* trans. by Richard Monges (New York: New York University Press, 1970); see also, J. A. Symonds, *Giovanni Boccaccio as Man and Author* (1895; New York: AMS Press, n.d.).

[20] A. S. Bernardo, *Petrarch, Scipio and the Africa: The Birth of Humanism's Dream* (Baltimore: Johns Hopkins Press, 1962).

[21] Franco Gaeta, *Lorenzo Valla: Filologia e Storia nell'Umanesimo Italiano* (Napoli: Istituto Italiano per gli Studi Storici, 1955).

[22] C. M. Ady, *Lorenzo De'Medici and Renaissance Italy* (New York: Macmillan, 1966).

[23] Johan Huizinga, *Erasmus of Rotterdam,* trans. by F. Hopman and Barbara Flower (London: Phaidon Press, 1952).

[24] E. L. Surtz, *Praise of Pleasure: Philosophy, Education and Communism in More's Utopia* (Cambridge: Harvard University Press, 1957).

[25] F. C. S. Schiller, *Studies in Humanism* (1912; Westport, Conn.: Greenwood Press, n.d.).

[26] Irving Babbitt, *Democracy and Leadership* (Boston: Houghton Mifflin, 1924) and *On Being Creative* (1912; New York: Biblo & Tannen, 1968).

[27] C. F. Potter, *Lost Years of Jesus Revealed,* rev. ed. (New York: Fawcett World Library, 1970).

[28] A. McC. Lee, *Multivalent Man* (New York: George Braziller, 1966).

vast and integrating society? Why does an avowed humanist, deeply concerned about human welfare, insist that the search for scientific knowledge is not to be confused with the search for practical ways of coping with specific social problems? Finally, he questioned my lack of respect for the magnificence of the powerful and the elegance of the academically prestigious. He perceived that my admiration is reserved for the simplicity of the scientist and the artist who may have little or none of what impresses so many in the short run in human society—the control of social power—but who have somehow contributed so much to humanity and to human values in the long course of social history.

He tried to counsel me on the errors in my ways. "Nonelitist sociology does not sell well," he contended. It is not what fellow professionals find rewarding, and they resist rewarding its practitioners.[29] Optimism about the future of man in a period of prodigal and wasteful international conflict, of disastrous neglect of human resources, struck my friend as scarcely warranted or tenable. A practical problem-solver is an instrument who may be both available and desirable to employers, but a scientist committed only to his own conceptions of human welfare and of curiosity strikes many subsidizers of research as irresponsible, even dangerous. Finally, he argued that the elegance of fancy terminologies and of even fancier methodologies is the academic robe with which many a social scientist is able to disguise himself and render himself impressive. Such elegant trappings set the proper social scientist apart from the merely wise journalist or belletrist. Only an occasional student or client will declare—amazedly, amusedly, or bitterly—that the social scientist (like the fabled emperor) is really naked.

After expressing gratitude for his concern, I turned down the advice of that sociologist. His was almost the same counsel I had received from another friend and had rejected three decades earlier with respect to the typescript of my first book, *The Daily Newspaper in America: The Evolu-*

---

[29] On this point, see "Willard W. Waller: A Portrait," by W. J. Goode, F. F. Furstenberg, Jr., and L. R. Mitchell, in *Willard W. Waller: On the Family, Education, and War* (Chicago: University of Chicago Press, 1970). The authors portray with some accuracy, but fail to appreciate fully, the motivations and contributions of a scientist who was a creative existential humanist. As they say (p. 48), "Waller knew that one managed one's career within a definite structure. One's place in the academic stratification system set limits, determined options, provided opportunities and forced compromises. Professors moved upward not only because their intellectual work was recognized and rewarded, but also because they made the correct strategic moves within the system." Waller failed to get adequate recognition during his life, not because (as they assume) he did not know how to make the "correct strategic moves," but because his dedicated curiosity and scientific integrity limited the compromises he would make. I say this on the basis of the many hours we spent together during which we sometimes discussed the "sociology of sociology." His refusal to compromise on matters he regarded as important is now bringing him wide posthumous recognition and acclaim.

tion of a Social Instrument.[30] Then the problem had taken the more specific form that newspaper publishers and certain allegedly scientific students of mass communications in the universities and in advertising and public relations agencies would not like an accurate treatment of that powerful mass medium, the daily newspaper. Similar comments were made down through the years about each of my other books. Fortunately, American book publishers provide the most free arena for ideas in the world today.

The ideas in the present book were brought together in response to the personal and social problems that have confronted me, my colleagues, and my students as citizens and as professional social scientists. I have interpreted these ideas in lectures and discussions before both nonprofessional and professional audiences, and I have discussed them with my students. They reflect so many exchanges with colleagues, students, and other friends that it would be impossible to indicate all of my indebtedness.

In addition to the acknowledgments in the references for each chapter, I wish to mention especially the following, who contributed knowingly, or unknowingly, but directly to this effort: C. M. Abraham, Denis P. Barritt, Abraham S. Blumberg, Herbert Blumer, Ronald H. Buchanan, William R. Burch, Jr., Leo P. Chall, Kenneth B. Clark, J. David Colfax, Kenneth H. Connell, Danilo Dolci, Franco Ferrarotti, Nelson N. Foote, Irving Goldaber, Lenore Turner Henderson, Mark Hutter, Helen Hall Jennings, Betsy Briant Jorgensen, Charles R. Lawrence, Jr., Hylan G. Lewis, Simon Marcson, David W. McKinney, Jr., Barrington Moore, Jr., Arthur Niederhoffer, Paul Oren, Jr., Holly G. Porter, Thomas P. Rootes, Jr., Joan Simon, Kenneth Simon, C. A. O. van Nieuwenhuijze, Morton O. and Jeanne Wagenfeld, Phyllis A. Wallace, and Leonard S. Zoll.

Very special thanks are due to another group of friends for their concern, encouragement, and aid. Charles H. Anderson, Milton L. Barron, Stanley Hastings Chapman, Norman K. Denzin, Howard Henderson, Glenn Jacobs, John Kosa, Elizabeth Brown Little, Jerre Mangione, Peter K. Manning, S. M. Miller, and Edwin Seaver all read the typescript and made useful comments that were fresh, probing, and incisive. Edward H. Stanford and Adrienne M. Neufeld of Prentice-Hall, and Daniel Kennedy most helpfully facilitated the publication process.

Sadie Altstein and Elizabeth Fournier of Brooklyn College and Joseph Bender and E. T. Solomon of the Graduate Center, The City University of New York, helped in many ways with the production of the typescript. The staffs of the libraries of Drew University, the Graduate Center and Brooklyn College of The City University of New York, and the Yale Club

---

[30] A. McC. Lee, *The Daily Newspaper in America: The Evolution of a Social Instrument* (New York: Macmillan, 1937; Octagon Books, 1973).

of New York City, and the staffs of the Millburn, Summit, and Chatham (New Jersey) Public Libraries have kindly aided my searches for materials.

As always, my wife and fellow sociologist, Dr. Elizabeth Briant Lee, has read critically each of this volume's many versions and has decidedly enriched each and every one of them. My sons, Alfred and Briant, have listened to my ideas, have read them, and have freely and helpfully criticized them.

A. McC. L.

Short Hills
New Jersey

Man Is Not a Tool;
Society Is Not a System

American public spokesmen talk a lot about freedom, autonomy, and independence. They call these sterling values. They say they are essential to the individual and to society.

But the young now contend they are asked to conform to models of man that are depersonalized tools of remote interests. They perceive themselves as confronting powerful inducements and coercions toward conformity in schools, in military training and on the battlefields, in business, industry, and government.

RESISTANCES TO DEHUMANIZATION

Throughout the world, many young people have openly revolted against taking on dimensions they picture as those of a punched tabulator card or of cannon fodder. They believe they have human dimensions, and they want to develop and express those human dimensions. They insist that society must nurture human values and permit their expression.

Millions more have uneasily shown their sympathy with the young rebels.

Students caught up willingly in the regimenting routines of such specialized trade schools and colleges as those of business, engineering, and the military, appear to be heedless of their dehumanization. Only when such persons perceive that their precise and rigid conditioning is becoming obsolete are they likely—usually too late—to feel disillusioned.

Only then do they possibly come to understand something about their lack of adaptability, and thus their lack of continued vendability.

INSTRUMENTAL VERSUS
HUMAN VALUES

Print, radio, and television enthusiastically report the spectacular events in which superheroes, such as astronauts, participate, but astronauts are instrument-heroes. Their melodramas are contemporary equivalents of ancient Roman gladiatorial contests. They are peaks among the routine fare of commercialized athletics, horse races, TV soap operas, and comic strips.

Such glorifications of instrumentalism fail to do more than pleasantly entertain the masses. Within each of the millions who feel obliged to assume a role as a tool or an instrument (surely including the men in space suits), there is a human being, still resistant to dehumanization. That human being thrills to the magnification of human values in the lives of Thomas Jefferson, Albert Einstein, Mahatma Gandhi, John XXIII, Martin Luther King, Jr., and numerous other independent artists, scientists, thinkers, and leaders. Human fantasy is transported by the astronaut's perfection in programmed instrumentation, briefing, and teamwork, but human imaginations continue to be captured by those who through the individual creativity of their lives have glorified more obviously human materials.

UNDIMINISHED MAN

The twentieth century is not diminishing man, rather, it emphasizes the individual. Writers of "science" fantasies are prone to envision a future of absolute authoritarianism, but the day of the human ant hill is not at all in sight or even foreseeable.[1] More men and women than ever before in the history of the human race are now spending at least part of

[1] So-called "social" insects, such as ants, termites, wasps, and bees, by their perfection of organization can persist and flourish as long as propitious life conditions continue to be available. Their very perfection of organization, rigidly transmitted from generation to generation through genetic processes, delimits their adaptability to changed conditions. It blocks experimentation with novel adjustments to environment. Since man's adaptations to environment and to other men are largely cultural and approximate, to be learned and to be adapted by each generation, the processes of organizational continuation are both imperfect and tentative, and both permit and invite a degree of experimentation.

their lives actively searching for fresh answers to old and new problems. The attention widely given to creative hobbies, to stimulating paperbacks and library books, to challenging TV and radio programs, and to study and action groups concerned with environmental and public welfare problems, suggests the breadth and depth of human ferment.

Human yearnings and temptations are at least latent in every polished social instrument, whether astronaut, military commander, cleric, corporate executive, academic administrator, political manager, or whatever. Human values find vivid expression in youths' revolt against war and depersonalization, in black impatience with white racism, hypocrisy, and exploitation, in female rebellion against traditional sex roles and male sexism, and in the work of our vast numbers of dedicated scientists and artists, therapists and administrators. They also appear in the growing dissatisfaction with organized religion, education, environmental pollution, militarization, colonialism and imperialism, and "made-work" (replacements within sequences of contrived obsolescence and of arranged mechanical failure, needless and endless duplications of effort, and inflated bureaucracies that are ends in themselves).

Our unsolved social problems are staggering, but social pressures are gathering to cope with them more effectively. These social pressures spring chiefly from human dissatisfaction with depersonalizing demands made by those in control of social power in the so-called social "system."

Only those who permit themselves merely to be conditioned instruments accept racism, heedless pollution and destruction of the environment, the population explosion, and perpetual starvation and deprivation among millions throughout the world. Sensitive human beings cannot accept such conditions. Even though many business and government leaders notoriously abuse human values, more people are working to cope with such problems now than ever before.

WHERE WE CAME FROM

When we look only at the appallingly wasteful and degrading side of human life in the twentieth century, without considering it in the light of the social history of previous centuries, humanity appears to have little future. We only have to ponder records of our diseased, vermin-infested, uneducated, and badly nourished ancestors, most of whom were exploited European serfs and peasants, to take hope. Our history texts perpetuate a mythology by peopling our past with selected kings, nobles, and gentry—not too choice a lot at that—but it is the descendants of their forgotten serfs and peasants who have inherited the earth.[2] These descendants are incredibly numerous and often still appear to be faceless instruments, but they include millions who feel their human potential and are not about to surrender it. This is not to say, as have so many analysts of social history,[3] that there is a mandate of upward-and-onward "progress"[4] in human affairs. The fortunes of social change turn both in favor of and against mass man, both toward and away from democracy and other schemes of social organization. Disillusionment with existing controls, visions of opportunity, and the availability of means with which to struggle for change all make the difference.

ISSUES OF HUMAN CONCERN

The present book is an effort to focus on the following issues of human concern in social science: How are human values now threatened by instrumentalism both in society generally and within what is known as social science? How can human beings resist such dehumanization? How can concerned naturalistic humanists help men to fight back? How can social scientists help equip individuals to participate more autonomously, and thus more effectively, in society?

RANK-AND-FILE MAN. Here are other interrelated questions touched upon in this work: As a great many social scientists appear now to be turning more and more to the service of the would-be controllers and manipulators of society, how can social science also be brought to aid the individual, the rank-and-file man, the human condition? How can we understand, with as little compromise and bias as possible, the oppressions, brutalities, and destructions, the creativities, kindnesses, and

[2] As Eric R. Wolf notes, " 'the raggedy little bastards in black pajamas'—as United States military officers referred to their new enemies [in Viet Nam]—have not only fought to a standstill the mightiest military machine in history, but caused many an American to wonder, silently or aloud, why 'our' Vietnamese do not fight like 'their' Vietnamese, why ever new recruits replenish the ranks of an [enemy] army destroyed many times over in our dispatches and news communiqués." *Peasant Wars of the Twentieth Century* (New York: Harper & Row, 1969), p. ix.

[3] See especially the contrasting ideas on "progress" of Auguste Comte, *The Positive Philosophy*, freely translated and condensed by Harriet Martineau (London: George Bell & Sons, 1896), II, 522–40; Karl Marx, *Capital: A Critique of Political Economy*, translated from the 3rd German ed. by Samuel Moore and Edward Aveling, rev. in terms of 4th ed. by Ernest Untermann (Chicago: Charles H. Kerr & Co., 1906), Part 8, Chaps. 26–33; Herbert Spencer, *A System of Synthetic Philosophy* (London: D. Appleton & Co., 1862–1896), esp. VI–VIII.

[4] See J. B. Bury, *The Idea of Progress* (1932; Gloucester, Mass.: Peter Smith, 1960); Morris Ginsberg, *The Idea of Progress: A Revaluation* (Westport, Conn.: Greenwood Publishers, 1953); Raymond Aron, *Progress and Disillusion: The Dialectics of Modern Society* (New York: Praeger, 1969); Georges Sorel, *Illusions of Progress* (Berkeley: University of California Press, 1969).

nobilities of man in society? How does such an effort at understanding differ from the effort to solve specific social problems?

UNDERSTANDING AND AUTONOMY. How can understanding help us to cope with our problems? Of what is our season of violence symptomatic? How autonomous can man in mass society become and remain? How autonomous is it worthwhile for a man to be in his society?

MYTHS AND IDEOLOGIES. What are the personal and social services of our ideologies and myths? Why is it so common now to claim their "death" or "end"? Why is it so difficult to perceive the birth or rebirth of significant ideologies and myths? Who are likely to be the midwives of social change? How equal can women and men of different color and contrasting education, occupation, religion, and wealth become in the latter twentieth century? Can we, with any confidence, see the possibility of achieving a more humane society beyond our contemporary violence and confusion?

This book attempts to explore and to respond to such questions and problems.

POSSIBLY AN EXCITING ADVENTURE. Walt Kelly is one of our most perceptive contemporary cartoonists. He drew one of the most pessimistic "comic" strips I have seen for his "Pogo" series. In it, Porky looks across a bayou and muses, "Used to be a man could look off across there an' see the future." Pogo asks, " 'Smatter now? Don't believe in the future no more?" Porky replies, "No. . . . It doesn't last." [5]

That sounds more like a weary old man than a great humorist. The future continually unfolds. As the sociologist Herbert Blumer says, "The life of any human society consists necessarily of an ongoing process of fitting together the activities of its members." [6]

An existential humanist can always find himself involved in the midst of exciting adventure. He tries to make group experiences in which he participates bring more fulfilment to more people. He attempts to help the midwives of social change bring a more humane society into being. Although he knows how accurate Henry David Thoreau was when he asserted, "But lo! men have become the tools of their tools," [7] he also knows that men are never satisfied with being just tools.

---

[5] From "Pogo," a feature distributed to newspapers by Publishers-Hall Syndicate, Inc., December 2, 1968.

[6] Herbert Blumer, *Symbolic Interactionism* (Englewood Cliffs, N.J.: Prentice-Hall, 1969), p. 7.

[7] H. D. Thoreau, *Walden* (New York: New American Library, 1942), p. 30. The German sociologist Georg Simmel changes the emphasis of Thoreau's (and my) analysis of the relation of individuality to social problems: "The deepest problems of modern life derive from the claim of the individual to preserve the autonomy and individuality of his existence in the face of overwhelming social forces, of historical heritage, of external culture, and of the technique of life." (*The Sociology of Georg*

SOCIAL WISDOM AND
INDIVIDUAL POTENTIAL

The great challenge of sociology and of social science is not the concern with social equilibrium or stability commonly expressed with a repressive conservatism by the entrenched.[8] The challenge is not to provide intellectual instruments and perspectives to entrepreneurs and administrators in the hope that they will approximate the ideal of the philosopher-king or even the philosopher-actionist.[9] That is the elitist trap into which endless generations of intellectuals have all too often fallen. On the contrary, the great challenge of social science is the development and wide dissemination of social wisdom and social-action techniques that will enable more and more people to participate in the control and guidance of their groups and their society. In meeting this challenge, social science stimulates and nurtures the fuller development of individual potential.

Simmel, trans. and ed. by K. H. Wolff [Glencoe, Ill.: Free Press, 1950], p. 409.) Thoreau took the desire for autonomy and individuality as a basic human value, and he considered existing social influences and culture, instead, as the problems with which man has to cope. Such social complexities, he believed, as I also do, can be adapted to changing human needs and desires.

    [8] See Bernard Barber, ed., *L. J. Henderson on the Social System* (Chicago: University of Chicago Press, 1970); A. McC. Lee, *Multivalent Man* (New York: George Braziller, 1966), Chap. 14.

    [9] Plato, "The Republic," in *The Works of Plato,* ed. by Irwin Edman (New York: Simon and Schuster, 1928), Book V, p. 410; H. D. Lasswell, "The Policy Orientation," and R. K. Merton, "Social Scientists and Research Policy," in Daniel Lerner and Lasswell, eds., *The Policy Sciences* (Stanford, Calif.: Stanford University Press, 1951); L. T. and Janice M. Reynolds, eds., *The Sociology of Sociology* (New York: David McKay, 1970), esp. papers by Dusky L. Smith (#3, #19), S. M. Wilhelm (#6), Martin Nicolaus (#13), and Diana Crane (#21).

CHAPTER I

How Humanity Can Thrive
with Science
as its Instrument

In our daily rhythm, we distinguish easily enough between the promise of the sun's first rays and the declining glories of its last light. The freshness of morning and the relaxation of evening help give a pattern to our routines. But when we look for evidence of other beginnings and endings, the distinctions are far from being so clear.

Do we see the last rays of a passing era in our urban and campus rebellions, in our protests against war, violence, and starvation, and in our current speculations about how we might work for a better way of life? Or do these rebellions, protests, and speculations arise like rays from the sunrise of a more humane country and world? Are the confusion, decadence, and jerry-built social structures of our world symptomatic of forthcoming dictatorship and collapse? Or will democratic humanism replace these weaknesses and disorders in a world that has never before really tried either democracy or humanism?

Is political and economic giantism—what the late President Eisenhower called the "military-industrial complex" [1]—making a hopeless sham of democracy? Or is participatory democracy beginning to be even more possible than ever before? Have the impersonal theories of scientists— to the extent that they are impersonal—made the insights, speculations, poetry, and even autonomy of the human individual, suspect and possibly irrelevant? Must the Hellenic trinity of beauty, laughter, and love now be perceived and understood only through the holes in IBM tabulation cards? Or are the limitations of a dehumanized quest for knowledge and

[1] Farewell television address, January 17, 1961.

7

for manipulative tools now finally becoming more apparent to us? Under the leadership of blacks, women, and the young—confused and divided though it be—are human beings now starting to fight back more effectively for human rights and dignity?

SCIENCE AND SCIENTISM

The struggle for dependable knowledge about the world and man has been age-long. The systematization of the search for knowledge has increased its impetus and its efficiency even though many of its great breakthroughs have come from the unsystematic, from imaginative and courageous people who were unimpressed by established principles and procedures. The most successful participants in the quest place their confidence in their own fresh perceptions of natural happenings and of novel experiments. Thus they give us what we call "science," with its emphasis upon reason disciplined by observation.

From its remote beginnings, science has not been the exclusive property of physical and biological investigators. It was a search for dependable knowledge not only about physical and biological matters, but also about man and his society. Its implications were permeating social studies long before Auguste Comte baptized sociology more than a century ago.[2]

During the nineteenth and twentieth centuries came the great technological conquests by the physical and biological scientists. The prestige of their magic identified science more and more not with a general attitude and procedure for acquiring knowledge, but with oversimplified conceptions of the methodologies, symbols, and abstract theories of physics, chemistry, and biology.[3] For any other discipline to appear "scientific," it had to take on the trappings of a scientistic mathematics popularly identified with systematic investigation and experimentation. Thus, long before the latter decades of the twentieth century, many sociologists were taking grandiose quantification to be the one route to popular and academic repute. Too many sociologists today permit obscure language and heavy stylization, as well as computerization and complex mathematical formulas, to overshadow accuracy, novelty, scientific sig-

---

[2] Auguste Comte, *The Positive Philosophy*, freely trans. and condensed by Harriet Martineau (London: George Bell & Sons, 1896), esp. II, H. E. Barnes, ed., *An Introduction to the History of Sociology* (Chicago: University of Chicago Press, 1948), Chaps. 1–3; Howard Becker and H. E. Barnes, *Social Thought From Lore to Science*, 2nd ed. (Washington: Harren Press, 1952), I, Chap. 15; George Simpson, *Auguste Comte: Sire of Sociology* (New York: Thomas Y. Crowell, 1969), esp. pp. 1–23.

[3] P. A. Sorokin, "Physicalist and Mechanistic School," in *Contemporary Sociology*, ed. by J. S. Roucek (New York: Philosophical Library, 1958), pp. 1127–76.

nificance, and social importance in their judgment of the worth of contributions to sociological knowledge.[4]

THE SOCIAL IMPACT OF SCIENCE. The impact of science on man as a social creature has several different aspects. The most obvious evidence of its impact is in domestic gadgetry, health-care facilities, urban and industrial structures and mechanisms, and the omnipresent threat of an ultimate nuclear holocaust. However, the most fundamental product of science is social and mental: the modification of the mental patterns of man. The reformation now taking place in the manner in which man perceives and organizes himself, his groups, and his society, constitutes the greatest impact of science. This reformation stimulated the Nobel laureate biologist George Wald of Harvard University to announce bluntly: "Something has gone sour, in teaching and in learning. It's almost as though there were a widespread feeling that education has become irrelevant. . . . Unless we can be surer than we now are that this generation has a future, nothing else matters."[5]

Like many other well-informed people, Wald contends that the threats of nuclear annihilation and of widespread starvation consequent to the continuing population explosion combine with our irresponsible military-industrial complex to make human survival highly doubtful. "[Our] present military establishment . . . is corrupting the life of the whole country. It is buying up everything in sight: industries, banks, investors, universities; and lately it seems also to have bought up the labor unions. . . . Our government has become preoccupied with death, with the business of killing and being killed. . . . Are we to have a chance to live?"[6] Caught in this crisis, students are forcing their teachers to realize that much of their education looks like outworn ritual and rhetoric.

Surely we cannot just sit and wait for Armageddon to obliterate us! How can we cope with starvation and nuclear and militaristic menaces? All these menaces can be overcome, and can only be overcome, if we learn very shortly how to assimilate radical changes with grace into our

[4] R. S. Lynd, *Knowledge for What? The Place of Social Science in American Culture* (Princeton: Princeton University Press, 1939); P. A. Sorokin, *Fads and Foibles in Modern Sociology and Related Sciences* (Chicago: Henry Regnery, 1956); C. W. Mills, *The Sociological Imagination* (New York: Oxford University Press, 1959); F. W. Matson, *The Broken Image: Man, Science and Society* (New York: George Braziller, 1964); Herbert Blumer, *Symbolic Interactionism* (Englewood Cliffs, N.J.: Prentice-Hall, 1969); Glenn Jacobs, ed., *The Participant Observer* (New York: George Braziller, 1970), esp. intro.; Ernest Becker, *Lost Science of Man* (New York: George Braziller, 1971).

[5] George Wald, "A Generation in Search of a Future," a speech at the Massachusetts Institute of Technology, March 4, 1969, excerpted in "News and Comment," *New Yorker*, March 22, 1969, pp. 29, 31.

[6] *Ibid.*, as excerpted in *Harvard Alumni Bulletin*, April 7, 1969, p. 15.

cultural baggage. Many of us do not—in fact, many of us cannot—think at all clearly and accurately and with enough strategic foresight about these menaces. Too many of us still have minds tyrannically controlled by (1) outworn myths, (2) tribalism, (3) the prevailing and dangerous conception of news, (4) views we consider orthodox, and (5) relationships we take to be sanctioned and legitimized by the "social system."

Let us see how these five tyrannies currently distort the thinking of many people. Then we will touch on the more specific challenges of a social and sociological nature that arise from the impact of science upon man.

FIVE TYRANNIES

1. *Outworn myths* so clutter our minds that scientific thinking about anything more complicated than physical or biological problems is sometimes nearly impossible. We can play spectacularly with such adult erector sets as those we make into interplanetary vehicles. Then we try to handle urban disintegration by subsidizing the very political and business conspiracies that feed like cancers on slum dwellers. We try to handle educational failures, not by creating more workable educational procedures, but by subsidizing the very personnel and institutions that have so demonstrably resisted change and cheated their students.[7]

WHAT IS MYTH? *Myth* is not being used in a limited anthropological sense to mean traditional narratives that prescribe rites and other usages and furnish supernatural explanations for natural phenomena, the universe, and man. Such an anthropological definition tends to identify *myth* with *superstition*. Sociologists broaden its sense and make it apply to "the value-impregnated beliefs and notions that men hold, that they live by or live for."[8] In other words, myths are popular, treasured, traditional theories. Myths may or may not be verifiable. They carry a sanction derived from religion, family, state, business, science, or merely from frequent usage. Myths may persist long after they have lost their social or personal utility, and may even persist after they have become social and personal handicaps.[9]

What outworn myths are we referring to? They are all so entrenched

---

[7] Harold Taylor, *Students Without Teachers* (New York: McGraw-Hill, 1969), esp. Parts 1 and 2; John Dewey, *Reconstruction in Philosophy* (Boston: Beacon Press, 1957).

[8] R. M. MacIver, *The Web of Government* (New York: Macmillan, 1947), p. 4.

[9] Barrows Dunham, *Man Against Myth*, 2nd ed. (New York: Hill and Wang, 1962); see also W. E. H. Lecky, *History of the Rise and Influence of the Spirit of Rationalism in Europe* (1865; London: Watts, 1910), esp. I, Chap. 3.

in our minds that even to try to label some of them "outworn" may be very offensive or disconcerting. Life without myth is unthinkable. Many myths help us to deal with the complexities of life, and many are also beautiful. We can talk condescendingly and amusedly about the myths of other peoples or of our own grandparents, but we prefer not to look critically at our own myths. We do not want to recognize and sort out our own myths so that we can decide which to keep and which to replace. It is much more comfortable to rationalize and romanticize the retention of outworn myths than to reject them.[10]

THREE DISASTROUS MYTHS. Here are three of the outworn myths that are disastrous to teaching and learning:

"Peace Through War." "That we can develop a more peaceful world by converging more and more of our national energies upon the combined military-industrial complex," the far-flung international structure of what Henry R. Luce of *Time* called "The American Century." [11] In consequence, as the late President Eisenhower asserted, "the free university, historically the fountainhead of free ideas and scientific discovery, has experienced a revolution in the conduct of research. Partly because of the huge costs involved, a Government contract becomes virtually a substitute for intellectual curiosity." [12]

In sociology and the other social sciences this seduction takes the form of an increased "policy" orientation toward research and theorizing. This means in many cases that sociologists and other social scientists are less frequently viewing themselves as social critics. Now a great many of them are primarily, and hopefully, thinking of themselves as counselors to the established power-manipulators of our society.[13] On this point the academically sophisticated and constructive Senator J. William Fulbright takes the same position that dedicated social scientists have long held. He contends that "Pentagon-sponsored field [policy] research in counter-insurgency [is not] an appropriate activity for social scientists who ought to be acting as independent and critical commentators on their govern-ment's policies. Far from being victims of anti-intellectualism as some of these scholars complain when their activities are criticized, they them-

---

[10] On the persistence of myths and other aspects of culture, see M. J. Herskovits, *Cultural Dynamics* (New York: Alfred A. Knopf, 1964), esp. Chap. 9; A. L. Kroeber, *Anthropology*, rev. ed. (New York: Harcourt, Brace & World, 1948), esp. pp. 287–88, 346–47.

[11] George Seldes, *One Thousand Americans* (New York: Boni & Gaer, 1947), pp. 110–20, esp. p. 111.

[12] Farewell television address, January 17, 1961.

[13] A. W. Gouldner and S. M. Miller, eds., *Applied Sociology: Opportunities and Problems* (New York: Free Press, 1965), esp. Chaps. 1–9; I. L. Horowitz, *Professing Sociology: Studies in the Life Cycle of Social Science* (Chicago: Aldine Publishing Co., 1968), esp. Chaps. 10–11, 19–23; R. A. Nisbet, *Tradition and Revolt* (New York: Random House, 1969).

selves are perpetuating a virulent form of anti-intellectualism. They do so by contributing to the corruption of their universities, the militarization of American society, and that persistent degradation of values which goes by the polite name of 'credibility gap.' " [14]

Too many social scientists now want to be of service to generals and corporate executives rather than to students, GIs, housewives, and other rank-and-file citizens. We used to ridicule this emphasis by Nazi, Soviet, and Japanese intellectuals. Now we too often embrace it ourselves.

"Education Through Rote Learning." A second myth: "That science is the cook-book subject taught in most schools. That it is not the potentially radical and even revolutionary search that it can be to help make our society youthful and flexible and vital."

We teach the natural sciences—whether physical, biological, or social —chiefly as systems of established principles. On the contrary, such scientific findings should be seen for what they are—collections of the more or less accurate and inaccurate relics of past research. We need to teach science as an approach, an attitude, a quest for greater sensitivity, for keener perception, for new jumps into reality.

In what is called "science," entrenched principles can function as doors locked against innovation and innovators. The personal reminiscences of a black social scientist, Charles V. Hamilton of Roosevelt University, Chicago, vividly illustrate this point: "I graduated from Roosevelt, I got a law degree from Loyola University and I got a Ph.D. from the University of Chicago. And I'm going to tell you very clearly that my education over that twelve- to fifteen-year period was geared toward making me a middle-class black Sambo. Nothing devious in that, and I'm not blaming my professors. It's just that that was their orientation." [15] This perceptive black could see blandly formative principles and their significance in what he was taught. He could see, understand, and resist the pressure to become a middle-class version of "black Sambo." The principles and pressures that he resisted could have effectively shut many a door against his scientific curiosity. How many white graduate students are as perceptive? How many ever notice that they are being shaped into mere instruments of academic reproduction and aggrandizement, into white-Sambo technicians? How many fight against that distortion?

[14] J. W. Fulbright, "Militarism and American Democracy," (mimeographed) Owens-Corning Lecture at Denison University, Granville, Ohio, April 18, 1969, p. 7. See also Fulbright, *The Pentagon Propaganda Machine* (New York: Liveright, 1970), esp. p. 127; Walter Adams and Adrian Jaffe, *Government, the Universities, and International Affairs: A Crisis in Identity,* Special Report Prepared for the U.S. Advisory Commission on International Educational and Cultural Affairs, 90th Cong., 1st Session, House Document No. 120 (Washington, D.C.: U.S. Government Printing Office, 1967), p. 10.
[15] "Black Mood on Campus," *Newsweek,* February 10, 1969, p. 53.

Another American who met with and broke down locked doors of "science" is Stanford R. Ovshinsky. He terminated his formal education in 1941 with graduation from both high school and night trade school. "School bored me," he said. "I didn't find it pertinent to the world." [16] Like many creative people, he educated himself. He followed his curiosity into mathematics, physics, biology, medicine, and literature. His aggressive and unorthodox approaches to scientific problems and to the business exploitation of his more than thirty-eight patents have brought him foreign and domestic recognition as a scientist, inventor, and entrepreneur. According to Sir Neville Mott, director of the Cavendish Laboratory at Cambridge University, England, Ovshinsky's recent work in electronics is "the newest, the biggest, the most exciting discovery in solid-state physics at the moment." [17]

In addition to Ovshinsky's fortunate genetic and environmental background for his accomplishments, the following statement is a significant key to his important electronic discovery: "Ovshinsky may have been lucky to avoid the conventional crystal-oriented instruction dished out to solid-state physicists in the universities, for he was thus presumably better able to appreciate the possibilities of amorphous materials." [18] That is a summary of the opinion of Hellmut Fritzsche, a University of Chicago physicist who is also a vice-president in Ovshinsky's corporation. Dean Ernest Gardner of Wayne State University's medical school made the same point: "He would raise questions that made you stop and think about things you usually take for granted." [19] Gardner recalled that Ovshinsky had originated several researches in which Ovshinsky collaborated with medical professors, researches that were later reported in leading scientific journals. Sir Neville Mott adds that Ovshinsky is also "both charming and extremely cultured—a man of very, very wide interests." [20]

Regardless of future judgments on Ovshinsky's labors, the manner in

[16] P. M. Boffey, "Ovshinsky: Promoter or Persecuted Genius," *Science*, CLXV (1969), 674.

[17] *Ibid.*, p. 673. Mott later retreated from this extreme endorsement but only to say that Ovshinsky's work is "of very considerable interest," p. 674.

[18] *Ibid.*, p. 674.

[19] *Ibid.*, p. 675.

[20] *Ibid.*, p. 674. Note also the statement by T. R. Blackburn: "I have gone so far, in my own teaching, as to sacrifice a few laboratory afternoons for my students to contemplate . . . the colors, smells, textures, and changes of some substances on which they would do a rigorous and abstractly interpreted experiment the following week. . . . Most of the students . . . are, at best, tolerant of my efforts to let them really know something about equilibria in aqueous solutions. At the risk of judging them too harshly, I cannot but feel that, by the time I see them, their natural curiosity about the physical world has been corrupted by too many years of rules, abstractions, and quickie true-false tests." ("Sensuous-Intellectual Complementarity in Science," *Science*, CLXXII (1971), 1007.

which he bypassed the conservatizing influences of existing principles emphasizes the problems of scientists dedicated to the search for new knowledge. The difficult experiences of such well-known innovators in science as Charles Darwin, Albert Einstein, and Sigmund Freud in trying to revise or replace established principles need not be recited here.[21]

"Freedom Through Subservience." A third outworn myth that tyrannizes many minds is: "That we need men of action who get things done, who do not hesitate over lessons of history or counsels of scientists or the niceties of human rights and human dignity. They aren't Boy Scouts. They know how to play in the Biggest League."

We still follow and even worship such Caesars both in war and in peace. We pervert for the use of such Caesars the teachings of the Prince of Peace, as well as the utterances of those latter-day instruments of revelation—the scholars, scientists, and artists dedicated to humanity. For example, in attempting to explain why the United States "has spent around a thousand billion dollars on arms and men-in-arms" during the first twenty-five years after World War II, the seasoned commentator Eric Sevareid stresses "the brass's positiveness, their unending *certainty,* as they present their plans and estimates. They are trained that way. Civilian officials must summon the courage of their doubts; the military may be frequently in error but are never in doubt. This is a large reason why they have constantly carried the day in their presentations to wondering, doubting congressional committees." [22] Domestic programs for health, welfare, and education, for integrating underprivileged groups, lack such Caesar-like lobbyists—and corporations and campaign funds to back them up.[23]

Those who have read George Orwell's novel, *1984,*[24] may detect a certain parallelism between these three tyrannous myths and the three slogans he sardonically predicts for a dictatorship of the future: "War Is Peace"—spokesmen for our ever-expanding military-industrial complex

[21] Henshaw Ward, *Charles Darwin* (New York: New Home Library, 1943); Francis Darwin, ed., *The Life and Letters of Charles Darwin* (London: Murray, 1887), 2 vols.; Charles Darwin, *Autobiography,* ed. by Francis Darwin (New York: Schuman, 1950); Albert Einstein and L. Infeld, *The Evolution of Physics* (New York: Simon & Schuster, 1938); Sigmund Freud, *The Origins of Psychoanalysis,* ed. by M. Bonaparte, A. Freud, and E. Kris, trans. by E. Mosbacher and J. Strachey (New York: Basic Books, 1954); Sigmund Freud, *Letters,* ed. by E. L. Freud, trans. by T. and J. Stern (New York: Basic Books, 1960).

[22] Eric Sevareid, "American Militarism: What Is It Doing to Us?" *Look,* August 12, 1969, pp. 14, 16.

[23] Jack Raymond, *Power at the Pentagon* (New York: Harper & Row, 1964); U.S. House of Representatives, Subcommittee on Government Operations, 88th Cong., *Government Information Plans and Policies* (Washington, D.C.: U.S. Government Printing Office, 1963); H. L. Nieburg, *In the Name of Science,* rev. ed. (Chicago: Quadrangle Books, 1970); and F. J. Cook, *The Warfare State* (New York: Collier, 1964).

[24] George Orwell, *1984* (New York: Harcourt, Brace, 1949).

allege that their chief product is peace—albeit by the way of war. "Ignorance Is Strength"—don't ask questions; just memorize principles. "Freedom Is Slavery"—be "free" through subservience to the men who "get things done."

Just as human beings will continue to be more than Orwell's faceless and mindless party members, so too are more and more people becoming disenchanted with distorting, outworn myths, such as the three above.

EXPLOITING ETHNIC IDENTITIES

2. *Tribalism* is a tyranny we have inherited from the peoples of many lands, but its American pattern owes much to the class-snobbery and racism that is called White-Anglo-Saxon-Protestantism, or WASPism. This is a pattern the English developed and brought with them to all parts of Great Britain and then to their overseas colonies in Ireland, the Americas, and around the world.[25]

The contention that tribalism is an outworn tyranny is not to be interpreted as belittling other aspects of the cultural heritages we have received from our disparate ancestors and through borrowing. Our composite American culture is and should be a mélange of the cultures of all lands, forever invigorated by the complexities and contradictions of its segments.[26]

Under attack are both ethnocentrism, which is closely related to egocentrism, and the exploitation of ethnic identities in a tribal manner to obtain for the group special competitive advantages. Even when such an exploitation has not existed, myths about the tribal conspiracies of other groups are often developed and used to justify a counter-conspiracy as a "defensive" measure. Separatist WASPism has made other ethnic groups more separatist and militant.

UNSPOKEN CONSPIRACIES. Ethnocentrism often takes the forms of class-centeredness and of racism. It is both the overglorification of one ethnic group's customs and physical characteristics and the underrating or rejection of those of other groups. In peacetime we sometimes become aware of the extremes to which we have carried such ethnic propaganda

[25] V. G. Kiernan, *The Lords of Human Kind* (Boston: Little, Brown, 1969), esp. Chaps. 1–3; T. F. Gossett, *Race* (Dallas: Southern Methodist University Press, 1963); B. N. Schwartz and Robert Disch, eds., *White Racism* (New York: Dell, 1970), esp. Parts 1–2; R. A. Goldsby, *Race and Races* (New York: Macmillan, 1971), esp. Chap. 7.

[26] Gerhard Lenski, *The Religious Factor*, rev. ed. (Garden City, N.Y.: Doubleday, 1963), esp. pp. 327–30, 335–42; M. M. Gordon, *Assimilation in American Life* (New York: Oxford University Press, 1964), esp. Chaps. 2, 3, 7, 8; A. McC. Lee, *Multivalent Man* (New York: George Braziller, 1966), Chap. 17.

against wartime enemies. We are not nearly so sensitive to our common depreciation of other groups within our own society. In selecting business or political associates and employees, neighbors, and fellow club members, we too often enter into what is really an unspoken conspiracy against those different from ourselves and in favor of those with similar ethnic identity—"our own kind of folks." [27]

Many blacks are now reacting to white racism by becoming openly tribalistic. They dramatize the fraudulence of their alleged opportunities in our white-dominated society. They drive home how tribalistically the whites still treat each other, as well as the blacks.

For small isolated groups of people in a primitive world unjoined to other groups by modern means of transportation, communication, and trade, tribalism was the basis for organized survival. In the highly complex and interrelated world of today, tribalism pushes us along a pathway toward national disaster and international chaos.

One small corner of the English-speaking world, Northern Ireland, provides one of the vast number of vivid illustrations available in the world today of the calamity called tribalism. Since 1921, the six northeastern counties of Ireland, with a current population of 1.5 million, have been a somewhat autonomous province of the United Kingdom. Formed as a Protestant-controlled enclave, leaders of the Protestant majority—two-thirds of the population—use a variety of devices to retain control not only of the province, but also of its smaller governmental units and their perquisites, such as jobs and access to public housing facilities. With constant charges and countercharges of conspiracy, both Protestants and Roman Catholics preserve and strengthen their separatism and tribalism. Children attend church-oriented schools, play different types of games, affect different dialects, and join different scout troops and clubs. When they are grown, those on each side contend that those on the other are plotting to monopolize the province. Although both religious groups derive from roughly the same highly mixed racial stocks, extremists on both sides recite racist myths with which to flatter their own identities and to belittle those of the opposition.[28]

[27] U.S. National Advisory Commission on Civil Disorders, Report (New York: Bantam Books, 1968), esp. Chaps. 7–9; One Year Later: An Assessment of the Nation's Response to the Crisis Described by the National Advisory Commission on Civil Disorders (Washington: Urban America and the Urban Coalition, 1969); Philip Mason, Prospero's Magic: Some Thoughts on Class and Race (London: Oxford University Press, 1962); B. B. Epstein and Arnold Forster, "Some of My Best Friends . . ." (New York: Farrar, Straus and Cudahy, 1962); S. M. Miller and P. A. Roby, The Future of Inequality (New York: Basic Books, 1970).

[28] O. D. Edwards, "Ireland," in Edwards et al., Celtic Nationalism (New York: Barnes & Noble, 1968), pp. 1–209; L. P. Curtis, Jr., Anglo-Saxons and Celts: A Study of Anti-Irish Prejudice in Victorian England (Bridgeport: University of Bridgeport, 1968); E. A. Hooton and C. W. Dupertuis, "Comparison of Catholics and Protestants," Part 2 of The Physical Anthropology of Ireland, I (Cambridge, Mass.: Peabody Museum of Archaeology and Ethnology, 1955).

Time after time during the half century of the separation of Northern Ireland, armed conflict has broken out, with the Royal Ulster Constabulary (the provincial police) and even the British soldiers usually showing partisanship against the Roman Catholic minority. A respected moderate Roman Catholic leader put it: "It's hard to believe, but this is tribal conflict now [in 1969], and as far as the Catholics are concerned, the police are just part of the other tribe. There's no credible authority left." [29] Another Northern Irishman—who could have been either a Protestant or a Roman Catholic—asserted at that time: "We've all been stuck in our ghettos for so long that we don't quite know what to do without them. When the barriers are up, we all know where we are, and who we are. But when they come down, we're a bit lost in the new landscape." [30] They do not know how to face a society of competing human beings free of conspiratorial tribal ties.

Unemployment typically runs higher in Northern Ireland and wages average lower than elsewhere in the United Kingdom. Tribalistic conflict under ethno-religious banners serves as a distraction from more basic issues. If deprived Catholics and deprived Protestants were to combine, there could be a dramatic and democratic shift in political and economic power. Hopefully, international tides of secularism and of closely related ecumenicism, as well as of trade, will eventually bring a broader and more tolerant spirit. As one commentator notes: "The important new middle class of all denominations finds it advantageous to be broadminded. Younger-generation leaders are showing their impatience with the old shibboleths." [31]

Cultural pluralism [32] is a worthy ideal for our heterogeneous society. However, when cultural pluralism implies tribal pluralism and tribal conspiracy, we have to remind ourselves that the segments of a tribally pluralistic society never enjoy equal rights, that the more powerful tribal groups have always exploited the weaker. [33]

---

[29] Quoted by David Holden, "A Bad Case of the Troubles Called Londonderry," *New York Times Magazine*, August 3, 1969, p. 29. The best running, detailed accounts of these Irish affairs are provided by the Dublin *Irish Times* and the Belfast *Fortnight*. See also Andrew Boyd, *Holy War in Belfast* (Tralee, Co. Kerry, Ireland: Anvil Books, 1969); Bernadette Devlin, *The Price of My Soul* (London: Andre Deutsch, 1969); Liam de Paor, *Divided Ulster*, 2nd ed. (Harmondsworth, Middlesex, England: Penguin Books, 1971); Patrick Riddell, *Fire Over Ulster* (London: Hamish Hamilton, 1970); Russell Stetler, *The Battle of the Bogside* (London: Sheed and Ward, 1970).

[30] Quoted by Holden, p. 44.

[31] D. S. Connery, *The Irish* (New York: Simon & Schuster, 1968), p. 280. This statement is accurate even though tensions and disorders have continued in Northern Ireland.

[32] H. M. Kallen *et al.*, *Cultural Pluralism and the American Idea* (Philadelphia: University of Pennsylvania Press, 1956), esp. S. H. Chapman's essay, pp. 103–12.

[33] G. E. Simpson and J. M. Yinger, *Racial and Cultural Minorities*, 3rd ed. (New York: Harper & Row, 1965), esp. Chaps. 4–10; Celia S. Heller, ed., *Structured Social Inequality* (New York: Macmillan, 1969), esp. Part 6.

A DISTORTING MIRROR

3. *The prevailing conception of news* is dangerous because it involves tyrannous entrapment. In the guise of furnishing the people "all the news that's fit to print" or some approximation of it, the mass media try to give the impression that they mirror objectively the day's most important developments. On the contrary, their staffs select and present material "in the belief that by so doing [the media] . . . will profit," to quote a leading writer on journalistic practice.[34] Newspapers, like radio and television, are operated to attract and to hold the attention of consumers so that advertisers can sell them merchandise, services, and ideas. The media do not risk boring customers or offending advertisers. Thus, news reports are only as instructive and as representative of popular interests as they have to be.

What does such a conception of news do to our daily picture of the world? It seizes upon the exciting antics of extremists—warmongers; black nationalists; student rebels; women liberationists; hippies; yippies; users of marijuana, LSD, and heroin; domestic murderers; battle scenes abroad and in our own streets; small-time thieves; and members of the so-called Mafia. News accounts build them up. Reporters bring into focus only spectacular events and the running stories and incidents in adventures of glittering individuals. These latter are much like the episodes in comic strips, except that they deal with the Indochinese War, the Presidency, the very wealthy, English royalty, astronauts, and figures in the entertainment and sports worlds. Think of all the excitement, too, that the media developed in connection with prohibition, communism, Senator Joseph McCarthy's antics, and such indefinable conceptions as isolationism, internationalism, keeping the world safe for democracy, national commitment, a limited war, the iron curtain, and the bamboo curtain. News makes us think we are in touch with the "world" and equips us to talk entertainingly and knowingly about the same things other people can also discuss entertainingly and knowingly.

With certain exceptions, which are noted below, the current theory of news glosses over what the less spectacular people—the vast majority —do to make the continuance and vitality of society possible. For example, news stresses street battles between the Green Catholics and Orange Protestants in Northern Ireland rather than the sincere involvement of a wide variety of Catholic and Protestant groups and individuals

---

[34] C. D. MacDougall, *The Press and Its Problems* (Dubuque, Iowa: W. C. Brown, 1964), p. 98. See media advertisements in such trade periodicals as *Advertising Age, Editor & Publisher,* and *Sales Management.* See also A. McC. Lee, *The Daily Newspaper in America* (New York: Macmillan, 1937), esp. Chaps. 10, 16, 17.

there in the work of reconciliation.[35] Our current approach to news tends to push unrepresentative and often trivial extremists into the center of the passing scene. It makes them look typical, and it tempts others to imitate them. Sometimes it helps to build fads—often irresponsible fads—by denouncing them in instructive detail. It unnecessarily stirs the anxieties and antagonisms of overprotective parents and flag-waving officials. It distracts attention from big-time thieves and conspirators, from collusions between legal and illegal operators in business and politics, from manipulators of government on behalf of special interests, and from the wheelers and dealers using United States power to exploit people and resources in foreign countries.

If the media told the war stories as they are, we would see all too vividly for media interests that even though wars are senseless to humanity, they are not senseless in the short run for those with a stake in them. Unfortunately, too many people think they have a stake, whether large or small, in wars.

When students and blacks embroil themselves in social actions that are reported in the mass media, they often see how the media distort and trivialize their disturbing efforts.[36] Their experience has often verified, at least to their own satisfaction, their contention that news accounts ordinarily are oppressive and unrepresentative.

A few excellent newswriters and newscasters transcend the popular conception of news and thereby reveal its shabbiness and inadequacy. They demonstrate that a commercial mass news medium dedicated to public service is a viable possibility. They also demonstrate that it requires personnel with unusual courage, imagination, and dedication to make it a possibility.

A SET OF BLINDERS

4. *Views we take to be orthodox* are those apparently accepted as correct by the people that we think "count." A great many people, with pathetic earnestness, want to have the security of feeling that they are not only right-thinking, but that they are certified as such through their agreement with prestigious spokesmen.

But how can we be sure we are right when there are so many interpretations of orthodoxy's formulas? Isn't the quest for orthodoxy a quest for a set of blinders with which to simplify life's complexities?

[35] Arthur Booth, ed., *Orange and Green: A Quaker Study of Community Relations in Northern Ireland* (Brigflatts, Yorks., U.K.: Northern Friends Peace Board, 1969).

[36] Daniel Walker, Study Team Director, *Rights in Conflict: The Violent Confrontation of Demonstrators and Police in the Parks and Streets of Chicago During the Week of the Democratic National Convention of 1968* (New York: Bantam Books, 1968), esp. pp. 215–331.

White and black students hear ritualistic statements by institutional spokesmen about the moral premises upon which their institutions are said to be founded. The students then rebel against the failure of institutional functionaries to implement those principles that relate to equality of opportunity and service to humanity. They rebel against bland interpretations of the moral premises embedded in orthodoxy that ask them to conform to instrumental roles. They want to live and create, to reshape a decadent society into a more vital one that does not exclude them, or at least will not exclude their children.

If the implications of science were fully embraced in our formation of views on important issues, we would no longer accept or reject any judgment just because it aligns with some doctrinal or crystallized orthodoxy. On the contrary, we would try to find wise guidance based upon the tenable reports of others and upon our own personal experience. In other words, we would seek fresh and perceptive observations of relevant developments. This would particularly help us to shake off slavery to ideas transmitted to us from the past. Under critical examination, ideas should have more to recommend them than how respectable, prestigious, orthodox, or even beautiful they are.[37]

OUR PATCHWORK
"SOCIAL SYSTEM"

5. *Relationships we take to be sanctioned and legitimized by "the social system"* make up the last of the small group of tyrannies to be discussed here. Central to this tyranny is the widely accepted myth that there is an objective "mechanism" called "the social system." [38] That the *myth* of a social system exists can readily be verified. A very large percentage of any population will assure you that there is such a system, that they live in and by it—whether they like it or not. Asked to describe it, these same people will have great difficulties. They can give you many different descriptions of "the social system," but the descriptions will have little in common other than names, institutional façades, and certain obvious bits of material culture, such as streets, power lines, buildings, and sewers.

A "social system" is only a patchwork of many devoutly held myths. It is seen differently, and those myths are interpreted differently, in each

[37] J. H. Plumb, *The Death of the Past* (Boston: Houghton Mifflin, 1970); John Dewey, *Individualism Old and New* (1930; New York: Capricorn Books, 1962), esp. Chap. 1, and *The Quest for Certainty* (1929; New York: Capricorn Books, 1960), esp. Chap. 11; H. J. Muller, *The Uses of the Past* (New York: Oxford University Press, 1952); and J. W. Fulbright, *The Arrogance of Power* (New York: Random House, 1966).
[38] A. McC. Lee, "The Concept of System," *Social Research*, XXXII (1965), 229–38.

of a society's groups. Whether the "system" can legitimize something —can give a sense of security and stability by sanctioning one's status, influence, or career—depends upon what is happening to a particular myth in that patchwork. The notion of "system" is also, because of its enticements and its widespread acceptance, one of the tyrannies over our minds that we need to understand.

Here again, the nonwhites, students, rebellious women, and other dissident groups, through their clinical experiences in social action, have probed the flimsiness of our "system" and the networks of legitimized relationships that control social power. They have discovered other legitimacies, born of fresh interpretations of idealism, of mass action, and of oppression. They have seen that traditionally legitimized interpersonal controls are still another trap—like outgrown myths, tribalism, news, and orthodoxy—to ensnare the vast majority. Most Americans are stripped of most, or all, of their autonomy and creativity and are harnessed as docile and dependable participants in the bureaucratic "rat race."

Can we face our society without recourse to a belief that it is somehow organized into an integrated and compensating "social system"? Can we confront the problems of life without the delusory aid of dogmatic formulas drawn from some orthodoxy? [39] Can we organize ourselves and our society in such a manner that we will not feel it necessary to "buy" legitimation through subservience to the manipulators of social power? Actually, the question should be "How can we?" rather than "Can we?" The blacks and the young and, as always, our small but vigorous army of autonomous and creative innovators of all ages and ethnic groups and of both sexes, are showing us that we must.

The foregoing are five tyrannical controls over our minds that are packed into our cultural baggage and block our assimilation of the potentialities of a humane social science. With this discussion as background, let us turn to other aspects of the impact of science upon our lives. Let us discuss those aspects in terms of what have been called "our idiot machines," of our unnecessarily long postreproduction gap, and of our new human-service needs. These are offered as more specific instances of the problems science has helped to precipitate for man, as well as the problems that scientific thinking can help us to solve, if we only permit ourselves to be scientific.

GARBAGE IN, GARBAGE OUT

Our idiot machines. Americans used to be highly amused at caricatures of the robotlike behavior of English clerks and Prussian bureau-

---

[39] A. McC. Lee, "On Formula Liberalism," *Journal of the Liberal Ministry,* VIII, No. 3 (Fall, 1968), 47–50.

crats who could only behave, it was believed, in terms of precisely memorized formulas. With our glorification of technicianism in so many university curricula, not to mention our more obviously labeled trade schools, we appear to be repeating the errors of rigidification so dramatized by the English and the Germans. But we are compounding those errors to an extent only recently made possible by "idiot machines."

Admittedly, it is a distortion to call complicated contraptions with electronic circuits "idiotic." Some have often been termed electronic "brains," but, of course, they are not brains. Any human brain—even the "idiotic"—has something of the mystery, magic, and majesty of the human spirit at work within it. A human brain, given a chance, is flexible, adaptable to changing facts and conditions. A machine is just what it has been programmed to be, and nothing more or less. When an electronic data-processing machine makes a mistake, one hears it said, "Garbage in, garbage out!" This is because a machine gives out just what has been put into it, marred only by imperfections in programming and by mechanical gremlins over which our technology has not yet gained complete control. The programming situation, too, is sometimes weakened by the fact that the kind of people who like to work routinely with machines tend to be the relatively less imaginative and less flexible.[40]

Have you ever had a debate by letter with a large merchandising organization that depends upon computerized records? It takes patience, but, like other clinical experiences in our society, it can be quite instructive. It does not take many exchanges of notes until the human representative of the machine, or the machine itself, gets completely bogged down. On one occasion a friend of mine ordered and paid for twenty $100 Series E Federal bonds. He received in the mail twenty $1,000 Series E bonds and had the greatest difficulty convincing the representatives of the government that he had received them in error! They contended that machines could not possibly make such an error.

The great inventor of the geodesic dome, Buckminster Fuller, has such an oversimplified notion of human society and such faith in mechanical gadgets that he sees mankind's salvation in the computer. He asserts: "A new, physically uncompromised, metaphysical initiative of unbiased integrity could unify the world. It could and probably will be provided by the utterly impersonal problem solutions of the computers. Only to their superhuman range of calculative capabilities can and may all political, scientific, and religious leaders face-savingly acquiesce."[41] That the

---

[40] Simon Marcson, ed., *Automation, Alienation, and Anomie* (New York: Harper & Row, 1970), esp. Part 2; E. B. Shils, *Automation and Industrial Relations* (New York: Holt, Rinehart & Winston, 1963); B. B. Seligman, *Most Notorious Victory: Man in an Age of Automation* (New York: Macmillan, 1966); George Terborgh, *The Automation Hysteria* (Washington: Machinery and Allied Products Institute, 1966).

[41] Buckminster Fuller, *Operating Manual for Spaceship Earth* (Carbondale: Southern Illinois University Press, 1969), pp. 35–36.

prestige of "science" and of computers may give such vast power to the "solutions of the computers" is a frighteningly real possibility. That the control of such omnipotent computers could be and should remain "utterly impersonal" is absurd. Even if such control were to remain "utterly impersonal," that would in itself be no assurance that the control would represent human welfare and humane interests. Computers can have the same conservatism and lack of adaptability built into them that has been injected at times into hard-won constitutional guarantees.

If we continue to place more and more faith in the dehumanized technician and in the idiot machine, we can look forward to substantial catastrophes in the future triggered by formula-ridden programming and dull-witted machine-tenders. There is no substitute for the broadly and fundamentally educated human being—with all his imperfections.[42]

ON KEEPING ALIVE

Our unnecessarily long postreproduction gap. We talk a lot about the generation gap, but let us consider that gap in a different light. We have actually decreased quite amazingly the length of time it takes to reproduce most of the specialists we need in our society. Simultaneously, in a great many areas we have lengthened the period of time people must wait before they can fully utilize their training, before they can step into the kinds of responsibility for which they are equipped by maturity, education, and experience.

By many criteria, students of a given age today are perhaps two years more mature than were their parents at the same age.[43] Educational procedures can help students gain a well-rounded education more rapidly and more adequately than a generation ago. (Reference is to those who either have not had the handicap of military brainwashing and experience or have had it and have somehow succeeded in overcoming its consequences.) [44]

Admittedly, when young people step out into society, they still need

[42] Daniel Bell, *The Reforming of General Education* (New York: Columbia University Press, 1966); Theodore Roszak, ed., *Dissenting Academy* (New York: Random House, 1968); Harold Taylor, *Students Without Teachers* (New York: McGraw-Hill, 1969). See also the role of computers in A. C. Clarke, *Two Thousand One: A Space Odyssey* (New York: NAL-World Publishing Co., 1970), or in the cinema of the same title.

[43] This would be a difficult point to prove one way or another, but it appears to be the net implication of a number of educators' judgments. See titles cited in footnote 42.

[44] K. E. Boulding *et al.*, *The Draft?* (New York: Hill and Wang, 1968), esp. Chap. 2; Willard Waller, *The Veteran Comes Back* (New York: Dryden Press, 1944); Sol Tax, ed., *The Draft* (Chicago: University of Chicago Press, 1967); Eli Ginzberg *et al.*, *The Ineffective Soldier: Lessons for Management and the Nation* (New York: Columbia University Press, 1959), 3 vols.

periods of practical experience, and sometimes advanced training as well, but many times they are frustrated and driven to unwise recourses or compromises by what they see ahead. Beyond their starting jobs, they perceive employment ladders clogged with the obsolescent and the incompetent and not too ornamented by the competent. The obsolescent and incompetent have nowhere else to go and do not give up what they have.[45] They often even delay retirement on an adequate pension because they do not want to trade a secure, easy, and orderly routine for a more speculative challenge, for just doing nothing, or—more likely—for trying to develop new routines as untaxing and supportive as those they would leave behind.

Thus students often see incompetence and decay entrenched through the advantages of age or in consequence of lucky speculations. At the same time, many of those who now appear incompetent or decadent might have been kept "alive" had they been motivated to plan for more dynamic and changeful careers.

Does this mean that oldsters should retire even earlier than they do now? Does this suggest that somehow the older people should turn over the control of our society entirely to youngsters in their twenties or thirties? Should more men and women retire at an early age to give their undivided attention to golf, tinkering, stock-market speculation, health-food fads, and hypochondria? On the contrary, retirement is unwise for any but the incapacitated. Our society needs all the intellectual, artistic, and physical resources it can muster to meet its pressing problems. It will need all such resources in order to survive. It does not need the obstructions provided by those—the vast number under present conditions—who become walking zombies at an early age.[46] This brings us to the last point:

Our need to open up new opportunities for human service. Let us look at a very attractive suburb of New York City in which relatively successful business and professional people find homes for their families. My wife and I have visited their homes and have tried to understand their aspirations, accomplishments, and failures. A great many of them, both husbands and wives, very clearly give the following impression:

---

[45] On the rise and entrenchment of people in positions beyond their competence, see Laurence Peter and Raymond Hull, *The Peter Principle* (New York: Morrow, 1969). See also C. N. Parkinson, *Parkinson's Law and Other Studies in Administration* and *The Law and the Profits* (Boston: Houghton Mifflin, 1957, 1960); Robert Presthus, *The Organizational Society* (New York: Alfred A. Knopf, 1962); and Anthony Downs, *Inside Bureaucracy* (Boston: Little, Brown, 1967), esp. Chap. 21.

[46] M. L. Barron, *The Aging American* (New York: Thomas Y. Crowell, 1961), esp. Chap. 10; Juanita Kreps, ed., *Technology, Manpower, and Retirement* (New York: World Publishing Co., 1967); Harold Sheppard, ed., *Industrial Gerontology* (Cambridge, Mass.: Schenkman, 1969).

They have struggled and connived on their ways to the top, but where are they? Many of them go to ritualistic cocktail parties, avoid serious discussions of anything controversial, cluck about the iniquities of youth, tell tired jokes, flirt with other people's spouses, keep in touch with society's current fantasy life through television and a newspaper, fight exploitative tradesmen and artisans, grouse about the racketeers in the town hall, state capitol, and Washington, tinker in the yard, give conscience money to the safest charities they can find, and take only token responsibility for the deprived and depraved in nearby slums and institutions. They "run away from it all" several times a year, perhaps to a resort or on a cruise, where they meet a new set of the same sort of people as those back home of whom they had gotten tired. They sometimes vaguely wonder what it is all about, but they do not press this question. It is easier to let their rituals dull the nagging problem.

CAREERS IN HUMAN SERVICE. The following point is probably quite a simple one, but it is an urgent and a practical one with revolutionary implications and possibilities. Recalling Henry David Thoreau's immortal statement that "the mass of men lead lives of quiet desperation," [47] let us not assume that people need or want to lead such lives. Our career perspectives are too short and too concentrated on the "rat race" itself rather than on what people can do for society and on what society can do for people. Men and women in business, government, education, and other pursuits can usually make their maximum contribution in any one job in perhaps a decade at the most. Then they should be able to move on to new and freshly challenging opportunities for human service. Sometimes several such changes and more can be made within the same organization, but greater invigoration can come from changing organizations. Reference is not only to highly skilled artisans and professionals, but to people with all types of competence, experience, and education.

WHOLE LIFE PLANNING. The increasing attention women are giving to "whole life planning" is a step toward what is being urged. Such planning usually contemplates this sequence of major periods: (1) education, (2) employment outside the home until the first pregnancy is rather advanced, (3) child rearing, (4) refresher education, and then (5) employment outside the home again, hopefully of a more durable and responsible kind and with better chances for growth and expression than in (2). Opportunities for the fifth stage require a great deal of expansion beyond the routine jobs that so often are the only ones now made available to women.

If we should build this career perspective into our thinking, planning, and acting, our well-to-do suburbs could become hotbeds of novelty and

[47] H. D. Thoreau, *Walden* (1854; New York: Signet Books, 1942), p. 10.

reinvigoration rather than cemeteries of misplaced or exhausted hopes. Benefits would then accrue to all parts of society. On younger age levels, the shortening of the postreproduction gap could help the young to cope better with their frustration and could encourage them not to grow dull in response to the pressures to conform, to perpetuate outworn patterns of incumbent job-holders. This could encourage frustrated but clever youngsters not to become dropouts, not to find a personal solution by working at an old handicraft, becoming a subsistence farmer, or seizing upon some bizarre life pattern.

For implementation, what is suggested would require a radical re-thinking of our socialization procedures for youth, as well as a reconsideration of the available career patterns for everyone. What is contributing especially to our spectacular "generation gap" of today is the segregation of the young, their isolation from realistic participation in, or even observation of, adult affairs. The young generally come to terms with academia as a formal game they must play, but one that has only vague and arbitrary relations with "the world." In addition, they are deeply involved in informal youth organizations, activities, and rationalizations. In this artificial world, with its pseudo- or play-culture, largely supported both nostalgically and financially by parents, the young learn how to play sex games (dating), how to join in gang activities (adapted to their class level), and how to cope with the formal controls of family and school. They do not learn how adults work, make deals, get ahead or fail, and play around. Now that more and more mothers, as well as fathers, are working outside the home, this generalization applies increasingly to girls as well as boys.

Thus, young people come to assume that their play-culture is what societal culture should and can be. Not being able to share in the experiential basis of youth's play-culture, adults consider it shockingly unrealistic, even untenably pathological. Not being able to share in the experiential basis of adult cultural patterns and social organization, youth find their parental generation stuffy and decadent. As in so many other aspects of social life, segregation here creates a destructive situation.

TO USE ALL HUMAN RESOURCES

To sum up the final point in this chapter quite briefly, the generation gap has been aggravated as a problem through our failure to take a long enough, sufficiently service-oriented, and constructive view of career potentialities and of social needs. It has been widened especially by our failure to keep older people moving into freshly challenging positions.

Let the younger people run many of our current institutions, but create new jobs and institutions to be run by older people that will aim at solving the pressing problems of slums, inequality, pollution, under-developed and starving countries, the population explosion, international tensions, and warfare.

The length of the human race's day on this planet depends upon a wiser use of human resources. Let us all, young and old, men and women, people of all colors and ethnic backgrounds, convince ourselves of the magnitude of our opportunities and responsibilities. Let us help humanity to persist. Let us help men and women to lead lives much more satisfy-ing than ones of "quiet desperation."

The contention here is that humanity can thrive with science as its instrument if it takes the implications of science more thoroughly into its cultural patterns, into its ways of thinking. Scientific findings are so often applied to serve the aspirations of war-makers and industrial entre-preneurs that science and scientists appear to be dangerous threats to the future of humanity. The antidote to that hazardous distortion is not a return to superstition or an appeal to the revelations of "god," man, or computer. The antidote is to embrace more thoroughly the spirit of curi-ous observation, free inquiry, and critical theorizing, called "science," in our education and in our popular culture. The usefulness of this antidote can particularly be seen through an examination of how sociology can equip the individual to become a participating member of a participant society.

CHAPTER 2

How Sociology Can Magnify the Individual

RAPPING ABOUT SOCIOLOGY

Concerned students like to talk endlessly about what they are learning from sociology: "Can we really use the stuff we're getting? Does it work when you try it out 'in life'?"

Such discussions can become quite personal, even intimate. They were once called "experience meetings." The "flaming youth" of the 1920s called them "bull sessions." Now they are "rap sessions." Autobiographical bits and items concerning close friends and relatives serve as illustrations. The most intimate revelations are often disguised as experiences of some unnamed person. The subjects range from how to "make" members of the other sex without involvement or regret, to how to reform the university, stop the war, get a job, or build a fortune. Sociology students are often concerned with how our jerry-built world, with all its iniqities, inequalities, and brutalities, can be made into one that is more likely to persist and more likely to be worth living in. Many of them fortunately focus on short-run improvements—hopefully with constructive longer-term implications—to which they can contribute during their lives.

When a teacher of sociology, as a presumed expert, is involved in such "rapping," he suddenly finds himself thrown on a dissecting slab. He has to cope with imperious demands for his cooperation in self-revelation. The nature of social controls, exploitations, and mass communications makes for exciting reading and discussion, students admit, but they want to get down to "where we live and where we are likely to live." How did he convince himself that the mental stance he represents is that of a professional sociologist? The stance itself may or may not be a pose—on that they are not at all sure, and they want to know. At any rate, it is a stance so different from any they have known before that they just have to demand fuller and more adequate explanation. Is such an orientation of use only to a professional sociologist and perhaps just as a hobby or a luxury to anyone else? How is it that the stances of sociologists differ so much, as even a small academic department can usually demonstrate?

SOCIOLOGISTS' DIVERSE STANCES. All those questions are significant, but let us turn first to the last question. There are sociologists concerned about helping people to live more effectively and satisfyingly as fuller participants in society, and then there are others who lean more to the manipulative or just to the dilettantish. Some are games-playing statisticians and other precise methodologists who can show how to learn very little about society, but how to determine that little bit in a most correct fashion. There are also social theorists who offer a scintillating supermarket full of alternative explanations, subtle distinction, exact terminologies, and conflicting theoretical models of man and society. They can discourse most grandly about almost anything, well out of touch with actual starvation, disease, war, exploitation, and hopelessness. And then, not to make the list too long, there are the existential humanists to whom sociology and related disciplines (including history, philosophy, and literature) must yield knowledge for life and living or not be worth the struggle. What they ask you to consider may at times not be pleasant or romantic or flattering or elegant. It may mean delving into outrageous ways of life and repulsive events. But it often strikes students as being relevant to their futures, as constituting, in effect, a kind of initiation into "real life." It is an initiation that contrasts sharply many times with an introduction to the instrumentalism of such "trade" disciplines as business administration and engineering.

SOCIOLOGY THROUGH STUDYING
SLICES OF LIFE

When students learn that a given professor actually has involvements in some exciting events "out in the world," they become all the more insistent that he reveal the nature of those involvements. They want to know the risks, consequences, and tensions, the human drama of such experiences.

What is to be learned from taking part in a slum work party detoxifying walls covered with scaling lead paint that is poisoning poverty-stricken inhabitants? Why and to whom is such work controversial?

What insights are to be gained from participation in the work of Alcoholics Anonymous or Addicts Anonymous?

What do the members hope to achieve in such organizations as the Black Muslims, the Black Panthers, the Jewish Defense League, and the Ku Klux Klan? What is the stated and real, the voiced and unacknowledged, the consciously believed and the unaware point of membership in the Daughters and Sons of the American Revolution, the Chamber of Commerce, the Junior League, and the trade and professional associations? How do they work to get what they want? Are those organizations sometimes used for purposes their members do not comprehend and perhaps would not sanction? If so, how?

What happens when a "lily white" neighborhood is desegregated? What sort of people help? How? What kinds of actionists work against desegregation? How?

What is the nature of the various anti-war or pro-peace efforts? How do the objectives and tactics of the conscientious objectors to any war, the objectors to a specific war, the advocates of peace through preparedness, the advocates of peace through war, and the agitators of internal social revolution differ? What evidence can be marshalled to support each position?

Can scientific studies be made that contribute usefully to the efforts of socially constructive actionists? How can we evaluate the alleged constructiveness of an actionist?

Is concern with individual social problems worth the bother? Doesn't such concern merely lead to efforts wasted on attempting to prop up an outworn social "system"? Doesn't the whole "system" need an overhauling or replacement?

Students soon learn that the existential humanist classroom is not bounded by four walls and that its subject matter includes experiences more vivid than lectures, text assignments, discussions, term papers, and even spontaneous rap sessions. They begin to realize how much easier it is to listen, read, or talk wishfully, and thus selectively and defensively, than it is to participate in social events without confronting mind-changing observations. Protective and distorting thought-curtains often prevent us from assimilating mind-modifying facts and ideas as we hear or read them, but a close-up view of an actual event can tear great holes in such comforting curtains. Active participation in an event can be most stimulating mental therapy. Fieldwork in social action may suddenly and sharply bring students to the conclusion that a great deal in society is not what they had assumed it to be.[1] This constrains them to read anew, to re-

---

[1] See Lincoln Steffens' discussion of such experiences in *The Autobiography of Lincoln Steffens* (New York: Harcourt Brace Jovanovich, 1931), p. 47.

discuss, and to rethink their social perspectives. Thus does their fundamental education for mature social participation get under way.

"SOCIOLOGY" AS AN ESCAPE

Many students do not identify with any given professor in his intellectual and actionist exploits. Many future sociology professors, for example, would be "turned off" by the hearty worldliness of an existential
humanist. The Harvard professor of government Carl J. Friedrich, in
accounting for the elitism and cultism common among intellectuals in
our society, notes that "the intellectual is apt to be maladjusted in childhood and youth. Frequently he is ridiculed and even persecuted by his
more normal schoolmates. His superior mind becomes the avenue of
escape from his hostile environment." [2] Since the sacred academic pre-
cincts can be invaded successfully via elegant theory and glossy methodology, the language and tools of select cults, these intellectuals in effect
ask: Why reopen the sores of childhood and youth? Why not make a
career of escapism? As one professor in a prestigious graduate school likes
frankly to assert, "I was an avid stamp collector as a youth. I have enjoyed
thoroughly my graduate work and my research since then because they
are my psychological equivalents of stamp collecting." Whether philately's
loss was sociology's gain in his case depends upon what one expects a
sociologist to accomplish. For the humanistically inclined, this professor's teachings and example have dramatic negative value. Fortunately
other professors in that university demonstrate that sociology has made
them more effective social diagnosticians, theorists, and citizens.

ENTICEMENTS OF THE
LABORATORY

Many a striving sociologist looks enviously at the laboratory of an
archeologist, physical anthropologist, experimental psychologist, or entomologist. They note the "scientific" aura such an orderly workroom
gives to a discipline, the apparent authority it imparts to its inmates, but
let us look candidly at an experimental psychologist's problems and labors
and then at a sociologist's.

Even the most specialized experimentalist among psychologists leans
heavily on the studies of social and clinical psychologists, sociologists, and
anthropologists in order to learn the individual and social contexts within

[2] C. J. Friedrich, *The New Image of the Common Man* (Boston: Beacon Press,
1950), p. 247.

which his subjects live and within which he experiments. For all the precision of his testing instruments, measurements, and statistical manipulations, he cannot but realize how much significant information has had to come to him from outside his laboratory. Much of that data is no less useful just because it may have to be in the form of unmeasurable observations.[3]

When the psychologist goes beyond experimentation with individuals and attempts to deal with arranged group situations, the artificialities of the laboratory become all the more limiting and all the more dependent upon outside observation. He realizes that each of his subjects is a person torn out of many group contexts and that each experimental group is fitted by its members into many remembered contexts. Both sociologists and psychologists engage in this type of experimental social-psychological work focused upon a small group or upon several groups in a controlled environment.[4]

What these illustrations briefly highlight is that each scientist must take his science's subject matter—not his tools—as his principal preoccupation. The archaeologist has as his goal the reconstruction of part or all of an ancient way of life, not the mere piecing together of single pots.[5] The physical anthropologist tries to shed light on the evolving anatomy and functioning of human beings as they have lived through the ages, not merely the reconstruction of single skulls or skeletons.[6] The entomologist does not stop with an orderly display of variations in the form or color of a beetle; he attempts to relate his findings to those of others in the search for how beetles and other insects live, modify, and reproduce under changing conditions.[7] Thus the scientist must not be enticed into oversimplifying or otherwise distorting his data through the overuse or inappropriate use of gadgetry such as a computer or of stage sets such as a laboratory. Such artifacts can too easily become ends in themselves, ends that obscure the scientist's basic jobs.

[3] F. J. McGuigan, *Experimental Psychology*, 2nd ed. (Englewood Cliffs, N.J.: Prentice-Hall, 1968), Chaps. 6–7.

[4] Muzafer and C. W. Sherif, *Groups in Harmony and Tension* (New York: Octagon, 1966); M. S. Olmsted, *The Small Group* (New York: Random House, 1959); R. T. Golembiewski, *The Small Group* (Chicago: University of Chicago Press, 1962); A. P. Hare, *Handbook of Small Group Research* (New York: Free Press, 1962); B. J. Biddle and E. J. Thomas, eds., *Role Theory* (New York: John Wiley, 1966); Dorwin Cartwright and A. F. Zander, *Group Dynamics*, 3rd ed. (New York: Harper & Row, 1968).

[5] R. F. Heizer and J. A. Graham, *A Guide to Field Methods in Archeology* (Palo Alto, Calif.: The National Press, 1967), Chap. 2; James Deetz, *Invitation to Archeology* (Garden City, N.Y.: The Natural History Press, 1967), Chap. 1.

[6] F. S. Hulse, *The Human Species*, rev. ed. (New York: Random House, 1971); Marvin Harris, *Culture, Man, and Nature* (New York: Thomas Y. Crowell, 1971), Chap. 1.

[7] R. E. Hutchinson, *Insects* (Englewood Cliffs, N.J.: Prentice-Hall, 1966).

USES OF THE SOCIOLOGICAL
LABORATORY

The above is not meant to suggest that the sociologist is always a stranger to the laboratory. In his study of appropriate problems, a sociologist may well find a computation laboratory to be most helpful in processing complicated data that can be reduced to comparable units.[8] He may save many hours of library research through employing a mechanized data-retrieval system, such as that developed by Sociological Abstracts, Inc.[9] He may be able to interview informants more efficiently and accurately in a neutral "laboratory" environment, equipped perhaps with a recording instrument, than he could in the street or in their homes.[10] He may achieve special insights by arranging confrontations between groups of competitors or antagonists in a "laboratory" situation.[11] He may gain useful knowledge by the extended study of play groups or work groups placed in controlled environments.[12] In each case, however, the sociologist needs to be vividly aware that what he is doing in a workroom is artificially abstracted from society; it has to be maintained or brought back into accurate relationship with what takes place spontaneously in society. It also needs to be added that a great deal of highly important sociological analysis and synthesis has been done upon the basis of observations made only in the midst of life.

HOW INTIMATE MUST
SOCIOLOGICAL LEARNING BECOME?

Students usually agree that reports from a participant and observer in social action go beyond anything they are able to learn from a formal

[8] W. F. Ogburn, "Limitations of Statistics," *American Journal of Sociology*, XL (1934–35), 12–20; George Simpson and Fritz Kafka, *Basic Statistics* (New York: W. W. Norton, 1952), Chap. 22; F. S. Chapin, *Experimental Designs in Sociological Research*, rev. ed. (New York: Harper & Row, 1955), Chap. 11; W. L. Wallace, *The Logic of Science in Sociology* (Chicago: Aldine-Atherton, 1971), Chap. 2.

[9] Searches of sociological literature can be made through the annual indexes of *Sociological Abstracts*, its decennial indexes for 1953–1962 and 1963–1972, and, by special arrangement, its computerized data-retrieval system.

[10] R. L. Kahn and C. F. Cannell, *The Dynamics of Interviewing* (New York: John Wiley, 1958); A. V. Cicourel, *Method and Measurement in Sociology* (New York: Free Press, 1964), pp. 73–104; P. E. Hammond, ed., *Sociologists at Work* (New York: Basic Books, 1964), Chaps. 3 and 10.

[11] See the Porter-Goldaber illustration of this later in this chapter.

[12] T. M. Mills, *The Sociology of Small Groups* (Englewood Cliffs, N.J.: Prentice-Hall, 1967); R. F. Bales, *Personality and Interpersonal Behavior* (New York: Holt, Rinehart & Winston, 1970).

text, including the text of such a participant observer. A person—a human "document"—is so much more than printed pages. Students like to be able to cross-question the person, to probe into nuances of a social-conflict situation that might be especially meaningful to them personally. They have to make a special effort, perhaps even a painfully wrenching one, they say, to take ideas more clearly and creatively into their own thought processes so that they might challenge such an "expert."

Into a text—even a highly competent one by some unknown person—students can probe only to a limited extent because it is a fixed portrayal. They can and should take exception to what they read in any text and should go to other sources for data and theory, but that skepticism is not so immediately involving or so satisfying as being able to question, discuss, speculate, and be reminded of recalcitrant facts. In this face-to-face process, students appear to be able to convince themselves that social knowledge can help them to influence social decision making more effectively than they had previously suspected.

The chief improvement that can be made on the use of such personal documents in a classroom is to facilitate outside special experiences for the students so that they themselves become the instructive human documents. They return to class from having labored in volunteer slum work parties, been participant observers at a debutante ball or a fox chase, had firsthand experience in a factory assemblyline, worked in a prison, mental hospital, or tuberculosis ward, accompanied a social case worker on his or her rounds, or attended a Rotary or trade-union meeting. When students are so "loaded," they become the best of documents both for themselves and for their fellows. They make sociological findings as printed in books spring into life.

The chief merit of "live" classroom work over correspondence [13] or other solitary study is that it permits students to perceive many different personalities—both teachers and students—interacting with data, ideas, and other personalities. A long step beyond this in educational effectiveness and growth is field or project work under trained and permissive guidance—that is, under guidance that encourages and stimulates indi-

---

[13] As senior faculty member, I have supervised the organization of a comprehensive introductory independent-study course in sociology on the college level. I do not wish to belittle that effort. Many students may get more from its taped lectures (by many leading specialists), lesson materials, study guide, and tutorial correspondence than they would from courses in many mass-production universities. I am speaking more highly only of "live" classes of moderate size, conducted by trained, involved, and well-motivated teachers. To satisfy the commendable needs for huge "open enrollments" in higher education, the reinforced independent-study courses of many public and private universities and of the English Open University are preferable to the regular classes in many overstuffed and understaffed universities.

vidual work and creativity and does not dominate or exploit. The student is fortunate who is able to identify with at least a few of his teachers and some of his other fellow students. Identification does not mean idealization, however. Identification that is quite clear-eyed facilitates learning, while idealization may only block it.

In addition to necessary personal ambitions, such identification plus personal experimentation with what is being studied provide the greatest stimulants to personal growth. Empathizing with a "working model" of what may lie ahead in life, whether in school or out, makes the route appear more traversable. Personal experimentation with ideas in practical situations gives a realistic sense of taking steps along a route "into life," into autonomy.

This case for teachers with something more than teaching experience does not imply that courses should be of a "trade-school" character. Working with a professorial poet or essayist or sculptor might forever enrich the life of a future banker or advertising copywriter. Becoming involved in a professorial painter's studio or a biologist's laboratory might help a sociologist or anyone else to mature more than would several extra courses in sociology.

SOCIOLOGICAL WRITING AS
AUTOBIOGRAPHY

Very little sociological writing takes the form of frank autobiography even though such efforts have come more into vogue in recent years.[14] Such writing is still thought by some to be narcissistic or egotistical, but it takes some such quality to want to become a professor or an actor or some other type of public figure. On the other hand, it is difficult to find a sociological work that is not somewhat autobiographical in the sense of being an intellectual "strip tease"; this is the case even when specific events may be omitted.

Perhaps one of the most intriguing and instructive autobiographical statements by a sociologist is Charles Horton Cooley's candid *Life and the Student*,[15] which his biographer observes "might just as well have

---

[14] An interesting exception is E. A. Ross, *Seventy Years of It: An Autobiography* (New York: Appleton-Century-Crofts, 1936). Biographical treatments have been more common; see Samuel Chugerman, *Lester F. Ward* (Durham, N.C.: Duke University Press, 1939); Joseph Dorfman, *Thorstein Veblen and His America* (New York: Viking Press, 1934); H. E. Starr, *William Graham Sumner* (New York: Holt, 1925); W. J. Goode *et al.*, "Introduction," in Goode *et al.*, eds., *Willard W. Waller* (Chicago: University of Chicago Press, 1970), pp. 1–110.

[15] C. H. Cooley, *Life and the Student* (New York: Alfred A. Knopf, 1927).

been *My Life as a Student,* for it was, in a sense, his autobiography." [16]
Other sensitive autobiographical accounts include William Foote Whyte's
appendix to his famous *Street Corner Society* [17] and some of the searching
essays in John Kosa's symposium, *The Home of the Learned Man.*[18]

WHAT SOCIOLOGY CAN GIVE
TO PEOPLE

In sketching here how sociology can magnify the individual, there
is no point in pursuing further the esoterica or the technicianism of the
field. The esoterica do give a select few a sense of personal grandeur
and the accreditation in a cult on which they choose to base a career.
It is also granted that technicianism may equip many other sociologists
for employment by social manipulators. Other chapters discuss further
such trivializations and abuses of sociology as a science of and for man.
Here our concerns are with sociology as awakener and stimulant and as
intellectual equipment with which the individual can more effectively
cope with life and living.

Sociology *can* give people an ever-refreshing sensitivity to all kinds
of other people, groups, and problems. It *can* help to make people feel
that action and change are possible and even desirable, preferable to
anxious and habitual attachment to a stability that cannot and does not
exist. It *can* destroy enfeebling respect for, and fear of, charismatic persons and statuses; it *can* replace them with more accurate assessments. It
can reveal human dimensions and limitations of the so-called social
system and of its legitimacy and orthodoxy, which when accepted uncritically, are so destructive of individual autonomy and effectiveness.

Sociology *can* show people how the control procedures of the family
and other social agencies tend to push most of us—not just blacks and
other minority-group members—toward accepting roles as Sambos, as
willing and dependent instruments for others. It *can* substitute an accurate conception for an unthinking or sentimental conception of social
controls. It *can* demonstrate how the control of power in our society depends more upon loyalty than upon competence, and that therein lies
the controllers' greatest vulnerability. It *can* spell out the insecurity and
frailty of any one controlling social power, whether in finance, politics,
religion, entertainment, or knowledge.

Sociology *can* point to the omnipresent morass of controllers of power

[16] E. C. Jandy, *Charles Horton Cooley: His Life and His Social Theory* (New
York: Dryden Press, 1942), p. 76.

[17] W. F. Whyte, "On the Evolution of *Street Corner Society,*" in *Street Corner
Society,* 2nd ed. (Chicago: University of Chicago Press, 1955), pp. 279–358.

[18] John Kosa, ed., *The Home of the Learned Man* (New Haven: College &
University Press, 1968).

behind any individual who appears to control power in our complex and multivalent society. It *can* detail how habituation and power fatigue eventually benumb those in influential statuses, how they eventually fail to represent the interests of the people they presume to serve. This applies not only to those who appear to control political power; all power— whatever its seeming form—derives from the conscious or unconscious consent of those controlled. That consent, regardless of how it is given, can be withdrawn in any of a myriad of ways.

Sociology and other social sciences *can* inform people accurately about how mass-communications agencies attempt to influence them. They *can* suggest ways to analyze, compare, and otherwise deal with such manipulative procedures. They *can* also clarify the nature of groups and institutions so that people can relate group and organizational interests more accurately to their own interests. In other words, these sciences *can* provide "consumers" with ready ways to analyze propaganda, agitation, and social organization.

Sociology *can* suggest the relative merits of being even a modest power crystallizer rather than a servant or courtier of a power wielder or power group. If the crystallization process does not become too important, and consequently too much of an end in itself, sociology *can* help people keep accurate perspectives on persons and events.

Sociology and other social sciences *can* tell people how to penetrate a mass-communications network, even for purposes contrary to those held by a given medium's nominal controllers. They *can* furnish data on how to cope with and even how to use voluntary organizations to launch acceptable social projects. "Acceptable projects" may be projects that might not otherwise be launched but that actually can serve popular interests and can gain popular support. In trying to use either media or organizations, people may or may not succeed, but available data *can* increase their chances of effectively influencing decision making. The chief dangers confronting would-be reformers are, on the one hand, temptations to be too plausible or even compromising, and thus to be co-opted when they should stick to substantial proposals for change, and on the other hand, to fight so hard for proposals as to be labeled "impossible" for being too polarized and polarizing. In some contexts the latter "danger" may be an advantage.

"GUTSY" VERSUS BLAND SOCIOLOGY

Why does sociology rarely offer these services to people? Why are they seldom found in sociology textbooks, except perhaps under heavy veneers of obscure terminology and unconvincing or irrelevant fact?

Briefly, the reason is that this is "gutsy" stuff. This is not superficial high-school "civics" or "sociology" or their direct college successors. This kind of sociology means stripping the disguises from social controls and manipulations and understanding how they work. It infinitely complicates the work of those who have won high administrative positions in our bureaucracies because it changes the whole "game." It requires new types of administrators, more democratic types.

The sociology advocated here demands that the primordial promise of democracy in education actually be implemented so that its promise for society can also be implemented. It means that people must be given a chance to become responsible citizens by again being treated, as they have been under some frontier and rural conditions, as though they are responsible and respected creatures. In other words, this kind of sociology would help to equip people to make our society what it can well be—an egalitarian, participant society.

Some sociologists try to achieve these effects both in their classrooms and in their books and articles. In our society, this constitutes a calculated professional risk as well as a basic ethical commitment.

"SOCIOLOGY" AS A SOCIAL PROBLEM

The sociology practiced by the majority of sociologists cannot accurately be described as a way to help people to understand and cope with society. Their sociology is a part of society's current problems; it is an instrument of a rigidifying control structure. Instead of being focused on the dynamic relations of individuals and groups to social process for the benefit of people, they are preoccupied with the maintenance of "social equilibrium" in its ramifications—in other words, with how to maintain the status quo. Instead of perceiving campus, black, and female agitations as evidence of healthy ferment in society, possibly evolving towards more egalitarian relations, they help fearful power wielders to find ways to smooth over, buy off, or even co-opt the leaders of such efforts. Thus the usual sociology course or text all too often *automatically* rationalizes *what is* and devotes little attention to the problems facing the individual, to the magnification of the individual, to what society *can become,* and to how to help change society.[19]

Exceptions to these strictures are more likely to be discovered in courses and texts dealing with such devastating problems as those of

---

[19] Gunnar Myrdal, *Value in Social Theory,* ed. by Paul Streeten (New York: Harper, 1958), Chap. 7; C. W. Mills, *Power, Politics and People,* ed. by I. L. Horowitz (New York: Oxford University Press, 1963), esp. Part 4.

environmental pollution, *white-collar* crime, poverty, propaganda *analysis*, and overpopulation. Even these subjects, however, are not at all uniformly "consumer-oriented." [20]

SOCIOLOGY'S DEBTS TO
LITERATURE

Please note the deplorable lack of relations so often evident between the self-consciously "scientific" social scientists of a university and the specialists in literature.[21] Few social scientists realize the riches in societal understanding available in literature. An artist's perceptions and portrayals can give participant observation a kind of ultimate glory.

Think of Niccolò Machiavelli's magnificent satire, *The Prince* (1513), and his highly perceptive *Discourses* (1521) and *History of Florence* (1532). They are unequaled in opening doors to man and society. Sociologists have much to learn from the incisive mind of François Marie Arouet de Voltaire as revealed in his *Letters Concerning the English Nation* (1732), his philosophical novels *Zadig* (1747) and *Candide* (1759), and his historical works, such as *The Age of Louis XIV* (1751) and *Essay on the Customs and Spirit of Nations* (1753–56).

For that matter, who has portrayed the interrelationships and dynamics of a city as deeply and accurately as Honoré de Balzac in his immortal *The Human Comedy* (1829–50), his penetrating portrait of Paris life in forty-seven volumes? Who has probed human pathology more intimately than Fëdor Mikhailovich Dostoevski in his *Poor Folk* (1846), *The Possessed* (1871), and *The Brothers Karamazov* (1880)? Who has portrayed the relations of man and society as memorably as Anatole France in the novels of his *Contemporary History* (1897–1900) and in such other novels as *The Crime of Sylvestre Bonnard* (1881)? Who has captured the spirit of America's Midwestern and Western frontier as well as Samuel Langhorne Clemens in such magnificent works as *The Adventures of Huckleberry Finn* (1885), *What Is Man?* (1906), *Letters from Earth* (1938, 1962), and his *Autobiography* (1917, 1924, 1959)?

How often I have wished that my students would ponder the social wisdom of these writers, and the list can, of course, go on and on. Think of the plays of Henrik Ibsen, George Bernard Shaw, and Sean O'Casey, and the novels of Charles Dickens, Sinclair Lewis, and John Steinbeck.

[20] Note the variety of orientations of articles published in *Social Problems* since 1953.

[21] F. W. Matson, *The Broken Image* (New York: George Braziller, 1964), pp. vii–ix, Chap. 7.

SENSITIVITY AND ACTION

Let us look again at some of the points we have already made in the light of these two questions: How can sociology give people an ever-refreshing sensitivity? and, How can it stimulate action, especially participation in constructive social action, by providing realistic models of actionists and action strategies? These are lessons based on sociology that cannot be learned very handily just through textbook or classroom work. They are more effectively learned by intimate participant observation.

SENSITIVITY THROUGH MARGINALITY. Increased social sensitivity regularly becomes a significant byproduct of any active involvement in social-scientific investigation, even on a modest scale. Social sensitivity can arise from intimate participant observation in groups quite different from our own. They can be groups that differ in class or ethnic context, or they can be deviant or criminal groups. In any case, these groups force us to think in the terms of a subculture different from our own in order to understand them. It is like learning to perceive people through another person's glasses. It gives us a sense of "culture shock," a disturbing but unfolding and enlightening experience.[22] It makes us, at least for a time, into "marginal" people.[23] In other words, we are shaken loose from the cultural setting in which we were raised. Thus we are shown quite vividly and in detail how other people think and feel, and how we have to think and feel if we are to comprehend accurately how *they* think and feel. It expands our ability to empathize with other people.

CULTURE SHOCK. One of my most disturbing but gratifying experiences of culture shock happened daily during a year's tenure in Italy. Even though I came from a marginal American social background and had very congenial colleagues, I had to cope with a very different cultural milieu. They all thought and spoke in Italian. They had been educated in a very different culture and university from that which I had experienced. Since none of my staff could speak English, not to mention American English, I discussed everything with them in Italian, dictated all my letters and memoranda in Italian, gave my lectures and conducted class discussions in Italian, and tried otherwise to function as a quasi-Italian. In consequence, at the end of a day, my head would be aching from my effort to function in a different culture. At the same time, I realized that

22 Whyte, *Street Corner Society*, esp. pp. 297–98. See also C. M. Arensberg and A. H. Niehoff, *Introducing Social Change* (Chicago: Aldine, 1964), esp. pp. 185–89, and P. K. Bock, ed., *Culture Shock* (New York: Alfred A. Knopf, 1970), esp. pp. ix–xii.
23 A. McC. Lee, *Multivalent Man* (New York: George Braziller, 1966), esp. Chap. 18.

the struggle added appreciably to my social awareness and knowledge, and thus to my ability to empathize with Italians. It resembled but was more vivid and inclusive than experiences I had had in the United States with criminals, mental deviants, and members of class and ethnic groups other than my own. When I lectured in Italy a few years later, I was pleased at the extent to which I could again "put on" my Italian set of spectacles and feel somewhat "at home" there.

Once we have accurately realized as well as we can what intergroup cultural differences really mean by having gone through one or more intergroup cultural barriers, through having suffered the travail of culture shock and thus of becoming somewhat marginal, we can appreciate how relatively similar human kind can be, even though so differentiated culturally. More than anything else, this adds depth and scope to sociological wisdom.

TO STIMULATE SOCIAL CHANGE

The other point concerning how sociology can magnify the individual that requires further illustration and interpretation has to do with stimuli to social action. Above all else, research having to do with human interrelationships and social structure should yield knowledge of what it is possible to do to make society more livable. When sociology provides realistic models of actionists and of social strategies that achieved desired results, it helps to give individuals a realistic sense of what they might actually accomplish. Let me illustrate this point with a summary of the work of the successful Italian sociologist-actionist, Danilo Dolci, and with a brief account of the activities of two American sociologists, Irving Goldaber and Holly G. Porter, in the development of intergroup understanding. The earthiness and effectiveness of both these examples make them serve our purposes. At the same time, they suggest only two of a great many possible ways in which the individual—magnified by sociological knowledge—can engage in constructive social action.

Now that both Gandhi and Martin Luther King, Jr., have become victims of violence, Dolci is today perhaps the outstanding exemplar of nonviolent methods for the achievement of social change. A northern Italian, Dolci as a young man turned from being trained as an architect to begin what he calls his real education—working at Nomadelfia in Italy. That Christian community "gathered together in a vast family boys and girls left homeless by the war [of 1939–1945]." There he says he had his "first opportunity to acquire knowledge through direct experience. Hoeing weeds, building latrines in the camps, living with orphans, former petty thieves, many of them sick," he learned "what it means to grow together;

after several months of common endeavor, even abysmally stupid faces became more human, and sometimes beautiful." He observes that he "became deeply aware that even as each man must take stock of himself and learn to live according to his convictions, so the life of the group, community life, is an indispensible instrument for stock-taking and for individual and collective maturation."

Dolci did not feel that he was doing enough to forward his concerns at Nomadelfia. It came to be too much just "a warm nest that tended to breed complacency," so far as he was concerned. In 1952, therefore, he set out for "the most wretched piece of country I had ever seen," [24] Trappeto, a fishing village in western Sicily.[25] Together with a deep humility, a rich background in the humanities and in social studies, and a drive to learn ever more, Dolci brought to this area's problems a wealth of practical know-how. As Aldous Huxley said of him, "He knows what specialists in other fields are talking about, respects their methods and is willing and eager to take advice from them." [26] Always working with only a small staff in a limited area, Dolci has succeeded in creating an experimental situation in which techniques of social change are developed and demonstrated. He is a practical social innovator who seeks to show how even the most deprived and exploited can improve their lot.

Dolci wanted to help western Sicilians to find ways to obtain more jobs, adequate irrigation, better health facilities, better opportunities for their young, and better living conditions. First, however, he had to perceive the area and its problems as intimately and as accurately as he could. This took painstaking observation, study, discussion, and analysis. He also had to gain the confidence of the highly suspicious and secretive people he sought to help. This took involvement—for him, even marriage. And then he had to stimulate volunteer organizations to plan and to implement whatever programs they might develop.

To do this investigatory and educational job, Dolci faced Mafiosi, ecclesiastical indifference and even opposition, and political-business venality on many levels, as well as the deep-set fear of experimentation of those who had been exploited for centuries. He sought joint or communal decision making. He wanted to stimulate the people's own natural leaders to come forth and function. He did not want to "sell" people "answers"

---

[24] Danilo Dolci, "Tools for a New World," *Saturday Review*, July 29, 1967, p. 13.

[25] See also Dolci's *Outlaws* (New York: Orion Press, 1961), *Waste* (New York: Monthly Review Press, 1963), *A New World in the Making* (New York: Monthly Review Press, 1965), and *The Man Who Plays Alone* (New York: Pantheon, 1969).

[26] Aldous Huxley, "Introduction," in Danilo Dolci, *Report From Palermo* (New York: Hillman/MacFadden, 1961), p. vii. For a more recent brief assessment by a sociologist, see J. L. Albini, *The American Mafia: Genesis of a Legend* (New York: Appleton-Century-Crofts, 1971), p. 109.

to their problems. As he hoped, "The struggle must be nonviolent—taking the form of active or passive strikes; refusal to cooperate on what is deemed to be harmful; protests and public demonstrations in all the many forms that may be suggested by the circumstances, one's own conscience, and the particular need." [27]

Thus Dolci is basically a well-informed clinical sociologist.[28] His chief emphasis is learning about society through carefully observing the consequences of efforts to change it. He believes in human potentialities, in understanding as precisely as he can those with whom he can work and what the problems are, and in encouraging people to organize, to inform themselves, and to take responsibility for social action. As he summarizes it, "People learn rapidly when they find it is to their advantage. . . . Already a good part in this area has had clear proof that when a large enough group works together with determination and a spirit of nonviolence, some very important things happen, such as getting a dam under way. And one democratic development follows another. For example, for the first time in their lives the workers on this dam are organized into a trade union. And for the first time the sharecroppers and landowners, both of whom stand to benefit from the dam, are getting together to make certain they will get their fair share of water; not, as in the past, the share that the Mafia would or would not let them have." [29]

As a researcher and resource person for the oppressed, and as a teacher and facilitator, Dolci offers no miracles. "Such struggle carries penalties with it, and the people must know it. Those who want things to remain as they are, to preserve the present 'order,' will try to put out of the running anyone who promotes change. . . . It is naïve to be surprised or shocked by it. Instead, responsible men must diligently look for those methods and strategies which can be used by the weak to bring about the triumph of reason, i.e., effective alternatives to violence." [30]

Dolci thus counteracts traditional exploitation, brutality, and callousness, with cleverness, with facts, with a variety of methods and guises for social pressure locally, regionally, nationally, and even internationally, and with dogged persistence and abiding faith in common people. He constantly helps western Sicilians to find appropriate nonviolent social-action levers and the strategic times and places for using such levers to force change. These methods have included, in addition to fact-finding, fasting, organization of cooperatives and unions, lobbying, a "strike in reverse" (building a needed road in defiance of the authorities), the occu-

---

[27] Dolci in "Tools for a New World," p. 15.
[28] Lee, *Multivalent Man,* Chaps. 21, 22.
[29] Quoted by Jerre Mangione, *The World Around Danilo Dolci,* new ed. (New York: Harper & Row, 1972), p. 79.
[30] Dolci, "Tools for a New World," p. 15.

pation of a public plaza, demonstrations, long marches, stimulating support groups throughout Italy and in many other countries, and constant publicity through conferences, speeches, clandestine and regular radio programs, books, and items in magazines and newspapers. He says that "the struggle must be carried on, peaceably but energetically, until common sense and the sense of responsibility have won the day." [31]

That winning of the day is in a very long-term sense. In any short-term view, Dolci knows very well that winning the day is not victory. The only sense in which he or any other cleareyed clinical sociologist can see "victory" for a humane effort is in having maintained movement toward needed adjustments. As Dolci phrases it, "There are difficult moments, and one feels overwhelmed. But it's senseless to speak of optimism or pessimism. The only important thing is to know that if one works well in a potato field, the potatoes will grow. If one works well among men, they will grow. That's reality. The rest is smoke. It's important to understand that words don't move mountains. Work, exacting work, moves mountains." [32] It is thus that Dolci's western Sicilians have been getting some roads, sanitary facilities, democratic cooperatives of agriculturalists, vintners, and artisans, democratic trade unions, the Iato dam, voices in self-government, and much more—a realistic sense of growth and accomplishment.

Dolci's academically trained sociological associates, sent to him by various European and American universities, have systematically studied many aspects of western Sicily—Mafia murders, underemployment, living standards, educational procedures and needs, and agricultural arrangements. These studies have been helpful, but the accumulating knowledge of social strategies and their consequences—in other words, of clinical sociology—is the greatest local and exportable contribution of all these efforts. Dolci's talks on his clinical findings have inspired university students in many parts of the world. Those who have worked with him at his Center for Study and Action in Partinico are forever impressed by the accomplishments and ideas of the "practical visionary" who inspires and guides it.[33]

DOLCI AS PROTOTYPE. This example is not meant to suggest that young men and women who study sociology necessarily have to try to approximate Dolci's spectacular performance. There are many ways in which

[31] *Ibid.*
[32] Quoted in Israel Shenker, "A Pacifist Revolt Is Urged by Dolci," *New York Times,* October 11, 1970.
[33] See also Dolci's *Poverty in Sicily* (London: Penguin Books, 1966), *For the Young* (London: MacGibbon & Kee, 1967), *Inventare il Futuro, Il Limone Lunare,* and *Non Sentite l'Odore del Fumo?* (Bari, Italy: Laterza, 1968, 1970, 1971). Friends of Danilo Dolci, Inc., 100 Hemlock Road, Short Hills, N.J. 07078, publishes a *Newsletter* on Dolci's current activities.

sociology can magnify the social effectiveness of students, and through them, that of others. That Dolci is accomplishing so much among "gli ultimi" (the last) suggests how much more others can do with less heroic measures among people whose problems are not so entrenched and so desperate. As a prototype, he has encouraged many to learn and to face their local social realities, to find levers with which to facilitate change, and thus to contribute to human welfare. After reading and discussing books by and about Dolci, students often say how wonderful it would be to get a great many more people to function like Dolci in all sorts of ghettos and suburbs and other places with problems. How can they help more people to grow, to learn to understand, and to try to cope with their own problems? Such questions can lead to rewarding and important careers.

CLINICAL SOCIOLOGISTS IN
AMERICAN CONFLICTS

Our second example deals with the work of Holly G. Porter and Irving Goldaber. It demonstrates in the more complex American setting what the sociologically trained can do at the very focal points of crucial social tensions—in this case, interracial tensions. It is another illustration of a nondirective social therapy that democratically fosters social change.

Let us first look briefly at the interracial setting and then at techniques with which these sociologists facilitate nonviolent change.

INTERRACIAL STRUGGLES. Interracial violence constantly scars our social history.[34] When European colonists learned that they could not profitably enslave Amerindians, they set about exterminating them or driving them off the more desirable lands.[35] Racist rationalizations for such behavior reached their pinnacle in the common white saying that the only good Indian is a dead Indian.[36]

---

[34] Richard Hofstadter and Michael Wallace, eds., *American Violence: A Documentary History* (New York: Alfred A. Knopf, 1970); reviewed by A. McC. Lee in *Fellowship*, XXXVII, no. 3 (March 1971), pp. 21–22; Hannah Arendt *et al.*, "Is America by Nature a Violent Society?" *New York Times Magazine*, April 28, 1968, pp. 24–25, 111–14.

[35] John Collier, *The Indians of the Americas* (1947; New York: New American Library, 1959); Helen H. Jackson, *A Century of Dishonor*, ed. by A. F. Rolfe (New York: Harper & Row, 1965); Stan Steiner, *The New Indians* (New York: Dell Publishing Co., 1968); Alvin Josephy, *The Indian Heritage in America* (New York: Alfred A. Knopf, 1969); W. E. Washburn, ed., *The Indian and the White Man* (New York: Doubleday, Anchor Books, 1964).

[36] General P. H. Sheridan put it, "The only good Indians I ever saw were dead," in a remark at Fort Cobb, Indian Territory, in January 1869. Quoted in Dee Brown, *Bury My Heart at Wounded Knee* (New York: Holt, Rinehart & Winston,

Southern white folklore to the contrary notwithstanding, African blacks never did accept slavery or remain in it willingly. Revolts began in the slave-accumulation compounds of West Africa and continued across the Atlantic.[37] Black-white struggles have since gone through at least six significant phases: (1) the two hundred slave conspiracies and revolts prior to 1861,[38] (2) black cooperation with the Union armies in the Civil War, the "greatest and most successful slave revolt—a sort of general strike against slavery,"[39] (3) white repressive violence during the prolonged race riot of the so-called Reconstruction that took at least five thousand black lives,[40] (4) following Reconstruction, white lynchings of another five thousand and killings of uncounted others in terrorist raids on Negro areas,[41] (5) from the 1890s the development of a clearer two-sidedness in interracial clashes,[42] and (6) especially in the 1960s and 1970s, widespread disorders that represented black revolts against white oppression.[43] American whites have yet to permit Negroes to work openly, effectively, and without interference toward equal status. It must be added that what is needed is a great deal more than mere permission. What is needed is substantial aid, freely contributed as reparation for three and one-half centuries of degrading exploitation.

EFFORTS TO COPE WITH INTERRACIAL VIOLENCE. In response to the widespread interracial violence of the 1960s and 1970s that included Spanish-Americans as well as blacks and "majority" whites, city, state, and federal authorities have usually followed physical repression with recourse

---

1971), p. 170. See also T. F. Gossett, *Race: The History of an Idea in America* (Dallas: Southern Methodist University Press, 1963), p. 228; R. A. Billington, with J. B. Hedges, *Westward Expansion* (New York: Macmillan Co., 1949), p. 46; Louis Ruchames, *Racial Thought in America* (Amherst: University of Massachusetts Press, 1968).

[37] M. J. Herskovits, "Ancestry of the American Negro," *Opportunity*, January 1939, p. 30.

[38] Herbert Aptheker, *American Negro Slave Revolts*, 2nd ed. (New York: International Publishers, 1963), esp. Chaps. 6–14.

[39] M. R. Davie, *Negroes in American Society* (New York: McGraw-Hill Book Co., 1949), p. 45.

[40] *Ibid.*, p. 54.

[41] J. E. Cutler, *Lynch-Law* (New York: Longmans, Green & Co., 1905); A. F. Raper, *The Tragedy of Lynching* (Chapel Hill: University of North Carolina Press, 1933); Gunnar Myrdal *et al.*, *An American Dilemma* (New York: Harper & Bros., 1944), Chap. 27.

[42] Stanley Lieberson and A. R. Silverman, "The Precipitants and Underlying Conditions of Race Riots," *American Sociological Review*, XXX (1965), pp. 887–98; E. M. Rudwick, *Race Riot at East St. Louis July 2, 1917* (Carbondale: Southern Illinois University Press, 1964); Chicago Commission on Race Relations, *The Negro in Chicago* (Chicago: University of Chicago Press, 1922).

[43] A. D. Grimshaw, ed., *Racial Violence in the United States* (Chicago: Aldine Publishing Co., 1969), esp. Chap. 12; A. McC. Lee, "Race Riots Are Symptoms," in Lee and N. D. Humphrey, *Race Riot (Detroit, 1943)*, 2nd ed. (New York: Octagon Books, 1968), pp. vii–xxviii.

to the old political device of appointing a prestigious study commission. At best, the suppression of violence may buy time in which change can take place. Unfortunately, study commissions often fill that time with great promise but provide little more than a forum for public debate; they stimulate and publicize investigations that may have little more than academic use, and they write reports that are too quickly filed and forgotten.[44] Such stalling may solve no problems other than the personal ones of the politician who appoints the commission's members and thus contributes to his own political survival. From long experience and from schooling in political folklore, he is well aware that time's passing can often blunt issues or see them lost in some new crisis or turn of events.[45]

Any effective dynamic for change comes from outside "establishment" circles, chiefly by way of the deprived people themselves. Sociologists as sociologists can serve chiefly as resource persons and as facilitators. At best, they can furnish data to nondirective social therapists working democratically for social change. Above all, sociologists can help members of competing or conflicting groups perceive each other as persons. They can do this in such a way as to make the problems of competitors or antagonists, and their social context, vividly clear. Such clarification helps to relate thinking and planning for change to real people and real organizations rather than—as is too often the case—to stereotypes or caricatures.

In the 1960s and 1970s American social scientists helped to clarify and facilitate the resolution of tension in three significant ways. All were described as efforts to convert impact of interracial violence into gains toward an egalitarian society. They centered on (1) negotiation media and procedures,[46] (2) the improvement of pressure strategies for the deprived,[47] and (3) opening two-way paths to intergroup empathy through carefully organized confrontations. All such efforts benefited from the wealth of research monographs and papers developed at the same time. All sought to apply social-scientific insights to this crucial area and

[44] Anthony Platt, "Introduction," in Platt, ed., *The Politics of Riot Commissioners: 1917–1970* (New York: Macmillan Co., 1971), pp. 45–46. See also Lee and Humphrey, *Race Riot*, Chap. 10.

[45] A. McC. Lee, *How to Understand Propaganda* (New York: Rinehart & Co., 1952), Chap. 8, esp. pp. 217–19.

[46] As examples, the Racial Negotiations Project, funded by the Ford Foundation through the Institute of Labor and Industrial Relations at the University of Michigan and Wayne State University, and The National Center for Disputes Settlement of the American Arbitration Association.

[47] Such has been the most important thrust of MARC, the Metropolitan Applied Research Center, New York, N.Y., founded and headed by social psychologist Kenneth B. Clark whose research played a significant role in the 1954 U.S. Supreme Court desegregation decisions (Brown *et al. vs.* Board of Education of Topeka and related cases).

to areas related to it, but here we shall treat only the third. The first two involve technicalities and other complexities not germane to our discussion at this point.[48]

Many names are given to procedures that stimulate two-way paths toward intergroup empathy among members of disparate groups and then reap social benefits from such empathy. The "quiet" or "unstructured" meeting of the Religious Society of Friends (Quakers) is often cited as a tested and durable folk model for such activity.[49] Scientific terms include "tension reduction" through "intergroup problem solving," [50] through a "group conversation method," [51] and through "Laboratory Confrontation."

"LABORATORY CONFRONTATION." The Goldaber-Porter program, organized as the nonprofit Community Confrontation & Communication Associates (CCCA) of Grand Rapids, Michigan, adopted the latter term and method. Mrs. Porter is a serene and comely mother of four, the WASP wife of a successful WASP manufacturer. Goldaber, a sociology professor at Brooklyn College of The City University of New York, skilfully combines classroom theory with street lore learned as a poor Jewish boy growing up in Brooklyn's crowded Brownsville section and as a long-time executive of New York City's Commission on Human Relations. Concerning urban turmoil, they share the belief that antagonized factions really prefer talk to warfare and that conditions, attitudes, and behavior can be changed through dialogue.

As Mrs. Porter describes it, their technique of conflict abatement or conflict transformation was "originally designed to create a productive working relationship between a given community's black ghetto residents and police personnel—long-time adversaries but increasingly victims of similar society neglect." In that, and then in other types of community adversary relationships, "Laboratory Confrontation" became a means of nondirective group therapy and community decision making that "did the impossible: It dealt in the formerly dealt out. It designated as special resource to the community those individuals thought to be most deeply alienated from the general welfare and most destructive. And it gave responsibility for roles in future community direction to individuals who

---

[48] For discussion bearing on negotiation and pressure strategies, see Chaps. 6–8.

[49] Stuart Chase, with Marian T. Chase, *Roads to Agreement* (New York: Harper & Bros., 1951), Chap. 6, "Quaker Meeting"; R. L. Howe, *The Miracle of Dialogue* (New York: Seabury Press, 1963); John Sykes, *The Quakers* (Philadelphia: J. B. Lippincott Co., 1959).

[50] Usually subsumed under "group problem solving." See H. H. Kelley and J. W. Thibaut, "Group Problem Solving," in Gardner Lindzey and Elliot Aronson, eds., *The Handbook of Social Psychology*, 2nd ed. (Reading, Mass.: Addison-Wesley Publishing Co., 1969), IV, Chap. 29.

[51] Rachel D. DuBois and Mew-Soong Li, *Reducing Social Tension and Conflict Through the Group Conversation Method* (New York: Association Press, 1971).

formerly had had little or no say and no basic information about why things were as they were." [52]

PLANNING AND ORGANIZING. How does the "Laboratory Confrontation" program of CCCA work? In each case, a "facilitator team" spends considerable time on advance planning and arranging with appropriate local sponsors and with leaders of adversary groups. These CCCA facilitators try to assure themselves that participants will be leaders representative of, and chosen by, the significant adversary groups in the tension situation, "groups who find it difficult to work with one another although they are in some way mutually dependent upon each other." This planning and organizing stage is crucial to the effectiveness of the whole program. The group-selected leaders—for each confrontation project usually a total of six to ten from each of the adversaries—must be ready to resort to an egalitarian confrontation.

EYEBALL-TO-EYEBALL CONFRONTATION. Then comes the most dramatic phase, "a closed-door, issue-oriented, eyeball-to-eyeball group dialogue . . . conducted in a neutral setting over a three- to five-day period." For this actual "Laboratory Confrontation," there has been advance agreement on the following simple "ground rules":

Anything is on the agenda; nothing is taboo.
Everyone participates and one-at-a-time.
Facilitators will not be involved in content-input.
Facilitators' process direction will be followed at all times.
There shall be no weapons in the laboratory.

Only those who witness or participate at length in such a confrontation can appreciate the skills and knowledge of human relations such ground rules require of facilitators. This is equally the case of all other phases of this nondirective social therapy.

At the outset of each confrontation, homogeneous groups of participants are asked to segregate themselves and to write the agenda for discussion in the form of their own specific grievances. In consequence, "the hostilities of members are expressed. Specific complaints are identified, explanations are offered, communication skills are developed, trust is built up, and, as feelings are altered, forces are joined to formulate common objectives and to prepare a scheme for implementation." [53]

[52] Holly G. Porter, "Laboratory Confrontation: A Viable Alternative to Political Violence," MS. presentation (Grand Rapids, Mich.: Community Confrontation & Communication Associates, October–November 1971), pp. 3–4.
[53] *Ibid.*, pp. 23–24. See also Donald Bouma, *Kids & Cops: A Study in Mutual Hostility* (Grand Rapids, Mich.: W. B. Eerdmans Publishing Co., 1969), esp. pp. 149–57.

"Laboratory Confrontation" is something different from the much-discussed "sensitivity training" and "T-grouping." [54] The latter attempt to modify individual personality in more basic and rather comprehensive ways. On the contrary, "Laboratory Confrontation" focuses practically upon "issues and problems affecting the relationships between groups of people." It seeks to modify such behavior "in mutually desirable ways." It provides "reinforcement for continuing that modification and benefiting from it by means of community-organized follow-through." [55] As Goldaber concludes, "Most of their grievances are based on mistrust and misinformation." [56]

Goldaber and Porter thus provide "a setting of minimal threat in which the participants move from positions of polarized antagonism to collaboration through a process which encourages 'gut level' ventilation of hostilities." [57] They admit that they have only "imprecise methods of identifying 'destroyers' " (disrupters, irreconcilable persons) who might be included in a confrontation and that the "tolerance level of the process is unknown." After many confrontations in many cities, however, they report that "somebody from the group always saves it from destruction." [58]

THE ASBURY PARK EXAMPLE. Porter and Goldaber do not pretend that one "Laboratory Confrontation" of twelve to twenty people during three to five days will permanently alter the course of an organization's or of a community's intergroup relations. Working from October 1970 through the summer of 1971 to cool the very tense interracial situation in the mile-square seaside resort of Asbury Park, New Jersey, they arranged repeated confrontations that eventually involved a large number of "individuals known to be 'opinion leaders' in the various factions represented in the city . . . people known to be critical of the 'status quo' and of the activities of other groups." [59]

Asbury Park had had disastrous rioting in July 1970 in which 180 persons were injured, 167 were arrested, and $4 million were lost in property destruction. The once-thriving vacation spot was in trouble. No one wanted to be city manager. The Chamber of Commerce had col-

54 L. P. Bradford et al., T-Group Theory and Laboratory Method: Innovation in Re-Education (New York: John Wiley & Sons, 1964); A. J. Marrow et al., Management by Participation (New York: Harper & Row, 1967); E. H. Schein and W. G. Bennis, eds., Personal and Organizational Change Through Group Methods (New York: John Wiley & Sons, 1965).

55 Porter, "Laboratory Confrontation," pp. 23–24.

56 Don Maley, "Photographers Urged to Shoot In-Depth Conflict Pictures," Editor & Publisher, July 26, 1969, p. 17.

57 Irving Goldaber and H. G. Porter, Notes on "Laboratory Confrontation" (Grand Rapids, Mich.: Community Confrontation & Communication Associates, n.d.), p. 2.

58 Porter, "Laboratory Confrontation," p. 32.

59 Ibid., p. 34.

lapsed. Businessmen commuted to homes outside Asbury Park. Whites were dismayed by rising taxes, muggings, and robberies. Blacks could find few year-round jobs and had to contend with high slum rents and omnipresent drug dealers and junkies. "Twenty-nine percent of the city lived on welfare. Racial antipathies were fast acquiring the face of hatred, particularly between the blacks and the hard-pressed, clannish Italians, the largest white ethnic bloc." [60] Rumors had it that on July 4, 1971, there would be another riot, one even more devastating than before.

The 1971 riot did not take place. As repeated "Laboratory Confrontations" involved more and more leaders of all types, ripples of consequences spread through the city. The Chamber of Commerce arose from the dead and developed a program to help the whole city, blacks as well as whites. The City Council yielded to joint black-white pressures and obtained state support for additional "Laboratory Confrontations." In the ten additional sessions, policemen confronted black and white teen-agers, senior citizens, businessmen, and street-wise ghetto dwellers who labeled themselves Brothers of the Mud Hole. Summer jobs were found for needy teen-agers. "Local planning stimulated a Model Cities grant, including funds for a swimming pool in the black area and a youth-development program." [61] Many other details might be given, but most convincing to the community was the favorable comparison of 1971 with 1969 figures for crime rates, for business levels of downtown merchants and beachfront concessionaires, and for applications for employment as police officers from both blacks and whites.[62] Full credit for all such developments can scarcely be given to the "Laboratory Confrontation" series, but it is accepted in the community as having had a key role in redirecting community energies.

WHO CO-OPTS WHOM?

Some critics belittle the Porter-Goldaber method, as they do the Dolci method. They say it is a way of co-opting the exploited, that it makes the oppressed come to believe that the "going system" works, that it buys them off with tokens. Such critics are people who look upon current society as a fixed configuration that only a violent revolution can modify. They do not perceive how that apparently fixed configuration changes. They do not understand how much more sweeping and construc-

---

[60] Fletcher Knebel, "A Cop Named Joe," *Look*, July 27, 1971, p. 15.
[61] *Ibid.*, p. 19.
[62] Data compiled by Irving Goldaber. See also Norman Sinclair, "Bridges to Understanding," *Engage* (United Methodist Church), May 15, 1969, and J. P. Adams, "A Confrontation That Wasn't," *Engage*, July 15, 1969.

tive are the gains that can be achieved by nonviolent aggression rather than by violence.

The powerful enter into a confrontation arrangement because they have learned that the less powerful groups are far from powerless. The "underdogs" enter into such talks as a possibly useful recourse. Both sides know that they can reserve their other strategies to use in case "Laboratory Confrontation" breaks down.

MUCH MORE THAN JUST "INTERESTING"

These examples suggest something of the range of social actions for which individuals can be responsible. They both illustrate how precise knowledge of social dynamics and methods of exploiting social leverages can facilitate social change nonviolently. Quite appropriately, both stress the significance in their efforts of helping people to grow. Both suggest specific ways in which sociology can help magnify the effectiveness of the individual through nondirective social therapy. Far less spectacular ways, but nonetheless workable ones, are available to all in everyday life—at school, at work, in voluntary organizations, at home.

Sociology is thus much more than just another "interesting" subject in the curricula of liberal arts and sciences colleges. With it, the ancient David could have achieved far more than he did with his fabled slingshot. It is a powerful and nonviolent weapon with which the Davids of the twentieth century can successfully cope with many of our society's Goliaths.

CHAPTER 3

Social "Therapy"
Versus
the Search for Knowledge

Absorbing into our education and popular culture more of the spirit of curious observation, free inquiry, and critical theorizing called science will continue to be a longtime process. This is partly because the miraculous and even awesome products of scientists so often obscure the scientific spirit.

THE RETAILERS AND RETELLERS

In the case of social science, the process of absorption is even more impeded and complicated because the most prestigious bearers of the label "social scientist" in popular thinking often are actually not scientists at all. They are those who devote themselves to being retailers, or retellers, of "scientific findings." In doing so, they find themselves impelled to play to their audiences. Thus, many times they offer social nostrums rather than interpretations of social-scientific findings. They try to dramatize their nostrums as being comparable to those of other "healing arts." These "therapists" are called sociologists or clinical sociologists or applied sociologists, and they counsel individuals, groups, and organizations personally or through their speeches and publications.

PREOCCUPATIONS OF "THERAPISTS." Social "therapists" may wish to use scientific knowledge to the greatest extent possible. When they find they need "answers" that scientists have not furnished, however, they quite often fail to limit themselves to scientific findings. Thus their "diagnoses" often depend upon both the scientific findings and their own educated guesses in unspecified proportions.

In other words, when functioning as therapists, these specialists do not have the concerns of scientists. They are preoccupied with serving their clients or audiences and with relating themselves therapeutically to those clients' or audiences' problems. As the sociologist Alvin W. Gouldner notes, "The experience of other applied disciplines also suggests, unfortunately, that the utilization of their findings is by no means entirely dependent upon their validity." [1] A most pressing criterion is whether or not a given procedure is likely to work in a specific case. At best, practitioners may be learned in the findings of scientists (to which they themselves as scientists may previously have contributed), but they assimilate such knowledge and then as therapists use it to authenticate their artful procedures and guidance.[2]

CONTRASTING STATEMENTS

Perhaps two parallel columns will suggest the chasm that may separate the statements found useful by social engineers and therapists from those made for the sole purpose of communicating as accurate a conception of a situation as possible. The first column below contains a selection from what many would-be social engineers or therapists now look upon as our society's chamber of horrors. The second column offers comments of a quite different sort, even though they deal with the same situations. The second series are statements made to reflect available evidence as accurately as possible.

The "horrors" cited in the first column are discussed at some length in the rest of this chapter. They are frightening assertions attached in the mass media to social developments. They are scare expressions popular today among social practitioners, popular writers, and their publics. They are tag-lines that such persons seize upon in their efforts to achieve quick importance, to gain reputations as elegant exemplars of fashionable intellectual magic available for social manipulation, and to win approval from

---

[1] A. W. Gouldner, "Explorations in Applied Social Science," in Gouldner and S. M. Miller, eds., *Applied Sociology* (New York: Free Press, 1965), p. 15.

[2] This characterization of the "therapy-minded" does not gainsay the fact that the "clinical study" of social events has yielded our greatest sociological insights. The difference lies in the highly significant matters of motivation and emphasis. The sociologist participating in "clinical study" is concerned with scientific investigation and assessment. He does not permit desire to serve a client to warp his findings or his judgment. See A. McC. Lee, *Multivalent Man* (New York: George Braziller, 1966), Chap. 22.

the magnificent ones, the wielders of social controls over the businesses, agencies, and foundations that subsidize much of so-called scientific social research and therapy.

The statements in the second column are in a more human and humane dimension. They are efforts at accuracy in a humanist and existential tradition, at its best a tradition unabashed by the magnificence of the powerful, uninfected by the elegance of prestige-seekers, and discouraging to the purposes of panacea-peddlers. It is a tradition concerned with searching for accurate understanding useful to people, rather than with the sensationalization of problems and with claims of having created pat solutions for them.

Social "therapists" diagnose our problems thus:	*Relevant scientific research*[3] *can be summarized thus:*
Modern man is alienated and alone.	Man is increasingly autonomous, perceptive, and sensitive to his own needs, desires, and relationships. No longer faced in this country with a primitive struggle for existence, a great many are learning that their fate is social, linked with the fate of others.
Man's privacy is nearly at an end.	In spite of prying investigators, in many areas of life man is winning his longtime struggle for greater privacy.
Man's excessive leisure time is a menace to himself and to society.	Man has no more leisure time (and probably less) than his forebears, but he finds his privatized way of life absorbing and rewarding.
Mass culture is degrading humanity.	The best literature and other forms of art now have the largest active market in the history of the world, judged by any criterion. Those participating in the creation of art works constantly increase in quality and in numbers.
The mass media are twisting people's minds, wasting their time, and making them stooges of clever, unseen elites.	In spite of the increasing sophistication of those who control or gain access to the mass media and who attempt to control minds through the media, people appear to be more able to resist such efforts in our country now than in the past.

[3] Each of these points is discussed at greater length later in the chapter and supporting evidence is suggested or outlined.

Social "therapists" diagnose our problems thus:	Relevant scientific research can be summarized thus:
Our country will shortly consist chiefly of three vast seas of homes and businesses—Boswash (stretching from Boston to Washington), Chipitts (Chicago to Pittsburgh), and Sansan (San Francisco to San Diego)—that won't be worth living in.	Ecological projections toward Boswash, Chipitts, and Sansan neglect (1) our depressing birth rate, yielding to the pill, the IUD, and status-striving, and (2) the current potentialities of travel and communication. Our businesses and homes may well diffuse over a much greater area with a gain rather than a loss in efficiency and in other human benefits.
The American family today is a "massive failure," to use an expression of the anthropologist Margaret Mead.[4]	Evidence of family failure today should be compared with evidence from the past. Considered sociohistorically, the American family today is an amazing success, relatively stable, and quite productive.
Our people's drugged children on wheels have gotten entirely out of hand. The hippie generation threatens civilization.	There are drugged children on wheels, but they are statistically few, albeit stressed by the mass media. In spite of such exceptions, our youth are quite mature, probably the most mature of any generation since those who crossed (at various times) the Atlantic frontier.
"Knowledge" has gone hog-wild in an information explosion. Only data retrieval machines and their specialist-servants can make it possible for us to cope with that explosion.	The information explosion consists chiefly of stacks of technical reports presumed to be useful in modern society. Wisdom is hard won in any generation by the educated individual. Those who are not overawed by the servants of the data-retrieval systems can acquire at least as much useful knowledge today as ever. If need be, it is not too difficult to learn how to manipulate such systems, rather than be manipulated by them.
After the assassination of Robert F. Kennedy, the historian Arthur M. Schlesinger, Jr., asserted that Americans "are today the most frightening people on this planet." He claimed that we are a "violent people with a violent	Our society also produced those who were assassinated and many world heroes of peace and human striving. Our peaceful heroes are much more the authentic product of our society than are the twisted mentalities who

[4] Margaret Mead, "The Life Cycle and Its Variations: The Division of Roles," *Daedalus*, XCVI (1967), 871.

Social "therapists" diagnose our problems thus:	Relevant scientific research can be summarized thus:
history, and the instinct [sic] for violence has seeped into the bloodstream of our national life." [5]	stilled the voices of some of our leaders.

Racism, exploitative status differentials between men and women and among so many other social categories and groups, our obsolescent educational establishments, the Undeclared Indochinese War, the hideous brutalities attributed to our soldiers, and the wanton pollution of our environment—all these could be on both lists. They would be in a different focus on each list.

WHY THE CONTRASTS? Why do the two columns differ so dramatically? Both are products of people of good will, but the people have contrasting motivations and goals. The first column, the currently popularized chamber of "horrors," consists of excerpts from the sales pitches of social practitioners preoccupied with the merchandising of techniques or procedures or "answers." The second column consists simply of efforts to state understandings of what is happening to man in modern United States. The following illustrates this difference through a discussion in more detail of the contrasts listed.

"ALIENATION"

Start with the matter of "alienation," the first idea listed above. As used today, "alienation" appears to vary in meaning from "disenchantment" to "disinvolvement" to "isolation." Traditionally, and especially in legal usage, it was employed to refer to estrangement of an owner from his possession of real or other property. It also took on the sense of a person becoming separated from his reason, thus "insane." In a law court, a psychiatrist may still be called an "alienist."

ACCORDING TO HEGEL AND MARX. Many subsequent writers have accepted and toyed with "alienation" in the sense that Karl Marx selected from the writings of G. F. W. Hegel.[6] Concerned as he was with therapeutic leverages with which to motivate men to solve their social prob-

---

[5] Quoted by David Burnham, "Schlesinger Calls Violence a U.S. Trait," *New York Times,* June 6, 1968.

[6] G. F. W. Hegel, *The Phenomenology of Mind,* trans. by J. B. Baillie, 2nd ed., rev. (1807; New York: Macmillan, 1955). See also Paul Vinogradoff, *Outline of Historical Jurisprudence* (New York: Oxford University Press, 1920), I, 232–369; Kenneth Burke, *Attitudes Toward History,* 2nd ed. (New York: Hermes, 1959), pp. 216–20.

lems, Marx concluded in one of his earlier writings: "The *alienation* of the worker in his product means not only that his labour becomes an object, assumes an *external* existence, but that it exists independently, *outside himself*, and alien to him, but that it stands opposed to him as an autonomous power. The life which he has given to the object sets itself against him as an alien and hostile force."[7] A comment on this by one of Marx's translator-editors bears out the contention being made here. In his later writings, notes sociologist T. B. Bottomore, Marx did not use "alienation" because "his confidence in the possibility of making industrial work inherently interesting and satisfying had diminished."[8] For Marx, "alienation" had lost its promise of manipulative utility.

THE CURRENT VOGUE OF "ALIENATION." As with other fashionably controversial catchwords in social discussions, "alienation" during its current vogue sprouted a variety of meanings. None of them is too precise, but each appears to many to explain a great deal. These meanings are of two types. One includes the more psychological elaborations and projections of Marx's worker alienated from his labor and product. The other stresses social structure, the estrangement of society from its members. Whether or not these two types are different is mostly a matter of emphasis; they are two verbalizations of one conception that is inadequate for sociological purposes. Let us look at each of them in more detail.

The first type is popular among those who use sociological formulas in therapy for patients or in social action through mass communications. Marx's writings on this view of "alienation," as the sociologist Daniel Bell sees them, include two possible "readings." One is the "contemporary psychological meaning of feeling estranged from the world," and the other had "a philosophical, Aristotelian sense, . . . a departure from what men would ideally be in the historical future."[9] Mixing the two, the psychoanalyst Erich Fromm's description of individual alienation became

[7] Karl Marx, "Economic and Philosophical Manuscripts" (1844), in *Early Writings*, trans. and ed. by T. B. Bottomore (London: C. A. Watts, 1963), pp. 122–23.

[8] Bottomore, "Introduction," *ibid.*, p. ix. See also Simon Marcson, "Introduction," in Marcson, ed., *Automation, Alienation, and Anomie* (New York: Harper & Row, 1970), pp. 1–9. "Automation has reached its epitome of expression in the automobile industry, and the automobile employee should have been in the Marxist sense the best example of alienation. . . . Instead, the automobile worker has become the most devoted member of our society to the benefits of leisure and to the consumption of goods and services in an environment which certainly cannot be described as one of anomie." (p. 2).

[9] Daniel Bell, *The End of Ideology*, rev. ed. (New York: Collier, 1961), p. 360, note with attribution to Morris Watnick. See also W. A. Faunce, *Problems of an Industrial Society* (New York: McGraw-Hill, 1968), pp. 100–115; Melvin Seeman, "On the Meaning of Alienation," *American Sociological Review*, XXIV (1959), 783–91.

popular among sociologists: "Alienation as we find it in modern society," he asserts, "is almost total; it pervades the relationship of man to his work, to the things he consumes, to the state, to his fellow men, and to himself. Man has created a world of man-made things as it never existed before. . . . The more powerful and gigantic the forces are which he unleashes, the more powerless he feels himself as a human being." [10]

ONE PERSPECTIVE ON "ALIENATION"—MAN CUT OFF. The sociologist Robert A. Nisbet recounts how this idea came to the point of our first column's first claim. He states that in nineteenth-century sociological writings, those who held the first of the two perspectives on alienation came to view "modern man as uprooted, alone, without secure status, cut off from community or any system of clear moral purpose. Estrangement is sovereign: estrangement from others, from work, from place, and even from self." [11] This, it needs to be added, has much in common with the ancient and usual legal-psychiatric or alienist definition of "mental alienation" as "insanity" or mental illness. It was derived from the even more ancient conception of "alienation" as separation from title to a piece of property. Thus, the idea need not stem from an Hegelian or Marxian root.

Note that in the various versions of "alienation," the conception refers merely to separation—from property, from sanity, from identity with a group or with society. It does not refer to a process of change or a passage from something to something else. It neglects the fact that aloneness or disinvolvement or even a sense of being rejected can be a challenge to seek new human relationships or means of expression. Above all, it fails to recognize the processual character of personality and of interpersonal relationships. [12]

What are the implications of the sweeping definitions and allegations of the above formulators? These writers apparently do not try to understand us in relation to our historical background or in the light of the human possibilities suggested by cross-cultural comparisons. On the contrary, they stress our powerlessness and confusion as a basis for telling us how sorely we need their magic-working guidance. If we will accept their

[10] Erich Fromm, *The Sane Society* (New York: Rinehart, 1955), pp. 124–25. Melvin Seeman, "The Urban Alienations: Some Dubious Theses From Marx to Marcuse," *Journal of Personality & Social Psychology*, XIX (1971), 135–43.

[11] R. A. Nisbet, *The Sociological Tradition* (New York: Basic Books, 1966), p. 265.

[12] L. E. Hinsie and Jacob Shatzky, *Psychiatric Dictionary* (New York: Oxford University Press, 1940), p. 20. This is the same sense as that found in current general dictionaries. It owes nothing to Hegel or Marx. See also H. J. S. Maine, *Ancient Law* (1861; London: George Rutledge & Sons, 1906), Chap. 8; Deric Regin, *Sources of Cultural Estrangement* (The Hague: Mouton, 1969), Chap. 1; and Gerald Sykes, ed., *Alienation* (New York: George Braziller, 1964), I–II.

diagnosis and do as they tell us to do, they will somehow fix things up for us—make us less alien, help us to live with our alienation or to convert our alienation into something else, something presumably less disastrous.

ANOTHER PERSPECTIVE ON "ALIENATION"—SOCIETY INACCESSIBLE. The second type of "alienation"—that of society from the individual—is popular among those caught up in sociology as an instrument oriented managerially, usually in defense of societal, or at least institutional, stability. A wide sweep of writings avers that modern society is "inaccessible because of its remoteness, formidable from its heavy structures of organization, meaningless from its impersonal complexity." [13]

The vague and speculative nature of these assertions becomes all the more apparent when it is seen that alienation has now become for many both the successor and the antithesis of the idea of progress. This inversion of progress is presumably the faith that intellectuals now are overwhelmingly accepting as a successor to faith in "progress," held previously for several centuries.[14] Built upon "progress," it is another speculative, undefinable, and value-charged word. How anyone can call such usages of either "alienation" or "progress" scientific is unclear. Popular writers become involved in such ideas, but, hopefully, social scientists try carefully to avoid intellectual enmeshment in such notions.[15]

What are the implications of this sweeping second definition and of the allegations associated with it? Those who hold this second view of society, or one closely resembling it,[16] promote in effect a sense of social futility by claiming that man can do little to cope with the vast and uncontrollable societal behemoth.[17] The social scientist is surely concerned in his work with man and man's future, but his conceptual framework does not prejudge his data either optimistically or pessimistically. On the contrary, preconceptions of optimism and pessimism are merely curiously interesting and possibly significant parts of his data. This is not

[13] Nisbet, The Sociological Tradition, pp. 264–66.
[14] Ibid., p. 266.
[15] J. B. Bury, The Idea of Progress (New York: Macmillan, 1932); Morris Ginsberg, The Idea of Progress (London: Methuen, 1953); Seeman, "The Urban Alienations."
[16] As examples, see Max Weber, "Science as a Vocation," Chap. 5 in From Max Weber, trans. and ed. by H. H. Gerth and C. W. Mills (New York: Oxford University Press, 1946), esp. pp. 153–56; Georges Sorel, Reflections on Violence, trans. by T. E. Hulme and J. Roth (Glencoe, Ill.: Free Press, 1950); and Émile Durkheim, Suicide, trans. by J. A. Spaulding and George Simpson (Glencoe, Ill.: Free Press, 1933).
[17] Gunnar Myrdal, Value in Social Theory, ed. by Paul Streeten (New York: Harper & Bros., 1958), pp. 143, 151; Danilo Dolci, Waste, trans. by R. Munroe (London: MacGibbon & Kee, 1963), esp. Part 3, and The Man Who Plays Alone, trans. by Antonia Cowan (Garden City, N.Y.: Doubleday & Co., 1970), pp. ix–xiv.

to say, it needs to be added, that his conclusions might not appear to be optimistic or pessimistic about some aspect of man's lot.

Thus, "alienation" in one sense is a way of convincing individuals that they should depend upon the formula-peddling counselors. In another sense, it unconsciously or subconsciously becomes a device for persuading an individual that he alone, or working with others, can do nothing worthwhile about his social situation. If luck did not bless him with participation in the "establishment," he can only choose between being a grateful and uncritical consumer and instrument or being a social dropout, relegated to the parasitical or criminal fringes of "organized" society.

To state the matter otherwise, many assertions of "alienation" are simply and accurately translated as contentions that members of some "problem" group are at odds with the spokesman's value orientation or conception of societal legitimacy or ideas about appropriate social-action procedures. That those group members may have another value orientation that they regard to be more satisfying or useful (whether a "rational" or an "irrational" one) is not within the focus of "alienation." It tends to carry a judgment from one social viewpoint.[18] In other words, what is gained by cynical or blasé or even "professional" oldsters calling cynical or blasé youngsters "alienated"?

THE UTILITY OF THERAPISTS. Please note that this is not to oppose the development of a large variety of therapists and other practitioners who make themselves available to assist with personal, group, and societal problems. The healthful continuance of our society requires these many specialists and more, as they can be developed. Free communication and discussion demands that therapists and would-be therapists present their claims for serviceability as freely as possible, even in quite sensational terms. Fortunately, practitioners, among others, have seized upon such conditions as those some choose to call "alienation." The dedication of many of them in trying to help their patients or clients is admirable. They have brought together intellectual, emotional, and actionist procedures that at times appear to help unhappy and/or damaged and/or needy individuals and maladjusted, weak, and obsolescent organizations and groups. Hopefully, those who are charlatans or misinformed eventually will lose out in their struggles for support, even though they may do short-term damage.

What is opposed is regarding the practitioner's, the patient's, or the

---

[18] Eric and Mary Josephson, eds., *Man Alone* (New York: Dell, 1962), and Gerald Sykes, ed., *Alienation,* illustrate this from a variety of viewpoints. See also A. McC. Lee, *How to Understand Propaganda* (New York: Rinehart, 1952), Chaps. 3 and 7; and Chaps. 6 and 7 in the present book.

client's conception of reality as one necessarily acceptable as accurate by other people and for other purposes. A religion or Freudianism or group dynamics or "eupsychian management"[19] may appear to have valid therapeutic uses in our present stage of knowledge, but this alone does not verify its teachings as being scientifically accurate generalizations about human behavior. A scientist somehow develops a curiosity unbound by any obligation to cure a specific patient, to modify a specific social situation, to maintain a therapist-patient or a practitioner-client relationship,[20] or even to produce marketably intriguing ideas. At the same time, the scientist who is a sociologist certainly dedicates himself to the study of pressing social problems as his means of serving mankind. Through criticizing and reconstructing social knowledge, the social scientist improves the wisdom available to people generally and to the social practitioner in ways not likely to occur to the involved social actionist.

GLITTERING GENERALITIES AS DATA. Such ideas as those labeled "alienation" are data of concern to the social scientist because people believe in them. He then wants to know: How have people come to believe in them? What do people do with them? What individual and social problems do such glittering generalities tend to obscure and distort? To whose advantage is it that the ideas seem to clarify and focus?

A social commentator who is a social scientist and not a social practitioner—not a political and economic ideologist like Marx, not a psychoanalyst like Fromm, and not an applied "sociologist" employed by clients like so many "sociologists" today—can be concerned about many of the same problems as the practitioner. Because of the differences in orientation, the nonpractitioner's interviewing, observing, reading, and sharing of his perceptions with others often lead him to differ sharply with the practitioner on many aspects of man's lot in society.

In the case of the "purely" academic social scientist, part of his difference in viewpoint from the hired practitioner may arise from his associating so continually with students with their fresh, critical minds, their drives for discovery and accomplishment. A surprising number of

[19] A. H. Maslow, *Eupsychian Management* (Homewood, Ill.: R. D. Irwin & Dorsey Press, 1965).

[20] A. W. Gouldner in Gouldner and Miller, eds., *Applied Sociology* (New York: Free Press, 1965), p. 15. Louis Wirth, in "Clinical Sociology," *American Journal of Sociology*, XXXVII (1931–32), 49–66, emphasizes the possible contributions sociologists might make to the welfare of patients brought into a medical or psychological clinical situation and discusses the role of sociologists as therapists in such a situation. See also A. McC. Lee, "Sociology, clinical," in H. P. Fairchild, ed., *Dictionary of Sociology* (New York: Philosophical Library, 1944), p. 303, and "The Clinical Study of Society," *American Sociological Review*, XX (1955), 648–53, for scientific uses of clinical study. See the perceptive discussion in M. O. Wagenfeld, "The Primary Prevention of Mental Illness," a paper read before the Society for the Study of Social Problems, Denver, Colo., August 28, 1971.

university students can be and are autonomous, perceptive, and sensitive enough to be fellow investigators busily engaged in pursuing their own ideas and observations. Even the few who are somewhat disturbed, disorganized, or maladjusted mentally can sometimes be drawn into intellectual adventures—much to their own advantage, as well as that of society.

"WITH IT" RATHER THAN "ALIENATED." The popularity of student strikes and confrontations, the student crusade against the Indochinese Undeclared War, the Peace Corps, Operation Head Start, and other serious interests of today's university students do not suggest a dependent or an enervating sense of "alienation"; rather, they point to students' apparent belief in their relative autonomy and effectiveness. Even the dropouts include those who have more faith in themselves than in what they see as a maladapted educational "system" in an unadapting social "system."

In contrast with the generations of work-enslaved urban and rural workers from whom we are mostly descended,[21] a great many people are now amazingly autonomous, perceptive, and sensitive to their needs, desires, and relationships. Thus traditional allegiances are more subject to test, examination, and possible modification or replacement. Now that the vast majority in this country no longer face a primitive struggle for existence, many of us are learning that our fate is social in the broad sense of being tied to the fate of humanity. It is social in terms far more basic than the outworn patterns of relationship and sentimentality inherited from the past. It is also social in terms more pervasive and binding than the exploitative relationships of our worldwide market economy.

Thus, rather than being "alienated" from mankind or from our own society, many of us are learning that our future is linked in a very intimate sense with the future of the human race around the world. The prime concerns on this international agenda are increasing pollution, frightening waste of resources, and increasing overpopulation.[22] The immediate hopes of the depressed and oppressed in our own and other countries depend upon the growing sense of social responsibility among rank-and-file Americans. In a little longer time perspective, the future of all human beings depends upon such an awakening.[23] As students and blacks are demonstrating so well in spite of their confused leadership, any of us can

---

[21] See for example, Peter Laslett, *The World We Have Lost* (New York: Charles Scribner's Sons, 1965), esp. Chaps. 1 and 5.

[22] W. R. Burch, Jr., *Daydreams and Nightmares: A Sociological Essay on the American Environment* (New York: Harper & Row, 1971); Paul and Anne Ehrlich, *Population, Resources, Environment* (San Francisco: W. H. Freeman Co., 1970).

[23] A. W. Smith, "The Profit Motive and the Environment," *National Parks & Conservation Magazine*, XLVI, No. 1 (January 1972), i–iv.

disproportionately make "our weight felt" politically and economically— in a broader social sense, we can stimulate or facilitate social change. We just need to learn seriously how to do so, and then muster the courage to try.

"MARGINALITY" RATHER THAN "ALIENATION"

Some of the phenomena oversimply related to "alienation" are thus more precisely and usefully seen in other lights that require greater knowledge of societal processes and social history. Some of them might well be related to such conceptions as *relative* isolation, *relative* deprivation of socializing experiences during maturation, or "marginality" in the sense used by the sociologist Robert E. Park.[24] Such terms quite explicitly suggest process rather than a static "alienated" category.

"Marginality" means chiefly that a great many of us have been shaken somewhat loose from the customs in terms of which we were socialized and are partly assimilated into another culture or into one or more other group cultures. For a time this can be a most stimulating, albeit often a painful, experience. For some, it is debilitating or may lead to delinquency and criminality; for others, it is an incitement to creativity. To a great many it is a healthy push into an active and involved life. Marginality is thus an aspect of mobility—both horizontally and vertically, both of a migratory sort and up or down in social status—and it is also related to attendant personal and social disorganization and reorganization. A healthfully changing society benefits from risking the problems of marginality precipitated by migration, mind-stretching education, and status-striving.[25]

It is not necessary to treat exhaustively all of the contrasts mentioned in the two parallel columns. To a degree, what is said above about "alienation" as a catchword also applies to "privacy," "leisure time," "mass culture," and "unseen élites" as glittering generalities. They are similarly

[24] R. E. Park, "Human Migration and the Marginal Man," *American Journal of Sociology*, XXXIII (1927–1928), 881–93, reprinted in Park, *Race and Culture*, ed. by E. C. Hughes *et al.* (Glencoe, Ill.: Free Press, 1950), pp. 345–56. Compare with Helen M. Lynd, "Alienation: Man's Fate and Man's Hope," in J. F. Glass and J. R. Staude, eds., *Humanistic Society* (Pacific Palisades, Calif.: Goodyear Publ. Co., 1972).

[25] The foregoing discussion includes material originally published in A. McC. Lee, "An Obituary for 'Alienation,'" *Social Problems*, XX, No. 1 (Summer 1972), by permission of the Society for the Study of Social Problems. See also Lee, *Multivalent Man*, esp. Chap. 18. For a refreshingly different discussion of both "culture" and "estrangement" from it, see Deric Regin, *Sources of Cultural Estrangement* (The Hague: Mouton, 1969), esp. Chap. 4.

speculative and ill-defined or undefinable terms that are often employed manipulatively in the guise of having scientific utility.

In the following, the contrasts are joined together so that they may be discussed further under these headings: (1) privacy and leisure, (2) mind twisting, (3) the American home, (4) the information explosion, and (5) American violence.

PRIVACY AND LEISURE

As shown in historical series of crude figures, the average workweek in the United States appears to have diminished in a most impressive manner. For industrial workers it dropped from about seventy to about forty or forty-one hours per week between 1850 and 1970.[26] Thus, not to go into variations among types of employment, some twenty-nine or thirty hours per week are superficially presumed to have been freed for "leisure" in a little over a century. But were they "freed"? If so, what does "freed" mean?

After the hours "saved" are adjusted to take into consideration differences in bases of computation and increases in time for commuting, for necessary chores in and about the home, and for moonlighting, the hours of work per week for males are little less, if any, and for females are somewhat more, than they were a century ago. As C. Wright Mills notes, "Leisure time . . . comes to mean an unserious freedom from the authoritarian seriousness of the job." [27] Even though the American male may share his wife's duties of shopping for and preparing meals, washing clothes, and tending children in the time "freed" from wage-earning, these are activities outside of the "authoritarian seriousness of the job." They are things to be done in his own manner and at his own pace, in an environment of which he shares control, and with people of his own choosing.[28] In other words, the diminishing hours of work on the job have made possible a greater privatization of life.

PRIVATIZATION OF LIFE. Not only are the personal and family sectors of living consuming more time in relationship to gainful employment or necessary work. They are also extending over other interests and activities that had been more directly controlled by organized politics, entertainment, and religion. Printed communications media, radio, television,

[26] U.S. Bureau of Labor Statistics, Dept. of Labor, *Employment and Earnings and Monthly Report on Labor Force.*
[27] C. W. Mills, *White Collar* (New York: Oxford University Press, 1951), p. 236.
[28] A. McC. Lee, "Time Budgets in the U.S.A.," a memorandum prepared for the Istituto di Sociologia, Università degli studi di Roma, 1967.

recordings of sounds, and, increasingly, tape-recordings of television and other motion-picture materials, make privatized ways of life ever more attractive. They provide opportunities for individual and family choices of influences in a separate environment. Political mass meetings and picnics become increasingly difficult to organize and increasingly unnecessary. If it were not for the community-orientation function of religious congregations for those who have recently moved from one area to another in our highly mobile society, we would probably have as low a level of church attendance and adherence as the English.[29] Whether or not God has died is a fashionable theological ploy, but that current forms of ecclesiastical organization and ideology have not coped with adherence problems is no news in any denomination. As the sociologist Peter L. Berger suggests, the increasingly secularized churches in this country are reaching "the strange state of self-liquidation."[30] The solace and mystical identity that apparently cannot now be so readily discovered in churches is being found in the family and in solitude. In this, as always, fortunate individuals are aided by the products of all sorts of artists or by becoming an artist. Unfortunate individuals yield to the short-term and costly promises of druglike entertainments and of actual narcotics.

THREATS TO PRIVACY. A great deal is now made of how mechanisms and bureaucrats are invading our privacy. A law professor has predicted that "man's technical inventiveness may [by the year 2000], in terms of privacy, have turned the whole community into the equivalent of an army barracks." He adds: "It may be a final ironic commentary on how bad things have become by 2000 when someone will make a fortune merely by providing, on a monthly, weekly, daily, or even hourly basis, a room of one's own."[31] Once again, we are confronted with the scary warning of a practitioner available for magic-working purposes, this time a lawyer.

This is not to belittle our need to fight for our legal and actual rights of privacy. As the sociologist John Kosa points out, "With the Federal Data Center being planned in Washington, with the Social Security number demanded on numberless forms and questionnaires, any institutional

---

[29] Geoffrey Gorer, *Exploring English Character* (New York: Criterion Books, 1955); Michael Argyle, *Religious Behavior* (Glencoe, Ill.: Free Press, 1959); P. L. Berger, *The Precarious Vision* (New York: Doubleday, 1961); and Gerhard Lenski, *The Religious Factor*, rev. ed. (Garden City: Anchor Books, 1961).

[30] P. L. Berger, quoted in "A Bleak Outlook Is Seen for Religion," *New York Times*, February 25, 1968. See also Berger, *The Sacred Canopy* (Garden City, N.Y.: Doubleday, 1967), Chaps. 5–7, which discuss implications of the secularization of religious organizations. See also Berger, *A Rumor of Angels* (Garden City, N.Y.: Doubleday, 1969).

[31] Harry Kalven, Jr., "The Problems of Privacy in the Year 2000," *Daedalus*, XCVI (1967), 887, 882.

inquiry on income, religion, Marxism, or health becomes a danger to the citizen's right to be left alone. Indeed, the fight against the invasion of privacy must begin without delay and it must proceed by curtailing the inquisitive activities, not of the behavioral scientists but of the institutions." [32]

DEFENSES OF PRIVACY. In spite of all this, our actual control of our own privacy has much better chances than the law professor predicts. Privacy or lack of privacy is not a correlate of some particular size, degree of integration, or technological sophistication of a society. For every mechanism for the invasion of privacy, guards or shields against it are likely to be developed. For that matter, so-called freaks (hippie youth) are demonstrating that many types of deviant behavior, such as smoking "pot," can often be done in public without notice, apparently with less chance of detection than in private. The inefficiency and blundering of spy networks and of police "witch hunts" are more than legendary; they are also frequently verified in practice. In times of hysteria and repression, it must be added, police all too often strike out practically at random. [33]

Privacy, both individual and group, grows out of resistance to its invasion, out of a desire to control more and more of one's own way of life, out of the development of personal resources for the use of privacy, and out of suitable employment opportunities. Let us hope that this more privatized way of life strengthens people for necessary ventures into social action. Let us hope that our social inventiveness facilitates such contributions to social adaptation and improvement.

MIND TWISTING

"Propaganda" and "brainwashing" suggest manipulations of individuals and groups as mysterious and dastardly as black magic. "Mass culture" and "mass media" imply that we are all somehow caught up willy-nilly in mind-twisting webs of words, sounds, and pictures—that humanity is on its way to the human equivalent of ant-hill like-mindedness and authoritarian control. The influence of such devices is exaggerated by our mass communicators as they seek to magnify their own importance

[32] John Kosa, "Who Invades Privacy and Why?" American Psychologist, XXIII (1968), 138. See also A. R. Miller, The Assault on Privacy (Ann Arbor: University of Michigan Press, 1971), and Richard Boeth, "The Assault on Privacy," Newsweek, July 27, 1970, pp. 15–20.

[33] Arthur Niederhoffer and A. S. Blumberg, eds., The Ambivalent Force (Waltham, Mass.: Ginn and Co., 1970), esp. Chaps. 3, 6, 8; Blumberg, Criminal Justice, 2nd ed. (Chicago: Quadrangle Books, 1970), esp. pp. vii–xiv and Chap. 3; C. R. Sowle, ed., Police Power and Individual Freedom (Chicago: Aldine, 1962).

and as they serve our propensity to identify alleged devils and to scare ourselves with them.

As we grow up, our minds are "programmed"—to use a rough analogy to computer practice—by mother, father, siblings, friends, teachers, and mass media. This programmed or guided experience in social interaction etches upon our minds values delineated in our society's culture and in the mores of the various groups into which we are assimilated. This formal and informal conditioning is multivalent—that is, through it we learn to function within a variety of group situations even though values customary in each of these various contexts often contrast. These contrasting values build into our minds a degree of "natural skepticism"; they set limits of tolerance within which our responses may readily change in reaction to suggestions (including advertising and other propaganda) or changed conditions.[34]

Because of the great difficulty in modifying basic sentiments etched upon our minds during maturation, both propagandists and brainwashers attempt first to work with what already exists in the minds of those who are their targets. "Communications will be most effective—that is, will secure the response most in line with the intention of the communicator— when they are in accord with audience predispositions; when they tell people what they (most) want to be told." In other words, communications "are more effective in canalizing people's existing dispositions than they are in redirecting their responses into directions neutral or counter to their interests, social positions, and group memberships—in which case they encounter a good deal of resistance." [35]

LIMITS TO REPROGRAMMING. But propagandists and brainwashers— and psychotherapists as well—try to carry attitude modification beyond the reinterpretation of sentiments existing in people's minds. Each in his way strives to reprogram a significant part of his subjects' reactions to social stimuli. Each uses a variety of manipulative procedures. Each has been credited with sentiment changes, but even where the evidence may appear convincing—especially evidence relating to the work of certain psychotherapists with their voluntary patients—the case for substantial and maintained sentiment modification appears to be unclear or incon-

[34] W. J. McGuire, "The Nature of Attitudes and Attitude Change," Chap. 21 in Gardner Lindzey and Elliot Aronson, eds., The Handbook of Social Psychology, 2nd ed. (Reading, Mass.: Addison-Wesley, 1969), III, esp. 167–71, and Lee, How to Understand Propaganda, esp. Chap. 7. See also A. M. Meerloo, The Rape of the Mind (New York: World Publ. Co., 1956); Eleutherius Winance, The Communist Persuasion, trans. by E. A. Lawrence (New York: P. J. Kennedy & Sons, 1959); and R. J. Lifton, Thought Reform and the Psychology of Totalism (New York: W. W. Norton, 1961).

[35] Bernard Berelson and G. A. Steiner, Human Behavior (New York: Harcourt, Brace & World, 1964), pp. 540–41.

clusive. Many thoughtful psychotherapists contend that they cannot do more than aid their patients to understand better their existing sentiments (consciences, superegos) and thus to live more satisfactorily with them. Those who have been maturely socialized and have a secure sense of identity do not change their attitudes and sentiments in response to brainwashing or propagandizing contrary to their own habitual views of self-interest or group-interest. A healthily critical mind cannot be brainwashed and finds ways to cope with manipulative propaganda.[36]

DEFENSES AGAINST MIND TWISTERS. Our best defense against both brainwashing and propaganda contrary to our own interests could be education, but it is not the kind of education often provided in our current American schools. Our educational procedures are more often geared to the development of believers and technicians rather than independent investigators and thinkers. But our closeness as yet to a peasant- and urban-worker heritage has given even our middle-class intellectuals an earthiness and realism not to be found very often among their European counterparts. The tasteless trash associated with what is called "mass culture" is deadening, but our current "mass culture" also carries with it a surprisingly great literary and artistic curiosity. Often it also exhibits a healthy distrust for the pretentious intellectual games of traditional academicians as well as faith in man's ability to test theories against "common-sense" evidence, especially the evidence of observation and experience.[37]

Some intellectuals call this earthy heritage in our "mass culture" an anti-intellectual one because it rejects the overly abstract and finespun theorizing used to support some elite's social perquisites. It opposes going beyond what may be observed or otherwise experienced. It brushes aside opinions supported solely by elegance of expression or by allegations of societal or intellectual legitimacy. This is the part of our heritage out of which realistic social science grew in the United States, even though many sociologists would now contend that it is anti-intellectual to look upon social science as a revolt against traditional intellectualism.[38] On

---

[36] Walter Weiss, "Effects of the Mass Media of Communications," Chap. 38 in Lindzey and Aronson, The Handbook of Social Psychology, V; Jacques Ellul, Propaganda, trans. by Konrad Kellen and Jean Lerner (New York: Alfred A. Knopf, 1965), esp. Chaps. 4, 5, and app. 1; Abbie Hoffman, Revolution for the Hell of It (New York: Dial, 1968).

[37] D. M. White, "Mass Culture in America," in Bernard Rosenberg and White, eds., Mass Culture (Glencoe, Ill.: Free Press, 1957), pp. 13–21.

[38] This can be seen more clearly in biographies of leading sociologists than in the intellectualized treatises on the origins of the discipline. See for example, W. G. Sumner's views on speculative philosophy and especially on metaphyics in A. G. Keller, Reminiscences (Mainly Personal) of William Graham Sumner (New Haven: Yale University Press, 1933), pp. 18, 57–58, 60–61.

the contrary, these would-be legitimists try to carry about with them a baggage of philosophical footnotes and hair-splitting that is presumably useful to understand life but actually distorts or obscures it.

When sociologists try to derive their legitimacy from those successful parvenus of intellectualism, the physical and biological scientists, they construct mechanistic or organismic "models" with which to characterize human interrelationships. When they are more preoccupied with literary tradition, they may seize upon such a model as the dramatic.[39] Both are substitutes for the more antique preoccupation of trying to graft allegedly scientific formulations onto an academically established, powerful, or intriguing philosophical tradition. All in all, it is amusing that such pretentious fabrications should be called "scientific" at all.

THE EARTHY REALISM OF PEASANTS. But let us bring together in a recent illustration these comments about mind-twisting and about the earthy realism of peasants: Even among the embattled, simple citizens of Viet Nam who are trying to cope with a foreign invader, resistance to persistent brainwashing and massive propaganda is truly an object of wonder. Think of the problems of our United States soldiers in Operation Dragnet, a program to uproot the "Viet Cong infrastructure in the villages . . . one of the most frustrating tasks of the war." When a reporter asked why one woman had turned informer, a lieutenant replied, "Oh, she had a small baby, and I told her if she didn't show me where the men were hiding I would take her baby away." The woman cooperated in the anti-Communist and "prodemocratic" cause.

According to Lt. Col. James S. Oliver, the Air Cavalry's provost marshall, "Some of these hamlets will have to be hit a third, fourth and fifth time. . . . Root out that Communist infrastructure. That is the only answer to this war in the long run." [40]

To restate this American officer's position, he appears to recognize that practically nothing short of complete genocide is likely to accomplish the goal of any such effort as Operation Dragnet. Surely there are times when Oliver wonders at the resistance of the simple human being to a leviathan. On this matter, American strategists might ponder the failure

---

[39] P. A. Sorokin, "Physicalist and Mechanist School," in J. S. Roucek, ed., Contemporary Sociology (New York: Philosophical Library, 1958), pp. 1127–76; Michele Marotta, Organicismo e Neo-Organicismo (Milano: A. Giuffré, 1959); and Howard Becker and H. E. Barnes, Social Thought From Lore to Science, 2nd ed. (Washington: Harren Press, 1952), II, index, refs. to organic, organicism, organismic analogy. Recent examples of the use of dramaturgic models are Erving Goffman, The Presentation of Self in Everyday Life (Garden City, N.Y.: Doubleday, 1959), and P. L. Berger, Invitation to Sociology (Garden City, N.Y.: Doubleday, 1963), esp. Chap. 6.

[40] Lt. Col. J. S. Oliver, quoted in Newsweek, July 24, 1967.

of the English to root out the infrastructures of Welsh, Scottish, and Irish nationalism even after a millenium of costly and destructive efforts.[41]

INNOVATION VERSUS RITUALISM. As these brief comments can only suggest, minds are formed or twisted as they are socialized in whatever groups and society in which they mature. Our families, schools, and mass media operate in terms of cultural biases that reflect the values their functionaries hold. That such mass media as newspapers, magazines, radio, and television are further biased by characteristics of their owner-ship and operation is clear enough.[42] At the same time, however, those media exhibit a deadening ritualism, a dependence upon superficial enter-tainment appeals, and a persistent distortion of "reality" in terms of their conceptions of "news" that weaken what influence they may have for social change. A courageous spokesman such as Martin Luther King, Jr., or a crusading investigator such as Ralph Nader can often facilitate changes in opinion and policy even against the tidal conservatism of the periodical and electronic media. Well-led and needed voluntary organiza-tions—whether political, economic, religious, female, youth, black, or whatever—can make powerful thrusts toward policy formation in struggles against "establishment" media.

Thus the process of socialization can largely foreclose an individual's possibilities for changing his mental orientation and general courses of action, but such foreclosure is avoided by many. The individual's sociali-zation processes might have included experiences that gave him a sense of social marginality—in other words, a share in contrasting cultures, or at least group cultures. When so enriched, he can achieve more of a sense of autonomous choice with which to face more judiciously or creatively today's contradictory world. Fortunately the socialization processes of our multivalent society are sufficiently inconsistent and contrasting that, in-formally at least, we are aided toward greater flexibility in personal adaptation.

THE AMERICAN HOME

As a social instrument, the American home is seldom discussed objectively. It is usually seen either as the sentimental source of all our

---

[41] See O. D. Edwards et al., Celtic Nationalism (New York: Barnes & Noble, 1968). For more details on the Indochinese struggle, see P. G. Bourne, Men, Stress, and Vietnam (Boston: Little, Brown, 1970); E. S. Herman, Atrocities in Vietnam (Philadelphia: Pilgrim Press, 1970); S. M. Hersh, My Lai Four (New York: Random House, 1970); Daniel Lang, Casualties of War (New York: McGraw-Hill, 1969).

[42] Daniel Katz et al., eds., Public Opinion and Propaganda (New York: Dryden Press, 1954), Chap. 5.

virtues or as the "massive failure" to which we "must" trace the major woes of our children. This "failure" is said to produce our delinquents and criminals, neurotics and psychotics. Among nonwhites in particular, family "failure" is said to "cause" lack of initiative in self-improvement or group improvement.[43] Both sentimentalists and those who require scape-goats tend to see the family and the social environment of the home as the source—even the creator—of socialization processes rather than as integrally related to even more complex social processes.

The reactions against these two polar positions by special students of family life have produced a third viewpoint, one that is still modishly worrisome about the current family and sentimental about its potentialities. It locates the culprit, however, in the "anti-family society" that we are now said to possess. The national professional body of teachers and counselors on family subjects devoted a recent annual convention to the topic "Beyond an Anti-Family Society." In paper after paper these specialists outlined nostrums with which they contended they could help the family survive and also aid our society to become "pro-family." [44]

Let us try to avoid all three of these extremes—the sentimental, the pessimistic, and the professional. Let us look briefly at the American home's changing ecological setting and then at the quality of its chief products, our children.

PLANNING VERSUS SPRAWLING. The evolving designs of our major urban areas distribute American homes among the urban slums and the privileged high-rise apartments, the colorless suburban real-estate speculations and the more tasteful and more functional developments, the sprawling and varied exurbs and the rural areas. This mention of designs refers to products of social invention, competition, and conflict. They come into being in the minds of artists and engineers when they are working with planning committees and bureaus, under legislative directives, and influenced by pressure groups.

What ordinarily constitutes "success" for area planners and designers? First, they must assess realistically what exists. They must comprehend the relative importance of vested interests in streets, buildings, and open spaces that are nonrational products of competition, manipulation, and conflict. Then they are asked to suggest ways in which the vested interests represented by their employers can be preserved or magnified through some modernizing adaptation. By the very nature of their employment, as functionaries of government or of voluntary organizations most often

---

[43] Lee Rainwater and W. L. Yancey, *The Moynihan Report and the Politics of Controversy* (Cambridge: M.I.T. Press, 1967), deals with a controversy over this very issue.

[44] See National Council on Family Relations, *Newsletter*, XIV, No. 4 (October 1969).

controlled by private utility and real-estate interests, planners and designers cannot focus clearly upon creating physical facilities in which healthy human communities can readily develop. They must preoccupy themselves with problems and opportunities incidental to the maintenance of an existing power structure. They are constrained by obsolescent conceptions of "the public interest," of technology, and of the city.[45]

Thus even as our cities become less workable mechanically, governmentally, fiscally, and especially socially, as places in which to establish homes and raise children, vast fortunes continue to be spent and made on tinkering with them. Instead of being rationalized, mass transportation is merely patched in ways that delay its collapse. Vast superhighways continue to be built to dump ever more traffic into downtown areas. Mass parking facilities can only be constructed where they become feeders to increasingly inadequate mass transportation facilities. Slum clearance projects chase the underprivileged from one overcrowded place to another even more overcrowded, but hopefully less visible. Office buildings pile up higher and higher. Fabricating and assembling plants get as close to markets and cheap labor as possible. All this has its setting in increasingly polluted air, water, and land described and discussed in increasingly polluted educational facilities and mass communications media.

PRO-FAMILY INFLUENCES. The anti-family aspects of our present urbanized society can be detailed on and on, and thus easily make for overemphasis. The prospect can be made to look very bleak indeed, but we also need to look at offsetting developments and possibilities. Our increasingly educated and aspiring population has a falling birthrate. Such birth-control procedures as "the pill," the IUD (intrauterine device), and legal and illegal abortions are facilitating and stabilizing this trend. At the same time, mechanical developments have made huge concentrations of population unnecessary, unattractive, and too expensive. Led by scientific and technical research laboratories, pharmaceutical manufacturers, book and periodical printers and publishers, and by other employers of skilled and educated people, more and more businesses are finding that they and many of their employees can gain from a suburban or small-town setting. Employers of the less skilled are following suit. Thus our businesses and homes are diffusing over much greater areas with

[45] Jewell Bellush and M. Hausknecht, eds., Urban Renewal (Garden City, N.Y.: Doubleday, 1967); Scott Greer, Urban Renewal and American Cities (Indianapolis: Bobbs-Merrill, 1965); Jane Jacobs, The Death and Life of Great American Cities (New York: Random House, 1961); Suzanne Keller, Urban Neighborhood (New York: Random House, 1970); Jeanne R. Lowe, Cities in a Race With Time (New York: Random House, 1967); S. B. Warner, Jr., ed., Planning for a Nation of Cities (Cambridge: M.I.T. Press, 1966); W. H. Whyte, Jr., Cluster Development (New York: American Conservation Association, 1964); Martin Meyerson, ed., The Conscience of the City (New York: George Braziller, 1970), esp. Parts 4 and 5.

gains rather than losses in efficiency, in community, and in other human benefits. It now looks as though this population diffusion might well take on much more impetus.[46]

If our population becomes fairly stable and if employers utilize modern media of communication and transportation to decentralize their operations, American community life could grow again in widely scattered centers. Very few of them would need to be remote from economic, educational, cultural, and political facilities. The chief dangers such a development poses are ones we desperately need to avoid even more in the future than we do now. They are the dangers inherent in segregation, whether by class, ethnic group, or skin color, and in lack of community involvement in political and economic self-control. A society of tribalistic minorities contains the makings of continuous exploitation, deprivation, internecine conflict, and passionate resistance to change. We can avoid such a fate if we work much more rapidly than now along the assimilative lines available to us in education and other cultural activities, in housing, and in employment.[47]

THE SURPRISINGLY SUCCESSFUL FAMILY. When the current American family is labeled a "massive failure," with what is it being compared? Did our tribal, serf, peasant, and urban-worker ancestors do such a better job of child-rearing in their European and African, Oriental and Amerindian families? This is not to excuse our shortcomings, but it is to recognize that while idealistic criteria may have inspirational utility, they give no accurate sense of our comparative situation today.

Our news media titillate *each* generation of their constituencies with tales of juvenile waywardness and delinquency. In the 1920s, to cite but one instance, they recounted campus orgies of bobbed-haired and short-skirted "flappers" and their slick-haired "sheiks." Rather than using "pot" or "speed," those "fast ones" drank "bathtub gin," etherized beer, and other forms of "rotgut." The "waves of student suicides" reported in the media came to an abrupt halt with announcements of official statistics to the contrary. Then, as now, the media devoted little attention to the millions of students soberly preparing themselves to take over as the technicians, artists, scientists, politicians, administrators, mothers, and fathers of American society. Now, as always, we could do a better job of raising many of the younger generation, but on the whole they compare favorably with both their forebears and those growing up in other countries. Our university students somehow continue to come from an ever

---

[46] Jean Gottmann, *Megalopolis* (New York: Twentieth Century Fund, 1961); and J. K. Hadden, L. H. Masotti, and C. L. Larson, eds., *Metropolis in Crisis* (Itasca, Ill.: F. E. Peacock Publishers, 1967), esp. Part 4.

[47] Park, *Race and Culture*, esp. Chaps. 6, 16, 26–29, and M. M. Gordon, *Assimilation in American Life* (New York: Oxford University Press, 1964).

greater number of families. Thus our families continue to furnish society with organizational functionaries and specialists. While certainly in need of improvement, our families as judged by their current children are scarcely "massive failures."

THE INFORMATION EXPLOSION

A subject on which the sociologist as scientist currently has to try even harder than usual to keep his mind on his job is the information explosion. This makes it necessary to look briefly again at the nature of that job before returning to the "information explosion" as such.

THE SOCIOLOGIST'S JOB DEFINED. The sociological scientist's job is not the one envisioned for him by the neopositivists. It is not to erect a new conception of social reality a brick at a time,[48] nor is his job the synthesis, clarification, or amplification of the venerated theories of selected great writers, as attractive as such scholarly gymnastics might be to the pedantically inclined. On their merits and without trying to prove a point on the authority of a prestigious "brand name," parts of such works may well be relevant to the tasks of the sociological scientist. But his job is to examine and reexamine piecemeal and in various contexts the alleged knowledge from any source about social behavior. This should especially include the critical assessment of widely held folk knowledge. This critical study should be done in the light of available observational data and also in the light of the scientist's own experience and cultivated judgment.

A sociological scientist is not just a technician. He is not just a census taker or an opinion surveyor or a market researcher or a social tactician or a social therapist, even though such technicians can turn up significant data of use to the scientist, as well as more directly to society in general. He is a person who wants both to gather at least a part of his data through firsthand observation and to have enough firsthand experience with how all other facts he uses are gathered to be able to understand, criticize, and employ such data accurately. The techniques of the technicians are mostly derived from the way-breaking experimentation and specification of the scientist, and the scientist can and should criticize and modify alleged knowledge about how technicians can and should operate. As nearly as possible, however, the sociological scientist should be a free intellectual with no obligation to provide specific services other than the transmission

---

[48] In the manner advocated by G. A. Lundberg, *Can Science Save Us?* (New York: Longmans, Green, 1961), esp. Chaps. 2–3.

of his findings to fellow specialists, to students, and to others who can apply or disseminate his contributions. His prime task is thus to try to replace social nonsense with more dependable social knowledge.

VAST EXPANSION OF THINGS IN PRINT. The "information explosion," to return to that point, refers to the vast recent expansion of all sorts of data gathering and report publishing. The volumes of *Sociological Abstracts* [49] and *Psychological Abstracts* [50] by becoming fatter and fatter each year attest to the "explosion" in printed materials of interest to social scientists. New professional journals appear each year. The sociological catalogs of book publishers have never been so thick or so numerous.

In view of this "explosion," how can the sociological scientist operate freely in our society and without becoming an enfeebled dependent of subsidies, machines, and organizations controlled by special interests? Actually, if a scientist can maintain his sense of personal integrity and if he succeeds in jumping a few academic hurdles without losing his curiosity, autonomy, imagination, and sense of humor, he can be at least as free and productive on the staff of an American university as he would be anywhere in the world—if he really wants to be free and productive. After all, our universities did produce William James, John Dewey, W. G. Sumner, C. H. Cooley, Thorstein Veblen, G. H. Mead, W. I. Thomas, R. E. Park, E. H. Sutherland, Willard Waller, C. Wright Mills, and others, admittedly with substantial assists from their own personal backgrounds and from the great American humanistic tradition. Some sociologists, earlier and now, have had and will continue to have their difficulties with academic hierarchies, but they can manage to survive and be productive in one or another university community. The temptations of elegance and magnificence, of orthodoxy and legitimacy, can easily weaken a sociologist *as scientist* by making him into something other than a scientist, perhaps into an "operator," a plausible technician, counselor, or manager.

INFORMATION FOR WHOM? Basic, usable, and tested knowledge about how society functions is a rare and valuable commodity. The intellectual functionaries in many types of organizations devote great efforts, quantities of print, and vast funds to what amounts to the perversion of such knowledge in popular media. In other words, they devote themselves to short-term manipulations to protect the special interests to which they dedicate themselves. Such functionaries are everywhere. Few of us can escape from being such a functionary, whether consciously or unconsciously. Somehow the would-be sociological scientist must weave his way

---

[49] New York, I– (1953–). See also Gerald Jahoda, *Information Storage and Retrieval Systems for Individual Researchers* (New York: Wiley-Interscience, 1971).
[50] Washington, I– (1927–).

through the special pleadings of such functionaries and through frank assessments of his own value involvements in order to find answers to his questions about social behavior that will satisfy more accurately his own autonomous curiosity. This is no novel situation. It is as old as scholarship and as social struggle. It long antedates the information explosion, and even sociology so called. It has only had its terms somewhat modified by the explosion.

Since a great many of the results of the information explosion are available to the social scientist directly and through published compilations and related research instruments, in a sense the information explosion has made the independent scientist more free to examine data accumulations than ever before. It permits him to spend more of his time thinking critically about the implications of data, their contexts and relevances, about the probable accuracy of generalizations based upon them, and about means to push on to new, more accurate, and more useful types of knowledge.

AMERICAN VIOLENCE

Headlines and TV spectaculars thrive on violent events. The patient and creative accomplishments of those who have no recourse to violence are only occasionally "news."

Are Americans violent "by nature"? Is American society inherently more one of conflict among individuals and groups than other societies? Must other nations regard the United States as a military threat to their security and autonomy?

How VIOLENT ARE AMERICANS? Domestic and international violence of the 1960s and 1970s raised these questions with increasing insistence. Television screenings of citizens being attacked by police dogs, of armed conflict on American streets and college campuses, and of the battlefield horrors of Viet Nam made daily violence vivid, immediate, and even intimate. The National Commission on the Causes and Prevention of Violence reported 239 violent domestic outbursts in 1964–1968 that were sufficiently extensive to be termed "riots" by the police. Of the estimated 200,000 participants, 191 were killed and about 8,000 were injured. Property damages were said to have totaled hundreds of millions of dollars.[51]

During the same period the United States forces dropped 2,948,057

[51] National Commission on the Causes and Prevention of Violence, *Progress Report . . . to President Lyndon B. Johnson* (Washington: mimeo. press release, January 9, 1969), app., p. 11.

tons of bombs on North and South Viet Nam, almost one and one-half times the grand total dropped by Americans during World War II on all European, Asian, and Pacific targets.[52] Some of the bombs contained napalm. They were supplemented by defoliants with aftereffects on humans and their environment that were not then wholly determined.[53] The amount of damage inflicted upon this small nation caught between two superpowers can scarcely be estimated. American military deaths in this war total just a few thousand less than those of World War I.[54] It is the fourth most bloody war in United States history. It is an undeclared war.

Little wonder that 1964-1968 included 370 civil rights demonstrations and 80 counterdemonstrations with at least one million participants, hundreds of student protests involving the occupation of school facilities, rioting, property damage, injuries, and deaths, and some 700,000 participants in antiwar and antidraft confrontations on campuses and in towns and cities.[55]

But the principal ways in which Americans slaughter themselves and each other or get killed otherwise are not in riots and battles. During 1964-1968 about twice as many citizens (some 55,000) were murdered in the United States as were killed in Viet Nam. Accidental deaths totaled about 550,000: 250,000 in street traffic, 125,000 in the home, and 175,000 in other types of accidents. Just how many deaths reported as accidental were suicides and homicides is anyone's guess. In addition, about 106,000 deaths were officially recorded as suicidal.[56] Taken together, all these violent losses of life within the United States comprise more than the number of Americans killed in all of our wars.[57]

The record of these five years is a sample of American violence, but such a sample is scarcely new in human history. Seasons without violence are too uncommon. Few peoples do not have recourse to intergroup violence, but a great many peoples include great segments committed to nonviolent procedures.

WHO ARE THE NONVIOLENT? The nonviolent are often said to be only

---

52 Office of the Secretary, U. S. Dept. of Defense, news releases.

53 John Cookson and Judith Nottingham, A Survey of Chemical and Biological Warfare (London: Sheed and Ward, 1969). Russell Stetler, The Battle of the Bogside (London: Sheed and Ward, 1970), analyzes data on the use of "control chemicals," Chap. 4, app., and biblio.

54 Office of the Secretary, U. S. Dept. of Defense, news releases.

55 National Commission on the Causes and Prevention of Violence, Progress Report, p. 11.

56 U. S. Public Health Service, Vital Statistics of the United States (Washington: Government Printing Office, 1964–1968).

57 Office of the Secretary, U. S. Dept. of Defense, news releases.

peoples so isolated or so poverty-stricken that they need not defend themselves and cannot wage an open struggle against a neighboring people. On the contrary, the dedicated nonviolent efforts led by Mohandas K. Gandhi in India and by Martin Luther King, Jr., in the United States provide spectacular recent exceptions to such a viewpoint. They remind us that nonviolence is far from being the tactic only of the powerless. Even more important than those spectacular cases are the millions of people throughout the world who in their modest daily lives say "no" to power and whose autonomy and dignity limit the growth of dehumanizing controls over their actions and their thoughts.

THE EUROPEAN TRADITION. A brief summary of European participation in wars suggests that the United States is surely carrying on its Old World heritage. Writers have often contrasted the professed pacific ideals of Christian Europeans with the records of their countries. As the late clergyman Harry Emerson Fosdick said, "In the early days Christianity joined with the state, became sponsor for war, blesser of war, cause of war, and fighter for war. Since then the Church has come down through history too often trying to carry the cross of Jesus in one hand and a dripping sword in the other." [58] From the twelfth through the nineteenth centuries England and France were at war with one another or with some other country from thirty-six to sixty-five of the years in each century.[59] Citing similar figures for those and other European countries ranging from ancient Greece to modern Russia and for the United States, the sociologist P. A. Sorokin notes that peaceful periods have been unevenly distributed, have lacked periodicity, and those "as long as a quarter of a century have been exceedingly rare in the history of these countries." [60] Only Holland had a full century of freedom from international military conflict.

Sorokin stresses (1) "that frequency of war is considerably higher than most of us usually think," (2) *that nations differ little in their peacefulness or belligerency*, (3) "that democracies and republics are not more peaceful than autocracies and monarchies," (4) that more literacy, educational opportunities, scientific knowledge, and mechanical inventions have not diminished the time devoted to war, and (5) that there "is no per-

[58] Quoted in C. H. Ward, *Builders of Delusion* (Indianapolis: Bobbs-Merrill, 1931), p. 340.

[59] P. A. Sorokin, *Contemporary Sociological Theories* (New York: Harper & Bros., 1928), p. 324, based upon F. A. Woods and A. Baltzly, *Is War Diminishing?* (Boston: Houghton Mifflin, 1915), and G. Bodart, *Losses of Life in Modern Wars* (Oxford: Oxford University Press, 1916).

[60] P. A. Sorokin, *Society, Culture, and Personality* (New York: Harper & Bros., 1947), pp. 498–99. See also Sorokin, *Social and Cultural Dynamics* (New York: Harper & Bros., 1937–1941), I–IV, esp. III, Chaps. 9–11.

petual trend toward either a decrease or an increase of war. . . . The theories claiming a progressive pacification of the race constitute merely wishful thinking." The twentieth century's bloodiness "is sufficient in itself to refute such utopian theories." [61]

WHO WON WORLD WAR II? Sorokin's sweeping conclusions are perhaps less surprising today than before the dawn of atomic warfare. In World War II some 16,933,000 soldiers were killed or died of wounds, and 34,325,000 civilians were slaughtered, a total of 51,258,000. The "winning" Allies lost six-sevenths of that total; the "losing" Axis powers lost only one-seventh! When coincident warborne epidemics are also included, the grand total killed was perhaps 60,000,000 in the five-year period, one and one-half times that of World War I.[62] Our technological efficiency is now such that the same number of people or more could be exterminated in the first few days of a third world war.[63]

Do such unbelievable destructions of human lives accomplish the goals sought? It is possible that the mobilization and militarization of life did at least as much to nurture as to destroy authoritarianisms. Military action did not save the lives of six million Jews, Poles, and others in the Nazi extermination camps.[64] Effective coping with what became Nazism would have had to start at least as early as the Versailles "peace conference," preferably through steps that would have prevented World War I.[65] As the sociologist Willard Waller cogently pointed out on the eve of World War II, "Any valid theory of war . . . must consider the fact that it grows out of the totality of our civilization. . . . War settles nothing because defeated nations will not accept defeat. War is an arbiter

61 *Ibid.* See also Arthur Larson, ed., *A Warless World* (New York: McGraw-Hill, 1963); Hannah Arendt *et al.*, "Is America by Nature a Violent Society?" *New York Times Magazine*, April 28, 1968, pp. 24 ff.; Morton Fried, Marvin Harris, and Robert Murphy, eds., *War* (New York: Natural History Press, 1968); Larry Ng, ed., *Alternatives to Violence* (New York: Time-Life Books, 1968); Thomas Rose, ed., *Violence in America* (New York: Vintage Books, 1970).

62 Quincy Wright, *A Study of War*, 2nd ed. (Chicago: University of Chicago Press, 1965), pp. 1542–43.

63 Herman Kahn, *Thinking About the Unthinkable* (New York: Horizon Press, 1962); Linus Pauling, *No More War!*, enlarged ed. (New York: Apollo, 1962); Philip Green, *Deadly Logic* (New York: Schocken Books, 1968); S. M. Hersh, *Chemical and Biological Warfare* (Indianapolis: Bobbs-Merrill, 1968).

64 A. D. Morse, *While Six Million Died: A Chronicle of American Apathy* (New York: Random House, 1968); Telford Taylor, *Sword & Swastika* (Chicago: Quadrangle, 1969).

65 See esp. H. E. Barnes, "The World War of 1914–1918," in Willard Waller, ed., *War in the Twentieth Century* (New York: Dryden Press, 1940); E. L. Bogart, *Direct and Indirect Costs of the Great World War*, 2nd ed. (New York: Oxford University Press, 1920); S. B. Fay, *The Origins of the World War* (New York: Macmillan, 1928); Walter Millis, *Road to War* (Boston: Houghton Mifflin, 1935).

whose decisions the contestants refuse to accept as final, for there is always the chance that another trial will turn out differently." [66]

WAR GUILT. In the highly interrelated world of today, the blame—whatever "blame" might be determined to be—for a Hitler is shared so widely by those in power as to be well nigh universal. The trials of Nazi war criminals dealt only with a few obvious instruments. What about the Americans and Europeans who backed Hitler and Hitler's backers with funds, materials, and silence? [67] Americans too often prefer nationalistic (so-called "consensus") historians who carefully select events supportive of pleasant national myths rather than those who, like Charles A. Beard [68] and Harry Elmer Barnes,[69] insist that unpleasant facts about the American past and present be remembered, pondered, and hopefully used. The latter seek to reverse, at least for a few decision makers, Hegel's futilitarian dictum that "peoples and governments never have learned anything from history, or acted on principles deduced from it." [70]

How can we explain the depressing frequency of wars, rebellions, riots, and murders, not only in the United States, but throughout the world? No "instinct of pugnacity" needs to be assumed to account for them. "Peoples have always gone to war with various degrees of relish or repugnance; but such sentiments have been in their traditions and not in any inherited instinct, one way or another," [71] a great many comparative students of society have concluded.[72] Recourse to interpersonal violence varies so greatly in terms of ethnic (including "racial") and class

[66] Willard Waller, "War in the Twentieth Century," in Waller, ed., *War in the Twentieth Century*, pp. 13, 32. See also Stewart Alsop, "An Old Rule That Doesn't Work," *Newsweek*, May 12, 1969, p. 120.

[67] W. E. Dodd, Jr., and Martha Dodd, eds., *Ambassador* [W.E.] *Dodd's Diary, 1933–1938* (New York: Harcourt, Brace, 1941); Telford Taylor, *Nuremberg and Vietnam: An American Tragedy* (Chicago: Quadrangle Books, 1970), esp. Chaps. 6–8; R. A. Brady, *The Spirit and Structure of German Fascism* (New York: Viking Press, 1937), and *Business as a System of Power* (New York: Columbia University Press, 1943).

[68] See for example, C. A. Beard, *An Economic Interpretation of the Constitution of the United States* (New York: Macmillan, 1913), *The Navy: Defense or Portent?* (New York: Harper & Bros., 1932), and *The Idea of National Interest* (New York: Macmillan, 1934).

[69] See for example, H. E. Barnes, *The Genesis of the World War* (New York: Alfred A. Knopf, 1926), *The Twilight of Christianity* (New York: Vanguard, 1929), *Society in Transition* (New York: Prentice-Hall, 1939), and *An Economic History of the Western World* (New York: Harcourt, Brace, 1938).

[70] G. W. F. Hegel, *Lectures on the Philosophy of History*, trans. by J. Sibree from 3rd German ed. (London: George Bell & Sons, 1858), p. 6.

[71] W. G. Sumner and A. G. Keller, *The Science of Society* (New Haven: Yale University Press, 1927), I, 369. See also Sumner, Keller, and M. R. Davie, *ibid.*, IV, 115–52.

[72] Fried *et al.*, eds., *War* and M. R. Davie, *The Evolution of War* (New Haven: Yale University Press, 1929).

differences that it is traceable to social learning (culture) and to happenstance rather than to biologically inherited "instinct."[73]

WAR TO PRESERVE INEQUALITY. A large share of the organized violence in society is associated with efforts to facilitate or to prevent social changes that are going to take place anyway. Only through the use of physical coercion can any dominant group continue for long to maintain a given condition of intergroup inequality. A relationship of intergroup inequality usually begins with the use of force and is given its justification later. Masters flatter themselves or accept the flattery of their lackeys about the reasons for their superiority and their consequent higher social status. The dominated do not fail to find ways to resist the propagandas that assert and attempt to legitimize their inferiority and their consequent low status. In effect, the dominated promulgate their own counterlegitimacy with which to give themselves some degree of dignity. Intimate knowledge of those living in any deprived area, whether in Calcutta, Tokyo, London, Rome, or New York City, would provide vivid authentication of this and give pause to any curious-minded person enjoying power, privilege, and high status in that city.

Our justifications of inequality have become increasingly sophisticated and labored. The more widely held ones are no longer based openly on such disproven crudities as alleged racial superiority and inferiority or the special genetic virtues said to be "bred into" a social-status-group-defined human stock.[74] They are now more commonly couched publicly in terms of IQs, academic grades and degrees, and other types of achieved certification,[75] including the control of powerful social structures, such as those that do the certifying. But the dominated still remain just as "unreasonable" as always about accepting their "inferiority" as a justification for their low status and for their economic and political deprivation. That the criteria are "scientific" or "realistic" or "necessary" for the maintenance of "the system" based upon so-called "incentives" somehow fails to impress those excluded from a more proportionate share in what society controls and produces.

73 M. E. Wolfgang and Franco Ferracuti, The Subculture of Violence (London: Tavistock, 1967); Marvin Harris, Culture, Man, and Nature (New York: Thomas Y. Crowell, 1971), pp. 231–34; F. H. McClintock, Crimes of Violence (London: Macmillan, 1963).

74 V. G. Kiernan, The Lords of Human Kind (Boston: Little, Brown, 1969).

75 D. C. McClelland, The Achieving Society (New York: D. Van Nostrand, 1961), esp. Chap. 2. See also W. H. Whyte, Jr., "How to Cheat on Personality Tests," in The Organization Man (New York: Simon & Schuster, 1956), pp. 405–10; Reinhard Bendix and S. M. Lipset, eds., Class, Status, and Power, 2nd ed. (New York: Free Press, 1966), esp. Parts 3–4; and M. E. Olsen, ed., Power in Societies (New York: Macmillan, 1970), esp. Parts 3, 5, and 6.

Think what happens to our academic rationalizations for inequality when successful whites and the dwellers in our dark ghettos ponder the statement of the psychologist Kenneth B. Clark: "Children who are treated as if they are uneducable invariably become uneducable." [76] Despite the wealth of evidence supporting this statement, it is a most difficult lesson for the academically oriented and talented to learn, but somehow they have to assimilate it into their thinking. Belief in any child can accomplish educational wonders. On that lesson may hinge significant aspects of our society's future, especially whether or not we shall continue to use violence to keep the nonwhites "in their places."

WAR TO DELAY SOCIAL CHANGE. That violence is often used to try to delay social change is an old story. In the words of James Russell Lowell, two English soldiers buried on the Concord battleground "came three thousand miles, and died, / To keep the Past upon its throne." [77] Yet social change takes place, and the greatest American revolutions were nonviolent ones that followed the one of 1776–1783 and are still coming. For all the fireworks and dramatic shifts of apparent control in violent revolutions, they cannot bring about the sweeping changes that have marked social revolutions in which violence was either incidental or not present.

Why don't we learn how nonviolent change takes place? Why don't we learn the costly futility of trying to prevent changes already under way? Much change is facilitated or can be stimulated by nonviolent negotiation, aggression, resistance, courage in intergroup and interpersonal relations—by knowing how to force issues to a nonviolent decision or how to yield to the overwhelming current trend of social processes.

THE NEED FOR NONVIOLENT AGGRESSION. The traditional "middle-class" repression of violence through avoiding controversial issues has the effect of storing up resentment over unresolved issues, such as those associated with inequality and deprivation. When the middle class was relatively small in our society, it could anxiously and fruitfully devote itself to serving as a kind of social balance-wheel, to trying to compromise at all costs the aggressive and often violent thrusts of upper- and lower-class activists. [78] As the middle class absorbs more and more of society, its mores must somehow provide a workable substitute for violence. It

[76] K. B. Clark, *Dark Ghetto* (New York: Harper & Row, 1965), p. 128.
[77] From J. R. Lowell's poem, "Graves of Two English Soldiers on Concord [Massachusetts] Battle-ground," inscribed on their memorial there.
[78] Leonard Berkowitz, *Aggression* (New York: McGraw-Hill, 1962), esp. pp. 279–83; D. R. Miller and G. E. Swanson, *The Changing American Parent* (New York: John Wiley, 1958), Chaps. 4–5; Miller *et al.*, *Inner Conflict and Defense* (New York: Henry Holt, 1960), pp. 262–63.

must cease its anxious idealization of so-called "compromise at all costs" that succeeds chiefly in shoring up the status quo for a while longer. Our resistance to change may become catastrophically effective.[79]

Old theories of social change and revolution often sprang from old ideologies, not from a study of evolving human society. Herbert Marcuse's contention that the United States is and will remain a prerevolutionary society [80] is possibly accurate in a military sense, but more broadly it is a misreading of history, a misconception of the nature of social revolution. Our contemporary social revolution, of which our season of violence is an unnecessary symptom, is a phase of the continuing American revolution, that can continue as long as certain stimulating aspects of our social processes continue. Egalitarianism, literacy, and activism are becoming more and more integrated into our popular culture.

Violence is used to achieve goals for which no other *known* technique appears to the participants at the time to be as available and useful. The popular backlash against using Americans in foreign military adventures has even led the United States government to seek recourses "to give the appearance of peace while continuing its war." [81] These recourses include automation and Vietnamization or the use of the client army, an army trained, equipped, and guided by the United States. General Ellis E. Williamson summarized the services of both recourses by stating, "We are making unusual efforts to avoid having the American young man stand toe-to-toe, eyeball-to-eyeball, or even rifle-to-rifle against the enemy." [82] Since such procedures maintain or even expand the market for military gear and supplies, they "help wed industry to the military more firmly than ever before" while assuring "the aggressor that he need never see the eyes of his victim." [83]

As riots, revolts, and wars have become more frightful and more destructive, experimentation with alternatives to violence has gained increasing urgency and support. Faith in the expediency and necessity of alternatives to violence has given the search new force and drive.

More and more, only the emotionally disturbed, inexperienced, and

[79] For a perceptive description and analysis of the relations of actionists and others with social change, see Goodwin Watson, *Action for Unity* (New York: Harper, 1947), esp. pp. 87–92.

[80] In the sense that the United States is an "advanced industrial society . . . capable of containing qualitative change for the foreseeable future." If revolution should come, he asserts, it would be because "forces and tendencies exist which may break this containment and explode the society." Herbert Marcuse, *One-Dimensional Man* (Boston: Beacon Press, 1964), p. xv.

[81] From slide film prepared by NARMIC (National Action/Research on the Military-Industrial Complex), sponsored by the American Friends Service Committee, entitled "Automated Air War" (1971).

[82] *Quaker Service Bulletin*, Winter 1972, p. 1.

[83] *Ibid.*, p. 7.

incompetent among those in positions of leadership precipitate armed conflict. Such persons too often achieve great power in modern movements and states, and when they confront the more competent, the latter get led into treacherous spirals of retaliation or of "preventive" violence—fighting to "make the world safe for democracy." Chaotic and overtense social conditions, often carelessly or cynically maintained and stimulated by interests powerful in their own or other states, have provided opportunities for the Stalins, Hitlers, Mussolinis, Francos, and Japanese war lords, not to mention our own members of such a list.

To PLAN FOR NONVIOLENT SOCIAL CHANGE. Thus, rather than talk about "the violent American" or "the violent human," we need to face these facts and probabilities: a capacity for anger is inherent in human nature. When thwarted strongly in expression, anger may erupt in violence, but violence is not essential to human personality or to human affairs. To minimize violence requires realistic planning that covers many facets of socialization and intergroup and international relations. Inseparable as means and ends are in any social effort, the sacrifice of human lives and values in organized violence always builds repressive, antihuman, authoritarian power structures.

When considered oversimply, organized violence may appear largely as an effort to resist or to facilitate orderly change. This oversimplification sometimes even includes accepting the existence of some cosmic plan or pattern of change, but the character of such a pattern eludes both actionists and scholars. At the same time, we do need to face the inevitability of social change, to learn its current directions and dynamics, and then to adapt to it wisely, nonviolently. To be sure, change always involves alternatives. Violence is a choice among alternative courses of action in any given case that is likely—regardless of the "winner"—to serve chiefly to reinforce authoritarian procedures and controls. Organized passive resistance and pressure, on the contrary, can strengthen and help to elevate the condition of the common man.

A great deal of interpersonal violence arises either out of failures in social maturation or out of the persistence of violent subcultures within groups in our society. Interpersonal violence, like more large-scale and organized violence, need not be taken either as given or as "natural." It would yield to more determined and more realistic study, planning, and training.

SUMMARY

To sum up this whole discussion of social "therapy" versus the search for knowledge, these are the points to be emphasized. There are probably remedies for a great many social problems. For some of them, current practitioners are probably making some useful contributions, but the evaluation of plans and procedures should not be left in the hands of the vendors. Above all, the pictures of social reality put forward by social therapists should be treated as data for critical study and not as verified knowledge.

CHAPTER 4

Courtiers or Participants?

Human beings around the world often yearn for social controls more responsive to the needs and desires of their "own kind of people." When the possibility or the desire to have their own kind in control is lacking, the next best has often been a longing for an elite "on top" who will "do the right thing" or "listen to reason"—in other words, an elite who "will serve us." Reformist or revolutionary proposals for social reorganization take one or the other direction.

ELITISM'S TEMPTING GUISES

Intellectuals, even many "radical" ones, more than anything else share a faith in an elitism that would entrust controls to the "best"—that is, to their particular type of intellectual. Thus even a so-called "dictatorship of the proletariat" gets defined as a dictatorship in behalf of the proletariat. With a dynamic ideology assuring mass morale in the face of a collapsing *status quo ante*, those adroit enough to serve as midwives of revolt and as instruments of social reorganization take control in behalf of the co-operative, and thus co-opted, masses. To judge from available examples, promises of elites to expand decision making until it is well diffused throughout the masses never appear to get fulfilled unless such promises are frozen into a revered body of constitutional law.[1]

[1] W. H. Hamilton, "Constitutionalism," *Encyclopaedia of the Social Sciences*, IV (1931), 255–59; Zechariah Chafee, Jr., *The Blessings of Liberty* (Philadelphia: J. B. Lippincott, 1956); C. H. McIlwain, *Constitutionalism: Ancient and Modern* (Ithaca, N.Y.: Cornell University Press, 1958); M. R. Konvitz, *Bill of Rights Reader*, 4th ed. (Ithaca, N.Y.: Cornell University Press, 1968), esp. Chap. 2.

THE ALLEGED DANGERS OF "VULGARIZATION." Elitist intellectuals often speak with horror of "vulgarization." Somehow a cult's writ, methods, and initiation requirements must be protected from infection, often even from adaptation to changed life conditions. Above all, they distrust vesting decision making in the "common man," in the "masses." As one such intellectual put it in the late nineteenth century, "One of the great divisions of politics in our day is coming to be whether, at the last resort, the world should be governed by its ignorance or by its intelligence." The former "assuredly reverses all the past experiences of mankind. In every field of human enterprise, in all the competitions of life, by the inexorable law of Nature, superiority lies with the few, and not with the many, and success can only be attained by placing the guiding and controlling power in their hands." [2] Such a simplistic, monovalent conception of "superiority" leaves a great many questions unanswered even in the author's own terms.

PLATO'S DREAM. These views are not new ones now and were not new in the late nineteenth century. It must be admitted that they have a kind of overwhelming cogency for many people up to a certain point. In his *Republic*, Plato urged a resolution of the issue in favor of a self-perpetuating power elite made up of those who could excel in a prescribed educative process. [3] That such an educative process, even if it were a wise one at a given time, might disastrously resist adaptation to changed life conditions escaped the keen analyses of the ancient Greek. Few secular documents have been so widely acclaimed and admired by current winners in the intellectual accreditation sweepstakes at any given period.

DEMOCRACY AS LIBERATION. Such examples of social disaster as the Weimar Republic, the Kerensky Russian regime, and the Spanish civil war are often used as arguments against democracy. Yet Hitler's Germany and Mussolini's Italy can scarcely help make elitism appear virtuous. Arguments in terms of such extreme cases yield little on either side. To be more judicious, in the words of the political scientist Jack L. Walker, "Political stability is indeed a precious commodity; I do not wish to create the impression that I reject its obvious importance. But I do think that both the discipline of political science and American society have suffered from our excessive concern with the protection and maintenance of our political system. I believe that the time has come to direct our attention to the infinitely more difficult task of involving larger and larger numbers of people in the process of government. The theory of democracy beckons us toward an ancient ideal: the liberation of the energies of all our citizens

    2 W. E. H. Lecky, *Democracy and Liberty*, rev. ed. (New York: Longmans, Green, 1898), I, 25–26.
    3 *The Works of Plato*, ed. Irwin Edman (New York: Simon & Schuster, 1928), pp. 410–20.

in the common pursuit of the good society." [4] To be realized more than it superficially has been, this ideal must permeate as many facets of our society as possible.

The Revolting Masses as Arbiters. The rise of a "rebel mass" in recent centuries has made this whole matter appear not nearly as simple nor as categorical as it may once have been. During five centuries of ever cheaper and more efficient means of mass communication and of the accompanying intellectual awakening, population expansion, and geographical dispersion of the world's peoples, controlling elites throughout the world have had to confront a "vertical invader." An intellectual elitist [5] who is shocked at this mass-invader's questioning of established moral controls and authorities even calls him a barbarian or a primitive ruler though he may be educated for some status other than a ruling one.

BASIC ISSUES IN SOCIAL CONTROL

What are the basic issues in this ideological struggle for the control of the mind, the loyalties and activities of man? How is it that some intellectuals have given up elitism? For what alternatives? Is there some view of society that is tenable other than one dominated by one or a congeries of elites? In order to cope with society's power potentialities and susceptibilities, do we need to develop tiers of courtiers to those exercising power? Or can we become relatively autonomous participants in a participant society? How can we achieve such a participant society?

Significant points in the ideological struggles over the vertical invaders include the following five:

1. Social wisdom or truth does not belong exclusively or absolutely to any one type of intellectualism. Whatever wisdom or truth might be, it has so far eluded any one religious or secular group or even a series of such. Each intellectualism that we know depends for its power and influence upon group and societal support or acquiescence. This support then is often reinforced or distorted by such crystallizations of social power as custom, money, and people holding traditional social statuses. Thus many kinds of intellectualism coexist. They are *variously achieved and variously accredited,* and a great many of them can make useful positive and negative contributions to social processes. Less structured and less orthodox ones include some of the most dynamic and stimulating cultural influences.

[4] J. L. Walker, "A Reply to 'Further Reflections on "The Elitist Theory of Democracy,"'" *American Political Science Review,* LX (1966), 392.

[5] José Ortega y Gasset, *The Revolt of the Masses,* (1930; New York: W. W. Norton, 1932), esp. Chap. 9.

2. The contention that a certain group cannot rule itself is a self-fulfilling prophecy. Only those can rule themselves who have an opportunity to learn how to do so by doing so. The converse of that statement also holds: groups entrusted with or seizing self-control typically do much better than anticipated, if one evaluates their behavior in terms of their own interests and not in terms of interests other than their own.

3. Nothing is gained by lamenting a lack of formal educational preparation for governance or administration or participation. The art of serving representatively is learned intellectually and emotionally in a variety of ways. We are coming to comprehend better how to sensitize people to meet the demands of representative roles. We are also learning how to assure that the fulfilment of such roles is rewarded and that their incumbents are not tempted to push for more personal control of power. With leaders dedicated to maximizing participation by their constituents, technical specialists can adequately handle details of administration as long as they are prevailed upon to confine themselves to implementing policies determined representatively. Society is so complex that in all its activities it must give representation to a vast patchwork of intertwining and complementing levels, specialties of competence and of interest expression.

4. Only those exhibit a sense of social responsibility who have seized, been given, or earned responsible social roles. Those denied social responsibilities often become actively irresponsible. Actual responsibility is the key.

5. Outsiders many times can see quite clearly how unjustifiably elitist, as well as resented, is the control of one ethnic or allegedly "racial" group by another. Regardless of rationalization, controls based upon class status or upon some definition of intelligence are just as excruciating and unacceptable to those dominated as those based upon ethnic identity or "race." A rule by some "elect" is no practical substitute for the development of representatively adapting social functions and social functionaries.

Should the "ignorant" then be "entrusted" with the control of social organizations? This is not the thrust of my argument. On the contrary, since more and more people are effectively demanding participation in social decision making, and since society can gain from unlocking popular concerns and potentialities, we should cease trying to place special elites in control of our social destinies. We should devote our talents in all the social sciences to "the liberation of the energies of all our citizens in the common pursuit of the good society." [6]

[6] Walker, "A Reply," p. 392. See also W. G. Bennis and P. E. Slater, *The Temporary Society* (New York: Harper & Row, 1968), esp. Chaps. 1 and 6.

THE MANIPULATED AND THE
PARTICIPANT SOCIETY

In the manipulated society, the society of therapists, the society of elites and courtiers, the above points are ignored, perverted by definition, or only grudgingly and in part accepted. In the participant society that may now be evolving out of five centuries of increasing freedom in communication, discussion, education, and influence of the masses upon social decision making, elites and courtiers may be replaced by representatively oriented functionaries and other participants in the wide ranges of complicated modern living. Between the two rough types of society, the manipulated and the participant, there are many possible compromises. As in the past, vested elites will offer many rationalizations for their continuance. Who is really representative is a controversial matter. It can only be determined through actual tests of public support, and the plural is used here advisedly. Only repeated tests can overcome the consequences of short-term manipulations and popular confusions.

THE SWEEP AWAY FROM ELITISM. For what considerations are some intellectuals now giving up elitism with all its enticements, and for what alternatives? Is it possible that such intellectuals are symptomatic of a sweep away from elitism that is now gathering momentum? [7]

Mass education, mass suffrage, mass marketing, and mass warfare—hopefully, mass peacemaking also—insistently focus the attention of intellectuals, regardless of specialty, upon anti-elitist challenges. In this, debates over public opinion polls and over other sample-survey investigations have probably done more to deflate claims of would-be elitists and social therapists than any other controversy or development. How often the predictions of the latter have been incorrect! Thus, in a sense, one can paraphrase Karl Marx and Friedrich Engels' *Manifesto* and say that the specter haunting the world of the intellectuals is not so much communism

---

[7] Paul Goodman attempts oversimply and with apparent cynicism to identify the current anti-elitism of the young with "The Black Flag of Anarchism," *New York Times Magazine*, July 14, 1968, pp. 10 ff. To account for the lack of overt identification of American youth with anarchism, Goodman asserts that the "American young are unusually ignorant of political history." Since they are not more than spottily and superficially Marxian or communist, he contends they are really anarchists without knowing it. What he seems regretfully to detect—but will not admit—is that our young need no Proudhon to tell them to be tired of hypocrisy and manipulation. They want to make society participantly democratic and humanist. See also Robert Hoffman, ed., *Anarchism* (New York: Atherton Press, 1970), esp. essays by P.-J. Proudhon, Alexander Berkman, and Emma Goldman; Daniel Guérin, *Anarchism: From Theory to Practice*, trans. by Mary Klopper (New York: Monthly Review Press, 1970), esp. intro. by Noam Chomsky, pp. vii–xx.

as it is the common man, the rising masses. This specter even haunts communist elites who allege that they make policies in the name of the proletariat. Whether one speaks of the common man in terms of public opinion, the labor force, the electorate, the market, or even culture or society, that bulky aggregate has become an increasing threat to all power, control, and authority based upon special privilege. The end of this tendency is not now at all in sight.

EXPERTS ON THE COMMON MAN. Would-be therapists or manipulators can try to pose as experts on what the "common man" is thinking or doing. They can claim to be able to manipulate those thoughts and actions. Sometimes they can succeed in doing so, especially for short-term goals such as the sale of a particular candidate for the presidency, a brand of cigarettes or beer, or a clothing fad. But as we saw, students whose only object is to learn about human thoughts and behavior often reach quite different conclusions from those enunciated by would-be therapists. The misdiagnoses, and hence misguidances, of courtier-minded therapists help push the manipulated society towards failure. Their biases constantly help to nudge us either toward greater popular responsibility and participation or toward chaos-making efforts by elites to retain their controls. The choice between those alternatives will scarcely be a rational one based upon fact and logic. It will arise out of our ability in a collective milling process to destroy outworn vested interests in time and to substitute for them functionaries motivated by rewards that are more defensible and less socially destructive.

FACILITATION RATHER THAN MANIPULATION

How can any modern society persist without therapists of many sorts? The answer to this query is already in an advanced stage of social preparation: many therapists, especially those engaged in interpersonal consultation, have long had as their ideal a nonmanipulative stance toward clients. Their roles would be more easily perceived if they were more often called consultants, facilitators, or resource persons. They seek to provide clients with data and facilities with which the clients may solve their own problems as autonomously as possible in their own ways. Constituents, clients, inmates in all sorts of institutions, and members of many social categories are now organizing to achieve self-determination and to cope with their own problems. Prisoners, ex-prisoners, people in mental institutions and in other types of hospitals, people on relief, the blind, the deaf, the obese, the homosexual, and other people with problems are all clamoring for self-control and self-guidance.[8] Women, blacks, Spanish-Americans, Amerindians, other ethnic minorities, school pupils, college students, dropouts from school and from society, the socially experimental, and a vast array of other groups and social categories are all finding bases for joining in the general trend of the times toward self-determination. Members of political factions and parties, professions and vocations, trades and industries, and religious sects and denominations had long preceded them. All are questioning policies to which they have been subject. All are insisting upon policies that they themselves formulate or negotiate and that thus represent, as they see them and as nearly as possible, their own interests and needs more accurately and more authentically.

These many groups, factions, and categories of people are not at all averse to the use of factual data on which to base their policy reformulations, but they do not want specialists to use a group's need for data or service as a medium for its manipulation.

They make mistakes. They and their leaders may be quite unprepared as yet for participatory democracy. They want to find believable and dependable answers to their own questions as much as they can for themselves, with or without trained aid. If therapists can convert themselves adequately into consulting resource persons whom clients can trust, such specialists in all their variety can weather the changes now more and more upon us.

Even self-organization of the socially rejected—prisoners and inmates of mental institutions—promises long-sought dividends for themselves and society. The story of prisons as training schools for criminals and for sexual perversion, as brutalizers of guards, trusties, and other inmates, is well known to social investigators. The story of mental institutions, except for the notable examples of some constructive ones, is all too similar. They institutionalize staff and other inmates on a basis of persistence or even mere survival. The "cures" or even discharges after inmate-assimilation become few. Organizations of prisoners and ex-prisoners are beginning to bring a new realism to demands not only for the reform of prison living conditions, but also for improving the reassimilation processes available to such persons for their reentry into the "world outside." (In thinking about such activity, we need to realize that only a small percentage of those who break any criminal law ever even see the inside of a jail!) [9]

---

[8] See for example, American Friends Service Committee, *Struggle for Justice: A Report on Crime and Punishment in America* (New York: Hill and Wang, 1971), prepared by a working party of prisoners, ex-prisoners, criminologists, lawyers, and educators.

[9] M. B. Clinard, "Criminal Behavior Is Human Behavior," *Federal Probation*, XIII (1949), 24; E. H. Sutherland, "Is 'White Collar Crime' Crime?" in M. E. Wolfgang *et al.*, eds., *The Sociology of Crime and Delinquency*, rev. ed. (New York: John Wiley & Sons, 1970), pp. 20–27; J. H. Skolnick, *Justice Without Trial* (New York: John Wiley, 1966).

REWARDS IN THE PARTICIPANT
SOCIETY

A more participant society means a society in which the rewards for enterprise, artistic and scientific creativity, and managerial services become less confiscatory. It means a society in which such rewards prominently stress private satisfaction and public recognition for public service rather than the creation of huge private estates of a wasteful and unnecessary sort. The useful accomplishments achieved through foundation grants can now be subsidized at least as well by voluntary organizations and out of decentralized tax resources and other publicly controlled funds. Privately endowed foundations have too* typically nurtured, and even exacted, elite-favoring policies in return for their grants.

In all my depth interviews with entrepreneurs, artists, scientists, technicians, and managers, I found none who values excessive financial rewards above (1) his fun in what he is doing in his work and (2) the sense that he is helping to make society a better place for the living. In spite of what are often excessive incomes, they themselves often live quite modestly and express their discontent at the destructive influence of their affluence upon themselves, their wives, and their children. Entrepreneurs admittedly have to have access to funds or to other crystallizations of social power in order to achieve their innovative goals. They do not appear to regard it as too important to them, however, that those assets should actually be theirs or merely that those resources should be made available to them in some secure manner for their operations. In other words, as numerous biographies [10] of civil servants and politicians clearly indicate, public entrepreneurs can be far more constructive social instruments in the employ of the state than they would be for a financial or industrial corporation, even in our plutocratic economy.

THE RISING COMMON DENOMINATOR. Would a participant society mean one in which all organizations and operations are reduced to the lowest common denominator of taste, thought, behavior, efficiency, and controls? Quite the contrary. Our manipulated society commonly perverts educational processes quite automatically and thus maintains chimerical social controls useful to vested elites. To an appalling extent, it impounds rather than enlightens our youth. It debases literacy. It contains pressures

[10] P. P. Van Riper, *History of the United States Civil Service* (Evanston, Ill.: Row, Peterson, 1958); Herman Finer, *Theory and Practice of Modern Government,* 4th ed. (London: Methuen, 1961). The notable contributions by professors and research people in public colleges and universities are not ordinarily separated from those in privately controlled institutions, but their records in the United States are distinguished.

that make popular thinking conform to noncontroversial patterns. It encourages unconscionable advertising and other "public relations." It permits the disastrous wheeling and dealing of a financial-industrial complex at home and abroad. It wastefully exploits our talent and labor. It commercially glorifies the banal in the arts. It appears constantly to strive to depress popular standards of taste, thought, and behavior, even though it fails to do so.

THE "UNSTRANDING" OF THE
COMMON MAN

At the same time, the vertical invasion of the masses continues. The intellectual variegation and sophistication of the masses increases. The creativity and agitation for greater shares in social control by the masses does not abate, and the spreading awareness of our environmental crisis is giving the vertical invasion even greater urgency.

As the political scientist Carl J. Friedrich concludes, "Marx, Freud, and Pareto left the common man stranded. . . . They (and most of us with them) saw the average human as tossed about on the seas of class struggles, emotions, and drives, without the faintest chance of making head or tail of what is going on—except for those who happened to agree with the particular revelation." [11] In spite of such sophisticated ideologists, the contrary is taking place: the common man is "unstranding" himself, as it were, and he is influencing intellectuals to accept his more dynamic roles.

The sort of society we have now results from how we have traditionally permitted controls over social power to be distributed within it. The kind of society we can now have depends upon our ability and our willingness to redistribute such controls. How powerful are financiers to remain? Must blacks, Puerto Ricans, Amerindians, Chicanos, and "poor whites" continue to be so segregated and so powerless? How are we to define the controls entrusted to men and women, to the various age levels? How bureaucratically rigid and unyielding to changed life conditions will our professionals be permitted to remain or to become?

SOCIAL SCIENCE AS THE SCIENCE OF SOCIAL POWER. What has such talk about the control of social power to do with sociology? Isn't the control of power a problem of political science and of economics? Many have taken that position, but on the contrary, social science as a whole can well be considered basically as the science of social power, whatever else it might

[11] C. J. Friedrich, *The New Image of the Common Man* (Boston: Beacon Press, 1950), p. 28.

be. None of the special disciplines deals with more than a phase or aspect of controls over power, and power needs to be seen broadly, in its complicated ramifications, for its nature to be at all clear.

THE POSSIBILITY OF A
HUMANE SOCIETY

As a consequence of mass pressures, of the shrinking of the world's apparent size, and of the threatened extinction of the human race through the growing overpopulation and pollution of the whole terrestrial environment, we are beginning to see more clearly how a society dedicated to human service rather than to personal profit through manipulation would unlock floodgates of creativity, whether entrepreneurial, artistic, scientific, technical, or managerial. The trend of human events and developments is more and more decisively forcing that view and its consequences upon intellectuals and society as an alternative to chaos.

To put the matter otherwise, more and more people as they now grow up in our society are learning that subservience is not necessary. Subservience depends more upon intellectual and emotional acceptance of subservience than upon anything else. People are comprehending that they do possess autonomous human dignity. It is theirs to keep, to nurture, to use. It involves some risks, some experimentation with techniques and etiquettes, but the spirit of the times is providing opportunities for mutual reinforcement in autonomous participation that have not existed so readily and so widely before.

The awakening and rising masses are fragmented, diverse, confused, and often poorly motivated and led. Their ferment and their efforts at self-direction and self-organization, however, are giving people ways to express themselves and to participate in cooperative self-determination. Thus they are exhibiting their autonomous human dignity to an extent hitherto not thought possible.

NO STATIC BLUEPRINT FOR
THE FUTURE

When reference is made to the kind of society we might have, there is no thought of furnishing a static blueprint for what we might achieve at some future time. All societies change. Societies are social arrangements in process, not fixed edifices. The concern is therefore with directions of change and with leverages that may be exploited to achieve more humane social interrelationships. Admittedly, it is a struggle in which there can be no clear-cut victory, and in which only eternal vigilance can protect human gains from the selfishly aggressive and manipulative. There can be goals, however, and social assets can be assessed and exploited for human gains rather than for the gains of antisocial elites.

THE SOCIETY WE CAN NOW HAVE

With that caveat in mind, the society we can now have can offer its members opportunities to participate more effectively and with more satisfaction in significant community life. It can present both sexes and all age levels with challenges to involve or engage themselves in significant social tasks. It can help us sense our interdependence upon one another not just within a limited neighborhood, region, or country, but with all humanity. It can foster conceptions of equality that glorify human personality and thus free both the exceptional and all other human beings to make their contributions to human welfare—not for exploitative purposes, but in gratitude for life and human fellowship.

TYPES OF "SOCIALISM." The society we can have can thus reflect our collective recognition that a mass society needs to be a humane society of participants, even a society that will frankly be called "socialistic." Both Republican and Democratic leaders in politics and their counterparts in finance and industry have been giving this conclusion grudging recognition more and more in recent decades. The problem has become not whether or not we shall have a socialistic society, but whether it shall be a plutocratic one ruled by an economic elite (often called state or national socialism), a demagogic one ruled by a political elite on the Soviet model, or a democratically participant one. The extremely ideologized examples of national socialism in Nazi Germany and Fascist Italy included in their baggage pompously charismatic leaders, militarized political parties, and racist excesses that might not be so clearly apparent in the early stages of such a development in English or American society. Similarly, the disastrous elitist-dictatorship potentialities of demagogic socialism on the Soviet pattern are not always apparent, even though Stalin gave them dramatic exemplification. Participatory democratic socialism might conceivably grow out of the demagogic type, and it has associations no more damaging than those in current Swedish experience.

STEPS AWAY FROM "FREE ENTERPRISE." The steps the United States has taken away from "free enterprise" toward either plutocratic or demagogic socialism obeyed no ideological mandate. They were steps their backers assumed in each case to be in line with social necessity, *i.e.*, economic and political expediency. Whether it was the federal government bailing out a sinking corporation, industry, or region, or setting up a "War on Poverty" (under the control of existing politicians) or a Medicaid program (on the terms of private medical practitioners), each step did have one hallmark in common with the others: it was assumed by the current power wielders to do more to strengthen than to weaken their own existing controls in our society.

This is not to say that those in crucial decision-making positions are always fully conscious of what they are doing and that they always know the precise significance of their acts. They cannot predict infallibly the consequences of their decisions—far from it. Perhaps in the very fallibility of their social knowledge and thus of their ability to predict—usually the case with entrenched elites—lies more of gain than of loss to society. Fortunately for the well-being of us all, the leaders of certain counterelite movements in society by reason of their peripheral or marginal position are more likely to recognize the expediency of accepting and acting in terms of daringly accurate social data than are those vested in positions of social control. Thus, peripheral though they be, they can have weight out of all proportion to their apparent power.

CHAPTER 5

The Many Faces
of Autonomy

QUESTIONS FOREIGNERS ASK

Students of mine in a European university, students deeply and sympathetically concerned about American affairs, have in effect asked me: "Professor, you Americans talk a lot about democracy and about the high values you say you see in individual autonomy. Your writers—Jefferson, Thoreau, Whitman, Woodrow Wilson, John Dewey, and John F. Kennedy among others—have written beautifully and convincingly about democracy and nonconformism and individuality. Why is all that? Do you really understand and mean it? Or is it just a pleasant and powerful but deluding verbal ritual? Why do not your people and your educational institutions demonstrate in their behavior an actual attachment to democracy as a way of life and to the development of autonomous individuals such as you say a democracy requires for its full and effective operation? Why do we in European universities get the impression that Americans are tremendously homogenized and fearful of nonconformism? Why do your institutions appear to us as being largely dedicated to human standardization?"

Such questions cannot be brushed aside with an abstract formula. Their implications require careful and dispassionate consideration. In a sense, the present book, especially this chapter, is a statement of my answers to them.

99

DEMOCRACY IN AMERICAN
PRACTICE

Unabashedly and in spite of the many cogent criticisms by social sophisticates in the United States and elsewhere who would undermine such a position,[1] I have faith in the practical virtues of the democracy of Thomas Jefferson and John Dewey adapted constructively to contemporary conditions. In my estimation, democracy can be a tenable and highly useful way of life for the individual and for society. I trust that we can learn how to implement it more fully for more people in the United States and elsewhere in the world. Certainly some of the wisest and most admirable Americans do much to exemplify democracy as a way of life and to help us to realize its potentialities in social policies. In spite of the elitism and conformism of many American writers and professional men, I am convinced that American professors as a group include some of the most free and democratic intellectuals in the world.

Though I have great faith in democracy, I am vividly aware of its spotty application, its denial in practice to many of our nonwhite citizens,[2] its abuse in the hands of those we belittlingly call politicians, the authoritarianism too typical of many of our voluntary associations and schools,[3] and our anxious devotion to influences that provide an apparent stability through conformism and bureaucratization. As a public-relations counselor recently asserted in a leading public-relations journal, "We pride ourselves on individualism, yet each day dissent is looked upon increasingly as a form of perversity or, at best, mental aberration."[4] We seem to believe that individual autonomy is fine as long as it is respectable, nonthreatening, and directed toward individual profit or enjoyment.[5] This is

---

[1] For explorations of the pros and cons of political and social democracy, see Alexander Hamilton, John Jay, and James Madison, *The Federalist*, with an introduction by E. M. Earle (New York: Modern Library, 1941); Bernard Mayo, ed., *Jefferson Himself* (Boston: Houghton Mifflin, 1942); Dumas Malone, *Jefferson and His Time* (Boston: Little, Brown, 1948–1951), I and II; R. B. Perry, *Puritanism and Democracy* (New York: Vanguard Press, 1944).

[2] U.S. Commission on Civil Rights, *Political Participation* (Washington: Government Printing Office, 1968); U.S. National Advisory Commission on Civil Disorders, *Report*, with an introduction by Tom Wicker (New York: Bantam, 1968), esp. Chap. 17; *One Year Later: An Assessment of the Nation's Response to the Crisis Described by the National Advisory Commission on Civil Disorders* (Washington: Urban America and the Urban Coalition, 1969).

[3] C. W. Merrifield, ed., *Leadership in Voluntary Enterprise* (New York: Oceana Publications, 1961); see also Robert Michels, *Political Parties*, trans. by E. and C. Paul (New York: Collier, 1962).

[4] R. E. Kingsley, "The Function of Controversy," *Public Relations Journal*, XI (1966), 7.

[5] See the ever-fresh comments on this by H. D. Thoreau in *Walden or, Life in the Woods* (New York: New American Library, 1942), esp. Chaps. 2, 18.

the vaunted sense of autonomy of the successful technician who habitually applies established policy. An example would be the autonomy of any carefully schooled social instrument—a successful football player or performing artist or statistician or insurance salesman or policeman. It is the sense of autonomy that a woman feels in selecting a new hairdo, new clothes, or a personal automobile, that a man feels in telling funny stories, getting a promotion in rank, making poker winnings, or hiring a new secretary.

THE STRANGE INNOVATORS. A great many of us, however, mistrust the strange sense of autonomy that permits artists, scientists, philosophers, and agitators to break with old forms, to cast doubt on familiar dependabilities of social life, and to offer new symbols, theses, observations, and organizational structures. Such innovators are rarely valued during their most creative periods, when their sense of autonomy is being given its greatest tests. After they have won their battles or have died, after they have become self-plagiarists rather than newly creative, after their impact upon their specialty and upon society has been absorbed, or at least handled, they can become heroes rather than freaks or cranks. But even then they are rarely the individuals we Americans hold up as models for our children. Their lives are much too speculative and even hazardous.

DEMOCRACY AS SOCIAL
PHILOSOPHY

Democracy is a philosophy of social organization and participation that maximizes tolerance toward, and benefits from, internecine disagreements, competitions, and struggles, even conflicts. It depends for its continuity and vitality upon the ability of its adherents to develop, tolerate, and exploit the talents and products of individuals and groups with a variety of degrees and types of autonomy. It is dedicated to equalizing opportunities without homogenizing aspirations.

Our compromisers who offer formulas for quick and quiet "action" are too often misunderstood and overvalued; they often serve chiefly to blunt the thrust of efforts toward social adaptation.[6] Democratic vitality comes from ferment, not from tranquility. From the standpoints of those with disproportionate vested interests of many sorts in our society, democracy is largely "negative"—and so it is, in a sense, contrary to what such critics would intend. Democracy resembles a disinfectant or a weedkiller. Both democracy and disinfectants can help human beings to survive and to thrive by offsetting or eliminating influences harmful to them.

[6] For keen insights into the nature of social action in the United States, see Goodwin Watson, *Action for Unity* (New York: Harper & Bros., 1947), esp. Chap. 3.

We Americans have yet to take the risk of developing a whole citizenry sufficiently autonomous, aggressive, and creative to implement democracy comprehensively throughout our society. To the extent that we have had and still possess such citizens, they are "thousand upon thousand common men,/ Cranks, martyrs, starry-eyed enthusiasts/ . . . And men with a cold passion for mere justice."[7] Before we preen ourselves with the accomplishments of these deviants, however, we should realize that a great number of them were developed elsewhere and fled to the United States to make their contributions.[8] How well are our natives performing roles as stimulating as our more productive immigrants?

A PARADIGM FOR SENSES OF AUTONOMY

As the foregoing suggests, the conception of individual autonomy, like many other conceptions used in the social sciences, is highly relative in degree and character, and thus quite diverse in its manifestations. As the psychologist Erik H. Erikson observes, such conceptions as "a sense of autonomy" are "at the same time, ways of *experiencing* accessible to introspection; ways of *behaving*, observable to others; and unconscious *inner states* determinable by test and analysis."[9]

One can readily expand these three aspects of a sense of autonomy into a more analytical instrument—a two-dimensional nine-box paradigm —by noting that each of these three aspects of autonomy can be evaluated (a) subjectively (in terms of the evolving, socializing self), (b) socially (in terms of the person's social interrelationships), and (c) objectively (in terms of actual and possible consequences of the person's thoughts, emotions, and actions).

Even this complicated paradigm, however, does not suggest at all adequately the major facets of the autonomy problem. In addition, the individual (self and person) has more than one social personality configuration, each keyed to a given type of social-situational context, and the criteria by which autonomy is evaluated are embedded in contrasting societal and group cultures. Somehow the tentative nine-box paradigm

[7] Stephen Vincent Benét, "Listen to the People," *Pocket Book*, ed. by Robert van Gelder (New York: Pocket Books, 1946), p. 384.

[8] M. R. Davie *et al.*, *Refugees in America* (New York: Harper & Bros., 1947); D. P. Kent, *The Refugee Intellectual* (New York: Columbia University Press, 1953); John Kosa, ed., *The Home of the Learned Man: A Symposium on the Immigrant Scholar in America* (New Haven: College & University Press, 1968).

[9] E. H. Erikson, *Childhood and Society*, 2nd ed. (New York: W. W. Norton, 1963), p. 251.

needs to be given far more boxes on other planes to bring into our analysis the full implications of the characteristic multivalence of both man and society.[10] And since I have perhaps unwisely spoken of "boxes," it needs to be insisted that the boxes are not categories; they are merely rallying points for phenomena resembling a selected ideal type, a way of bringing them together for comparison and other considerations.

To state Erikson's conceptions [11] of a sense of autonomy more fully, they may be seen as—

(1) an unconscious inner state (determinable by test and analysis, to be seen individually and socially in a mutivalent context);

(2) a way of experiencing (accessible to introspection and analysis, to be seen individually and socially in a multivalent context); and

(3) a way of behaving (observable by others, to be correlated with social-situational stimuli and thus set in a multivalent context).

To amplify the second dimension given for our nine-box paradigm, each of the Erikson views can be evaluated by self and others in relation to—

(a) the individual's self-history (adaptations to physical, biological, and social influences), the "subjective";

(b) the person's social life-history (including his typicality or deviance in terms of relevant personal, group, and societal patterns), the "social"; and

(c) objective consequences, both actual and possible (significance of levels of aspiration and of accomplishment, of special incidents making for goal-realization), the "objective."

To carry our paradigm into a third dimension, data on inner states and on ways of experiencing and behaving can be evaluated by the individual or for him by an analyst—

(i) in terms of his own somewhat unique criteria and characteristics considered in the setting provided by his life-history;

(ii) in terms of criteria arising out of social interaction within his variously defined cultural settings (group and societal); and

(iii) in terms of criteria selected for their relevance to probable objective consequences.

Such evaluations would deal with the qualitative characteristics and degree of autonomy as they arise from the cultural matrices and from other experienced influences of those exhibiting autonomy.

---

[10] This discussion applies theories brought together and developed in much greater detail in A. McC. Lee, *Multivalent Man* (New York: George Braziller, 1966), esp. Chaps. 14–21. The present chapter is not an extract from that book.

[11] Erikson, *Childhood and Society*, p. 251.

AUTONOMY ON DIFFERENT
STATUS LADDERS

To suggest further the complexities of this paradigm, let me discuss certain cultural (group-cultural rather than societal-cultural) differences in the patterning of a sense of autonomy. Let us consider the rather different senses autonomy takes among those performing social roles related to what is called social science. Let us look at the sense of autonomy of (1) *enterprisers,* absorbed in some version of what they often call "the game," (2) *bureaucrats,* absorbed in affairs related to "the organization," whatever their organization may be, including especially the status ladder associated with that organization, (3) *technicians,* especially those involved in their "science" (whether it be sociology, anthropology, political science, or whatever) and absorbed in the merchandising and utilization of their techniques, status and reputation, and related wisdom, and (4) *innovating scientists,* absorbed in searching for novelty under whatever conditions they find available. The social sciences include all four of these types, though few social scientists would wish to admit to an orientation other than that of an innovating scientist. Let me emphasize here that these social types do occur and are useful for analytical purposes despite the fact that individual social scientists often are not "pure" examples and certainly may change during their careers from one type to another. The types fit us all much better than most of us wish to admit.

THE MANY VALUE ORIENTATIONS OF SOCIAL SCIENTISTS. A social scientist's social-status-group background and other experiences provide him with a value orientation to his field. They equip him with preconceptions as to what type of status ladder is most worthwhile and available for him to try to climb. They give him a sense of whether it is more likely to be satisfying, at least at the outset, to try to get into the wheeling-and-dealing "game" of research grants or other entrepreneurism, or to put his faith in identifying with an organization through its bureaucracy, or to trust to his technique-centered abilities as a journeyman available for hire, or to try to assault the shortcomings of his science as directly, as wholeheartedly, and as heedlessly as possible. Success in any one of these emphases or types of status ladders requires a different conception of autonomy from the others. Each calls for more than an ordinary sense of autonomy as judged either subjectively or objectively. Whether or not it also demands an extraordinary sense of autonomy as judged socially depends on the status ladder involved. Some social groups are unusually supportive of efforts by their members at upward mobility. Many bureaucrats and professionals find it expedient not to appear too autonomous. Frustration, disillusionment, or an impression of greener fields may take a social scientist from one to another of these types of ladder and orientation, but the values associated with his initial type of striving are usually deeply set in the thoughts and emotions of every social scientist who is sufficiently impelled to distinguish himself on one or another of these ladders.

CONTRASTING SUBCULTURES. These four types of orientation to social science are different enough to constitute the bases for what amounts to four rather contrasting subcultures within each of our social-scientific fields. The adherents of each orientation have developed a rationale for their work rather different from the rest. These rationales—all publicly alleged to be those of innovation-prone scientists—figure strongly in clique formation, in educational policies for professional training and evaluation, in practical criteria for personnel selection, and in internecine quarrels within social-scientific fields. Thus in studying the roles of autonomy in the sociology and psychology of social-scientific knowledge it is important not to stop with surface statements about attachment to scientific investigation, but to pry into the evidence of these four major types of orientation as well as the evidence of other more or less subtle ethnic, class, national, and more personal value configurations and adhesions.

THE BIASES OF SOCIOLOGISTS

Much of sociology is alleged to be value free.[12] In the case of studies in any given field, the less important socially the social or sociological problems with which a piece of research deals, the more likely it is to appear to be value free.

THE ENTERPRISER'S BIASES. In spite of such routine allegations of their being "value free," some sociological writings are entrepreneurially biased in one or more ways. One need not go so far as some of the defensive statements surrounding the fall of Project Camelot to detect this flavor in monographs and in articles in learned journals.[13] Project Camelot was

---

[12] A. W. Gouldner, "Anti-Minotaur: The Myth of a Value-Free Sociology," in Maurice Stein and Arthur Vidich, eds., *Sociology on Trial* (Englewood Cliffs, N.J.: Prentice-Hall, 1963) pp. 35–52; R. W. Friedrichs, *A Sociology of Sociology* (New York: Free Press, 1970), esp. Chaps. 4 and 5.

[13] I. L. Horowitz, "The Life and Death of Project Camelot," *TransAction*, III, No. 1 (November-December 1965), 3–7, 44–47. See also the resulting comments, esp. III, No. 3 (March-April 1966), 2, 55–56, and III, No. 5 (July-August 1966), 54–56. A. McC. Lee, "Sociologists in an Integrating Society," *Social Problems*, II (1954–1955), 57–66, "Individual and Organizational Research in Sociology," in S. M. Lipset and N. J. Smelser, eds., *Sociology: The Progress of a Decade* (Englewood Cliffs, N.J.: Prentice-Hall, 1961) pp. 158–65, and "Items for the Agenda of Social Science," in A. W. Gouldner and S. M. Miller, eds., *Applied Sociology* (New York: Free Press, 1965), Chap. 33.

subsidized by the U.S. Department of the Army through the Special Operations Research Organization located at American University and was guided by high-echelon Army officers who worked through a prestigious academic staff recruited from a variety of American universities for the purpose. The Project's "scientific" mission was the analysis of leftist movements in Latin America in order to spot situations that might become insurrectional:

> Two parallel but distinct vocabularies were maintained—one military with military justifications, the other sociological with social-scientific justifications—illustrating perhaps the sleight-of-hand manner in which role theory is able to transform military intelligence work into value-free social research without the slightest change in the activity itself.[14]

Fortunately for the restoration of a more defensible balance of influence among the four orientations to which sociologists adhere, Project Camelot died of exposure, although Camelotism in the sense of entrepreneurism in sociology marches on.[15]

The Bureaucrat's Biases. In spite of the routine allegations of their being "value free," many other sociological writings leave the bureaucratically oriented quite comfortable and admiring. This has been the great appeal of both the innovating Max Weber and the rationalizing Talcott Parsons.[16] Both provide academic bureaucrats with abstract, and consequently vague, "systems" of social thought that seem to order all significant aspects of society. Both have aided bureaucratic aspirants with endless possible starting points for elegant degree dissertations that are socially noncontroversial. Appropriately enough, during World War I at the age of fifty, Max Weber "was commissioned as a disciplinary and economic officer, a captain, in charge of establishing and running nine hospitals in the Heidelberg area." During more than a year in that capacity, Captain Weber took a "social apparatus . . . of dilettantes . . . and . . . worked for and witnessed its transformation into an ordered bureaucracy." [17] Parsons exemplified similar talents and enthusiasms when, after

---

[14] Friedrichs, A Sociology of Sociology, p. 122.

[15] R. V. Bowers, "The Military Establishment," in P. F. Lazarsfeld, W. H. Sewell, and H. L. Wilensky, eds., The Uses of Sociology (New York: Basic Books, 1967), Chap. 9; Gouldner and Miller, eds., Applied Sociology, esp. Chaps. 5–9 and 21.

[16] Franco Ferrarotti, Max Weber e il Destino della Ragione, 2nd ed. (Bari: Editori Laterza, 1968), esp. Chap. 2. See also papers on Max Weber by Talcott Parsons, Reinhardt Bendix, P. F. Lazarsfeld, Edward Shils et al., American Sociological Review, XXX (1965), 171–223.

[17] H. H. Gerth and C. W. Mills, "A Biographical View," in Gerth and Mills, eds., From Max Weber: Essays in Sociology (New York: Oxford University Press, 1946), p. 22.

serving as president of the American Sociological Association, he took over as its secretary in a reorganization and then became during 1965–1967 the first editor of its "trade" journal, *The American Sociologist*.[18]

THE TECHNICIAN'S BIASES. To continue my illustrations of bias due to orientation in spite of routine allegations of its being "value free,"a great deal of sociology is technique-centered or frankly concerned with methodological rather than substantive problems. Of all types of sociological writing, this is presumably the most carefully insulated from "contamination" by uncontrollable complexities of social life. It is, at any rate, easily kept clear of unfashionable value involvements.

THE DEDICATED INNOVATOR'S BIASES. Sociologists who are oriented entrepreneurially, bureaucratically, and technically often regard those oriented solely or principally toward innovation and revision as irresponsible, negative, and, of course, unscientific, biased, or perhaps value-laden. These "irresponsible" devotees of curiosity and innovation in sociology, with their characteristic irreverence toward established techniques, theories, and data, have not been numerous in American sociology, even though United States sociologists are the most numerous in the world. These innovators also have their biases. Their predominant bias usually derives from the drive motivating their quests. This leaves them unwilling to permit things to remain the same after they have worked on them. This bias helps to explain, for example, why William Graham Sumner is such a bitter pill to either admirers or opponents of "social Darwinism" when his later and more mature writings are read extensively and with care. He could once be called a social Darwinist, but he evolved into a keenly probing social scientist.[19] This bias also helps to explain the dissatisfaction and disillusionment of Marxians with many of the papers of C. Wright Mills.[20] Not to provide an exhaustive list but merely some examples, we

[18] For candid statements by Parsons on his activities as Secretary of the American Sociological Association, replies, and an assessment, see A. McC. Lee, reports as A.S.A. delegate from the Society for the Study of Social Problems, *Social Problems*, IX (1961–1962), 289–92, 400–401; X (1962–1963), 97–100, 293–97, 409–11; XI (1963–1964), 319–21; XII (1964–1965), 356–60. See also reports by Parsons as Secretary in *American Sociological Review* and his editorial column in *The American Sociologist*, I and II (1965–1967).

[19] Reinhardt Bendix, "Max Weber and Jakob Burckhardt," *American Sociological Review*, XXX (1965), 176–84, writes of Sumner's work as "a defense of the 'Gilded Age,' sanctioning the success of the few and the deprivation of the many as inevitable outgrowths of the struggle for survival" (p. 179). This generalization could be based on Sumner's *What Social Classes Owe to Each Other* (New York: Harper & Bros., 1883), but it could not at all be derived accurately from his more mature writings, such as *Folkways* (Boston: Ginn, 1906) and his later essays. See M. R. Davie, *William Graham Sumner* (New York: Thomas Y. Crowell, 1963).

[20] I. L. Horowitz, "Introduction," in C. W. Mills, *Power, Politics and People* (New York: Oxford University Press, 1963), esp. pp. 14–20.

have also such "irresponsible" social-scientific innovators as Charles
Horton Cooley, Robert E. Park, W. I. Thomas, Thorstein Veblen, Willard
Waller, and those imports, Pitirim A. Sorokin and Florian Znaniecki. A
great many recognized by Americans as outstanding innovators in sociology have been Europeans—for example, Émile Durkheim, Karl Mannheim, Herbert Spencer, Vilfredo Pareto, and Max Weber; and many were
not to be called sociologists strictly speaking at all—for example, Franz
Boas, Sigmund Freud, William James, A. L. Kroeber, W. E. H. Lecky,
Niccolò Machiavelli, and Karl Marx.

COMPARATIVE UTILITY OF THE
FOUR TYPES OF ASPIRATION AND
AUTONOMY

The foregoing discussion may have given the impression that only
those social scientists who are dedicated to innovation are to be considered
seriously as sociologists and are to be emulated. In spite of this implication, sociology and other scientific disciplines require specialists with each
of the four outlined types of aspiration, identification, and autonomy, as
well as a range of ethnic, class, national, and more uniquely personal
differences in orientation. Entrepreneurs develop support for novel types
of investigation, for new trends in a discipline, and for new applications
of scientific findings. They upset vested interests and offer new inducements to productivity. Bureaucrats make possible the programs of our
academic departments, research institutes, colleges, and professional
societies. They provide necessary administrative and organizational
knowledge, dedication, and stability. Technicians, skilled in social-scientific procedures and findings, make possible the replications of research,
the applications of findings, and the training of more technicians who
provide the principal media for the polishing, transmission, and use of a
field's products. The innovators not only develop the great bulk of fresh
"merchandise," largely to be used by others, whether accepted or rejected
by them, but they also share responsibility with the entrepreneurs for
keeping a field somewhat shaken up and thus vital and relevant to the
needs of society.

No one needs to feel downgraded by these labels. The labels can
merely be brushed aside, as they constantly are in practice. At any rate,
the lion's share of prestigious jobs, titles, and other rewards goes to the
entrepreneurs, bureaucrats, and technicians in any social-scientific field.
As in the churches, the innovators receive their rewards from the enjoyment of their work or in anticipation of recognition in a hereafter that may
never come.

THE RECOGNITION OF SOCIOLOGY'S
MULTIVALENCE

The two principal concluding points to be made here are these: 1. A greater mutual understanding, tolerance, and recognition of mutual usefulness among the adherents of these four diverse value-orientations in our social-scientific and other learned fields would eliminate a lot of unnecessary wear and tear in professional planning, would assure each discipline of more dynamic development, and would certainly serve better the interests of society. 2. The stimulation of a greater sense of autonomy for members of each of the four groups could be achieved much more readily after a recognition of a discipline's multivalent motivational and organizational needs. The intolerance among the adherents of these four orientations in any field is at times quite shocking.

Let us develop this second point a little further.

THE NEED FOR INNOVATORS. At the present time in our society we do a rather good job of developing vast numbers of well-trained and well-motivated bureaucrats and technicians. They are "normal." As the latter-day and vastly expanded Rome of our century, we need both bureaucrats[21] and technicians in great quantities and in many disciplines in order to operate our huge and complex society. We also need enterprisers and innovators in our disciplines. Many of our spokesmen admit this, but we often get them chiefly by accident, by mistake, largely in spite of our efforts to make instruments rather than to nurture autonomous leaders of our people. Our most dependable sources of enterprisers and of innovating scientists and artists sufficiently autonomous to succeed in their difficult careers are individuals and groups who have been wrenched away from their social matrices and forced to cope with new social situations, new cultural patterns, and new social challenges. Marginality, chiefly due to such forced cultural mixing, gives us much of the invention, novelty, borrowing, and thus adaptation, to be found in society. At the same time, it needs to be added, it also stimulates less desirable and even disastrous individual and social deviations.[22]

As long as our latter-day Rome is able to siphon off the creative marginals from its own depressed ethnic pockets and from other countries, perhaps the stimulation of the kinds of autonomy that foster scientific,

---

[21] See H. H. Stroup's justification of the bureaucrat in his *Bureaucracy and Higher Education* (New York: Free Press, 1966).

[22] R. E. Park, "Introduction," in E. V. Stonequist, *The Marginal Man* (New York: Charles Scribner's Sons, 1937), pp. xiii–xviii; A. L. Kroeber, *Anthropology: Culture Patterns & Processes*, rev. ed. (1948; New York: Harcourt, Brace & World, 1963), pp. 226–29; Lee, *Multivalent Man*, Chaps. 18–19.

artistic, and other sorts of innovation may be left somewhat to accidents and mistakes. The time may well come, however, as it did in ancient Rome, when the "systems [of Plato and Aristotle, of Zeno and Epicurus], transmitted with blind deference from one generation of disciples to another, precluded every generous attempt to exercise the powers, or enlarge the limits, of the human mind. The beauties of the poets and orators, instead of kindling a fire like their own, inspired only cold and servile imitations: or if any ventured to deviate from those models, they deviated at the same time from good sense and propriety. . . . A cloud of critics, of compilers, of commentators, darkened the face of learning, and the decline of genius was soon followed by the corruption of taste." [23]

The growing pall of orthodoxy over course work in the social sciences suggests that we also may already have developed too uncritical a deference to established methods and theories.[24] We, too, are inspiring many "cold and servile imitations." [25] Our compilers and commentators create a sense of activity with their vast piles of books and papers, but are we attempting well enough to exercise the powers and to enlarge the limits of the human mind?

Fortunately, for all the efforts of the established elites to maintain the hegemonies of their cults, the pressures outlined in the previous chapter are democratizing social science and society. The vertical invasion of the masses, the shrinking and integration of the world, and the environmental threat of mankind's actual extinction are all joining to make the risks of autonomy less important than its challenging opportunities. The young and the young at heart realize more vividly than ever that it isn't even safe to "play life safe."

[23] Edward Gibbon, *The History of the Decline and Fall of the Roman Empire*, ed. with notes by H. H. Milman (Philadelphia: Porter & Coates, 1845), I, 107–8. See also A. L. Kroeber, *Configurations of Culture Growth* (Berkeley: University of California Press, 1944).

[24] Note the vast number of reprint collections for text use advertised in sociological journals and the relative sameness and superficiality of introductory texts. Note also the extreme but symptomatic criticisms of the field in such "radical" sociological periodicals (more or less transient) as *Berkeley Journal of Sociology* (University of California at Berkeley), *Catalyst* (State University of New York, Buffalo, N.Y.), *Eastern Union of Radical Sociologists Newsletter* (Brandeis University, Waltham, Mass.), *Heuristics* (Northern Illinois University, De Kalb, Ill.), *The Human Factor* (Columbia University, New York, N.Y.), *The Insurgent Sociologist* (New University Conference—Radical Sociology Caucus, University of Oregon, Eugene), *Leviathan* (San Francisco, Calif.), *Ripsaw* (Columbia University, New York, N.Y.), and *Sociologists for Women in Society Newsletter* (Notre Dame University, Notre Dame, Indiana).

[25] See the penetrating analysis by Gunnar Myrdal, *Value in Social Theory*, ed. by Paul Streeten (New York: Harper & Bros., 1958), esp. pp. 44–45, 54. See also Friedrichs, *A Sociology of Sociology*, esp. Chaps. 10 and 12; P. A. Sorokin, *Fads and Foibles in Modern Sociology and Related Sciences* (Chicago: Henry Regnery, 1956), esp. Chaps. 8–10; C. W. Mills, *The Sociological Imagination* (New York: Oxford University Press, 1959), esp. Chaps. 3–5.

SUMMARY

What began as a discussion of questions about autonomy in the United States raised by students in a foreign university has evolved first into a consideration of the ramifications of a sense of autonomy and of the many criteria by which autonomy might be judged. Then it proceeded into an analysis of our indebtedness to deprived groups in our own society and to foreign countries as sources for creatively autonomous people.

As it was with the foreign students, the institutions of other countries always seem to foreigners to be dedicated largely to homogenization. To learn about the life of a society and its vitality, however, do not look to the easily available reports on its activities. Look to its focal points of ferment and stimulation. The people at those foci in United States society today echo the creative impulses of Jefferson, Thoreau, Whitman, and other idealists of nonconformity and individuality. Members of all societies (and especially of our own) need to learn that same lesson for the understanding of their own as well as of other societies.[26]

[26] Some parts of this chapter appeared as "Institutional Structures and Individual Autonomy," *Human Organization*, XXVI (1967), 1–5.

CHAPTER 6

Ideologies in Social Struggles

Humanist sociology achieves a more decisive role in society through the growth of its values in popular thought, strategy, and action. Humanist sociology is not the exclusive intellectual property of an elite. It is not the kind of sociology an elite can exploit to seize and maintain special perquisites in society. With the help of dedicated sociologists, ideas about the mission and characteristics of a man-centered science of man, society, and human interrelationships will come to flourish more in a general way in our societal culture and in more precise ways in many of our group cultures.

Thinking more broadly about ideologies helps one to picture how humanist sociology may spread. Ideologies rise, change, sometimes merge, and disappear. Popular ideologies are the simplified bodies of doctrine by and with which people live, aspire, dream, succeed, and fail. Institutional functionaries, pressure-group spokesmen, and agitators constantly attempt to restate or reorient accepted ideologies for their purposes. In our day such publicists are forever subjecting ideologies to propagandas and to other pressures and manipulations aimed at modifying, activating, or replacing them. In considering the nature of ideologies in social struggles, let us look at the nature of popularly accepted ideologies and also at the nature of those being promulgated for acceptance—for example, that of an existential and humanist sociology.

IDEOLOGY'S PREMATURE OBITUARY

At the outset, it must be admitted that a fashionable sociologist has already announced "the end of ideology" as a consequence of the "tragic self-immolation of a revolutionary generation that had proclaimed the finer ideals of man; destructive war of a breadth and scale hitherto unknown; the bureaucratized murder of millions in concentration camps and death chambers." He also contends that "all this has meant an end to chiliastic hopes, to millenarianism, to apocalyptic thinking—and to ideology." He thus asserts that "ideology, which once was a road to action, has come to a dead end." Beyond what he calls "ideology" he appears to see and to hope for the growth of "intellectual maturity," for the "end of rhetoric, and rhetoricians, of 'revolution,'" but somehow not "the end of utopia as well. If anything, one can begin the discussion of utopia," he insists, "only by being aware of the trap of ideology." [1]

These sweeping dogmatisms were written before the beginning of the 1960s—before the renewal of black uprisings, before student revolts against militarism and educational irrelevance, before renewed women's liberation efforts, and before restless agitations against the pollution of our environment, urban decay, suburban isolation, and so many other problems. In order to understand the alleged "trap of ideology" to which the above quotation refers, however, one first has to comprehend the trap of definition in which he and so many other social-scientific students of ideologies appear to be caught.

AVOIDING TRAPS OF DEFINITION

The terms *ideology, intellectual,* and *propaganda* all have at least one significant characteristic in common. It is this: When they are employed in the generic senses suggested by their etymologies, they tend to bring into relationship phenomena with value adhesions that contrast sharply and that by such juxtaposition, point to undesired comparisons. These phenomena include ideas, activities, and persons that are esteemed and also ones that are hated or feared. They help to emphasize similarities between "their" and "our" ideologies, intellectuals, and propagandas. As a consequence, scholars, as more or less subconscious apologists for themselves and their kind, as well as other more obvious public apologists, often try to control such comparisons by giving these terms arbitrarily limited, value-laden meanings.

IDEOLOGY. For many social thinkers an ideology is not merely "a pattern for beliefs and concepts (both formal and normative) which purport to explain complex social phenomena with a view to directing

---

[1] Daniel Bell, *The End of Ideology*, rev. ed. (New York: Collier Books, 1961), pp. 393, 400, 399. See also C. I. Waxman, ed., *The End of Ideology Debate* (New York: Simon & Schuster, 1969).

and simplifying socio-political choices facing individuals and groups." [2] For them an ideology is a kind of infective growth, or even a poison, responsible for the distortion of facts and beliefs in ways they take to be either objectionable or even repugnant. "Ideology is the conversion of ideas into social levers. . . . What gives ideology its force is its passion." [3] Thus ideology creates, it is said, a "false consciousness," while philosophy can reveal a "true consciousness." [4] Thus, quite oversimply, "my philosophy" is "rational" and "true," and "his ideology" is "passionate" and "false."

INTELLECTUAL. Similarly, academic apologists are shocked by opposition from the nonacademic, those who think and speak without suitable accreditation. They develop, therefore, elegant ways to differentiate between "intellectuals" and "intellectualism" on the one hand, and types to be called "anti-intellectuals," "cynics," or "irresponsible agitators" and their "ideologies" or "propagandas" on the other.

Generically, the newspaper writer, the industrial technician, and the political strategist can each be as intellectual as the liberal-arts university professor. In the struggle for the minds of men, however, the professor is often more than tempted to glorify himself and to denigrate intellectuals lacking his formal institutional certification and status. When similar denigration of the academic is attempted by those pushing nonacademic intellectualism, it becomes an academic sin. *Anti-intellectualism* [5] is a term more than a little reminiscent of the more ancient one, *heresy.* [6]

PROPAGANDA. In the same vein, *propaganda* is defined generically as a way of conveying ideas rapidly to many people. Through combinations of symbols—words, personalities, music, drama, pageantry, and others —the propagandist attempts to use mass media to make impressions upon

---

[2] Julius Gould, "Ideology," in Gould and W. L. Kolb, eds., A *Dictionary of the Social Sciences* (New York: Free Press, 1964), p. 315.

[3] Bell, *The End of Ideology*, pp. 394–95.

[4] *Ibid.*, p. 394. These terms come from Karl Marx and Friedrich Engels, *The German Ideology*, trans. and ed. by R. Pascal (London: Lawrence and Wishart, 1939), and from Karl Mannheim, *Ideology and Utopia*, trans. and ed. by Louis Wirth and E. Shils (New York: Harcourt, Brace & World, 1936). See also D. G. MacRae, *Ideology and Society* (London: Heinemann, 1961); S. M. Lipset, *Political Man*, rev. ed. (New York: Anchor Books, 1963); and Charles Hampden-Turner, *Radical Man* (Cambridge: Schenkman, 1970), esp. Chap. 11, "The Crypto-Conservatism of Technological Thinking."

[5] See Richard Hofstadter, *Anti-Intellectualism in American Life* (New York: Alfred A. Knopf, 1963), esp. Chap. 1.

[6] W. E. H. Lecky, *History of European Morals From Augustus to Charlemagne*, 3rd ed. rev. (New York: D. Appleton, 1908), I, 98, and II, 40, and *History of the Rise and Influence of the Spirit of Rationalism in Europe* (London: Watts, 1910), esp. Chaps. 1 and 4; H. C. Lea, *History of the Inquisition of the Middle Ages*, 2nd ed. (New York: Harper & Bros., 1906), I–III; W. G. Sumner, *Folkways* (Boston: Ginn, 1906), esp. pp. 225–51, 253–59.

specific or general publics. The impressions may be wholly or partly "true," "confusing," "clarifying," or "false." When similar information is transmitted in our society in a detailed and accurate manner rather than in the stimulating short hand of the propagandist, few bother to listen. In moments given to decision, vividness and emotion quite often override common-sense demands for accurate facts and for an opportunity to question and discuss.[7] Consequently, literature abounds purporting to distinguish between *our* communications or *our* educational materials and *their* propaganda.[8]

To understand ideologies, intellectuals, and propagandas as social phenomena, we need to avoid confusing objective considerations with value considerations. Objective considerations include their nature, development, and social roles. Value considerations deal with their personal, status-group, and national involvements and uses. We need to try to perceive clearly and to compare many sorts of these social products, with many value orientations, and to try to discover as accurately as possible their cultural and social-interactional ingredients and functions.

TO UNDERSTAND CONFLICTING VIEWPOINTS

Aware of the "multiplicity of conflicting viewpoints," Karl Mannheim put forward his *dynamic relationism* as "the only possible way out." Each ideology, "though claiming absolute validity, has been shown to be related to a particular position and to be adequate only to that one. Not until he has assimilated all the crucial motivations and viewpoints, whose internal contradictions account for our present social-political tension, will the investigator be in a position to arrive at a solution adequate to our present life-situation." Mannheim called for a "total view" and said that this "implies both the assimilation and transcendence of the limitations of particular points of view." This would have as "its goal not

[7] See A. McC. Lee, *How to Understand Propaganda* (New York: Rinehart, 1952), p. 2, and *Che Cos'è la Propaganda* (Torino: Casa Editrice Taylor, 1961), pp. 27–28. See also Umberto Benigni, "Propaganda, Sacred Congregation of," *Catholic Encyclopaedia*, XII (1913), 456–61; C. D. MacDougall, *Understanding Propaganda* (New York: Macmillan, 1952), esp. Chap. 4, *The Press and Its Problems* (Dubuque, Iowa: W. C. Brown, 1964), esp. pp. 264–76; Clarence Schettler, *Public Opinion in American Society* (New York: Harper & Bros., 1960), esp. Chap. 15; and Jacques Ellul, *Propaganda*, trans. by Konrad Kellen and Jean Lerner (New York: Alfred A. Knopf, 1965), esp. Chaps. 1–3.

[8] See discussions by S. S. Sargent and R. C. Williamson, *Social Psychology*, 3rd ed. (New York: Ronald Press, 1966), esp. Chap. 18; S. A. Stouffer *et al.*, *The American Soldier* (Princeton: Princeton University Press, 1949), I, esp. Chap. 9, 437–38; J. C. Clews, *Communist Propaganda Techniques* (New York: F. A. Praeger, 1964).

achievement of a super-temporally valid conclusion but the broadest possible extension of our horizon of vision." Thus even though we may "quest for reality" as a way "to escape ideological and utopian distortions . . . it is precisely the multiplicity of the conceptions of reality which produces the multiplicity of our modes of thought." [9] For that matter, as the sociologists Peter L. Berger and Thomas Luckmann point out, "Definitions of reality have self-fulfilling potency. Theories can be *realized* in history, even theories that were highly abstruse when they were first conceived by their inventors." [10]

One can share Mannheim's concern for "the profound disquietude of modern man" in the face of "the multiplicity of conflicting viewpoints" without oversimply interpreting this, as he does, as a crisis to be resolved, attributing this to the "disruption of the intellectual monopoly of the church," accepting *dynamic relationism* as "the only possible way out," or defining the "greatest exertion of mankind" in current society as "the attempt to counteract the tendency of an individualistic undirected society, which is verging toward anarchy, with a more organic type of social order." [11]

The multiplicity exists. Like all stimulating situations, it is disquieting, disturbing, even upsetting, but it is scarcely a crisis in the sense of our being at a decisive historical moment or turning point.

IDEOLOGICAL MULTIPLICITY. Ideological multiplicity appears to hold more promise than danger, except for those trying to find the alleged but delusory peace and quiet of a society more homogeneous ideologically, and therefore more monovalent culturally. Many influences other than the decline of imperial Rome and of ecclesiastical power helped to bring forth the modern multiplicity. Mannheim might have cited longtime Jewish, Muslim, heretical Christian, primitive magic, alchemical, astrological and astronomical, commercial, military, and other diversifying influences operative in Europe ever since the decline of Rome's *multiplicity*. [12]

Talk of a single "possible way out," like Mannheim's quest for a transcendent sense of reality raises such questions as these: A way out for whom? For society? For intellectuals only? Why only one way out? Society's multivalent culture provides and is likely to continue to furnish many perceptions of "reality," thus many bases for ideological formulations and interpretations. Certainly "each group seems to move in a separate and distinct world of ideas," but one neglects the social realities of

---

Mannheim, *Ideology and Utopia*, pp. 98–99, 106.

[10] P. L. Berger and Thomas Luckman, *The Social Construction of Reality* (Garden City, N.Y.: Doubleday, 1966), p. 118.

[11] Mannheim, *Ideology and Utopia*, pp. 13, 32, 98.

[12] A. D. White, *A History of the Warfare of Science With Theology in Christendom* (New York: D. Appleton, 1896), I–II.

cultural conditioning to say "that these different systems of thought, which are often in conflict with one another, may in the last analysis be reduced to different modes of experiencing the 'same' reality." [13]

What if the objective societal symbols, artifacts, and basic environment are the same for all, except for degree of availability? They are perceived and conceived differently by members of different social status groups in each society of which we know. Are there not strengths in ideological multiplicity, reflecting as it does cultural multivalence, when it is faced with frankness and tolerance?

Finally, Mannheim's apparent anxiety in the 1920s to replace an unplanned individualism with "a more organic type of social order" stresses a type of solution for living in a giant society well-illustrated by modern states in a variety of forms, but it is a type of solution that has scarcely proven itself in this war-torn century as a way to avoid anarchy more than temporarily. Our vast, centralized, integrated states, with their persistent conformist pressures to homogenize individuals and their values, may merely be more efficient ways to prepare for chaos.

These points are mentioned and criticized not to brush aside Mannheim's substantial ideas but to suggest weaknesses in his theorizing preparatory to building upon his contributions. An approach or orientation more receptive to the implications of cultural multivalence and more relative to change and diversity through time and space can add something to the positions Mannheim helped to develop.[14]

INGREDIENTS OF IDEOLOGIES

The principal ingredients out of which potentially or actually successful ideologies are constructed are notable for their lack of novelty. They typically include symbols for generalities drawn from a societal culture which are long embedded in moral preachments. The conceptions (of "reality," of deprivation, need, and challenge, of tactics) and referents associated with such symbols, as well as the general integrating symbol and theory binding them together, derive from the subcultures of the groups to whose concerns an ideology is chiefly related. Messianism, regal divine right, egalitarian aspirations, puritanical devotion to entrepreneurism, and class conflict, are folk theories that long antedated

[13] Mannheim, *Ideology and Utopia*, p. 99.

[14] See Franco Ferrarotti, "Introductory Remarks on Ideology and Sociology," prepared for the Working Group on Ideology and Sociology, International Sociological Association, Evian, France, September 4–11, 1966, and his *Max Weber e il Destino della Ragione*, 2nd ed. (Bari: Editore Laterza, 1968), esp. Chap. 7. My chapter, particularly the discussion following, applies theories developed in A. McC. Lee, *Multivalent Man* (New York: George Braziller, 1966), esp. Chaps. 3–6 and 23.

Christianity, absolute monarchy, democracy, the so-called protestant ethic, and Marxism. The contribution of the formulator of a given version of an ideology lies chiefly in pattern, relative emphases, topical applications, and rhetorical artistry. The formulator may be an individual writer, a drafting committee, or the impersonal and continuing discussion processes of a group or society, which gradually crystallize a folk ideological position with some clarity and influence. When an ideology is to be mass-communicated in whole or in part, it is often applied to a specific competitive or conflict situation. The same ideological ingredients become those of the related propaganda. In a sense, propaganda is ideology on the march. Much of the continuing impact of a legitimated ideology is through its permeation of a society's formal and informal educational processes.

BRIDGES OF SYMBOLS. Among other things, ideologies, like propagandas, are bridges of symbols. Their bridgelike character depends upon the socially traditional, and thus individually habitual, hold of the symbols through the variety of group-entrenched concepts and referents subculturally associated with those symbols. They promise much to followers and potential followers, often in diverse groups with contrasting interests. They penetrate organizational and propaganda media through which a ruling oligarchy may gain and maintain a degree of control and direction. In order to make them viable, ideologies contain claims to be related to one or more sources of authority and thus to power, whether theological, popular, military, economic, historical, scientific, or, better, a combination of several of these.

An ideology nominally deals especially with religious, political, economic, familial, or scientific problems and has its assertedly related goals. It is often used, however, for purposes other than those for which it was presumably developed and given popular acceptance. For example, "Christianity (originally a lower-middle-class ideology if anything) was harnessed by powerful interests for political purposes with little relationship to its religious ingredients. . . . There may be large elements in an ideology that bear no particular relationship to the legitimated interests, but that are vigorously affirmed by the 'carrier' group simply because it has committed itself to the ideology." [15] Thus Freudianism has been used to combat Marxism. Darwinian evolutionism has been seized upon to give intellectual support to unbridled free-enterprise capitalism. Naively moral literalists disrupt such appropriative efforts; they are nuisances to would-be manipulators of prestigious ideological materials.

[15] Berger and Luckmann, *The Social Construction of Reality*, pp. 114–15.

TO TYPIFY IDEOLOGIES

Rather than by their subject matter, it would appear more practical to typify ideologies in terms of their stage of development or vogue (folk, somewhat formulated, crystallized, decadent, modifying), in terms of the groups to which they are related (societal, stratum, ethnic or ethnoid, interest), and in terms of their current social role (revolutionary, reformist, legitimated). Interrelations among these three sets of typings could give us sixty possible combinations in a three-dimensional paradigm if we were to feel inclined to do such diagramming. There are, for example, emerging folk-societal ideologies that are reformist, such as some of those now being formulated by black action groups for the modification of United States society. The ideologies we most commonly discuss are those that can be characterized as societal, crystallized or modifying, and revolutionary, reformist, or legitimated. Some of the ideologies most influential in the subtle coloration of the thoughts of intellectuals in largely unrecognized fashions are those of strata, ethnic or ethnoid groups,[16] and interest (especially occupational) groups, which are often of a folk nature or are only partly (often inaccurately) given a literary form. These ideologies are rationalized with, and are made to work within, the overall, legitimated, societal ideological patterning.

ADAPTABILITY OF IDEOLOGIES. In offering such a typology as a way of characterizing ranges of ideological phenomena, it is insisted that actual examples of ideologies are usually typologically "impure." Other dimensions of ideology are also subsumed under the types given—for example, relative absolutism, inclusiveness, exclusiveness, or relative charisma, authority, or pathos. What is principally implied in this suggested typing is that the characteristics of ideologies are relative to their social purposes and roles and to their degree of aggressiveness or establishment. As their social purposes and roles change, ideologies constantly modify, but less in symbolic representation than in associated concepts and referents. What is also implied by this suggested typing is that rather than announcing or even seeking an end to ideology or to the influence of ideologies, it would be more useful to study the amazing persistence and adaptability of ideologies, their many guises, and the deep roots of even the most disastrous ones in the family life and multivalent person-

---

[16] S. H. Chapman, "The Spirit of Cultural Pluralism," in H. M. Kallen *et al.*, *Cultural Pluralism and the American Idea* (Philadelphia: University of Pennsylvania Press, 1956), esp. footnote, p. 110.

alities, especially in the prototypical and successor roles and groups in typical socialization patterns and in those subscribing to them.[17] Only after such studies have proceeded much further than now can social scientists offer data and generalizations upon which decisions might be made about the utility or lack of utility of ideologies to specific types of group or to societal welfare broadly considered.

In many ways the present stage in the development of the study of ideologies and of propagandas (mass communications to some) resembles the study of human sex life prior to the work of Havelock Ellis,[18] Sigmund Freud,[19] and the Kinsey group.[20] It is also reminiscent of the stage of development of such other social-psychological and more broadly social-scientific fields as criminology and mental disorder. In spite of excellent work in both fields, there are still a great many "social scientists" who boggle at the unpleasantness and threats to "social order" and to their own psychological stability in basic studies of crime, delinquency, psychoses, and neuroses, and thus reject the interrelationships of the "normal" and "abnormal" or "deviant." The principal problem in sex, deviancy, and ideology appears to be that of the student attempting to study an enticingly important field without having his research endanger his own habitual view of himself and his own groups. Emotionalism, adroitness and even trickery, irrationality, and the use of force, recur as one studies ideologies and phenomena related to them. Ideologies are part and parcel of social competitions and conflicts. They reflect the levels on which such competitions and conflicts are carried out, levels that will require much more than scholarly wishful thinking or social-scientific technique to brush aside and deny. It is also quite possible that our societal Augean stable requires its filth for its operation as much as a

[17] The conceptions referred to here are set forth in detail in A. McC. Lee, "A Sociological Discussion of Consistency and Inconsistency in Intergroup Relations," *Journal of Social Issues,* V (1949), No. 3, 12–18; "Attitudinal Multivalence in Relation to Culture and Personality," *American Journal of Sociology,* LX (1954–1955), 294–99; *La Sociologia delle Comunicazioni* (Torino: Casa Editrice Taylor, 1960), esp. Chaps. 2–6; *How Customs and Mentality Can Be Changed* (The Hague: Institute of Social Studies, Publications on Social Change No. 8, Uitgeverij van Keulen N.V., 1958); *Marriage and the Family,* 2nd ed., with E. B. Lee (New York: Barnes & Noble, 1967), Chap. 8, esp. pp. 102–12; and esp. *Multivalent Man,* Chaps. 11–13.

[18] Havelock Ellis, *Studies in the Psychology of Sex* (1900–1910; New York: Random House, 1936), I–II.

[19] Sigmund Freud, *The Basic Writings,* trans. by A. A. Brill (New York: Modern Library, 1938), and other works.

[20] A. C. Kinsey *et al., Sexual Behavior in the Human Male, Sexual Behavior in the Human Female* (Philadelphia: W. B. Saunders, 1948, 1953), and other works. See also Jerome Himelhoch and S. F. Fava, eds., *Sexual Behavior in American Society* (New York: W. W. Norton, 1955), esp. Chap. 33 by L. P. Chall and "A Selected Bibliography" by Fava and Chall.

garden requires manure and compost. This is one of the many possibilities that should be faced.[21]

IDEOLOGIES CHANGE;
IDEOLOGY PERSISTS

For all the alleged increase in popular sophistication in political and economic matters through expanded educational facilities—a development often more accurately described as increased brainwashing or homogenizing through expanded impoundment facilities for the excess labor supply—the numbers of voters, soldiers, and customers for massive political parties, armies, and mercantile operations continue to appear to be abundant and not too questioning. "The ideology operates not only as a unifying force and a guideline to action in ambiguous situations, but also as a *language,* a set of semantic guides, which makes possible rapid and efficient communication of the wishes of central authorities." [22]

Thus one must speak of the persistence rather than the end of ideologies as a characteristic of human societies of a massive and literate sort in the world today. Ideologies are the intellectual and emotional patterns in terms of which groups and individuals are provided with ways to organize their cultural symbols for use in communication and action. Ideologies come and go, but the end of ideology is scarcely in sight. In the world's larger societies men with admittedly mixed motives continue to accept ideologies as reasons or excuses for participation in wars and in other social conflicts and competitions, the irrationality of which their propagandas help to obscure and to justify.

When they are functioning as social scientists, men turn aside from the traditional roles of intellectuals as formulators, curators, disinfectors, and critics of ideologies. They forego being interpreters, redefiners, and obfuscators for those who employ them and whose social manipulations and exploitations benefit from their ideological construction. They try to see these social instruments more nearly as they are.[23]

[21] See the highly perceptive essays by Willard Waller, "Editor's Introduction" and "War in the Twentieth Century," in Waller, ed., *War in the Twentieth Century* (New York: Dryden Press, 1940). See also M. R. Davie, *Evolution of War* (New Haven: Yale University Press, 1929).

[22] E. H. Schein, "The Passion for Unanimity," in Bernard Berelson and Morris Janowitz, eds., *Reader in Public Opinion and Communication,* 2nd ed. (New York: Free Press, 1966), p. 608. See also Ellul, *Propaganda,* pp. 259–302; Schein, *Coercive Persuasion* (New York: W. W. Norton, 1961); Institute for Propaganda Analysis, *Propaganda Analysis* (periodical bulletin, New York, 1937–1942); and Lee, *La Sociologia delle Comunicazioni.*

[23] The preceding is based on A. McC. Lee, "Il Persistere delle Ideologie," *Critica Sociologica* (Roma), I (1967), 5–15.

CHAPTER 7

Ideologies Within Sociology

In view of what we have outlined about the nature of ideologies, of humanist sociology, and of an ideology promulgating values supportive of humanist sociology, what can be said about the possible future of humanist sociology? Helpful in throwing light on this question is the study of *The Structure of Scientific Revolutions* by Thomas S. Kuhn,[1] adapted more specifically to the context of sociology.

Let us look briefly at what Kuhn would call normal science in sociology at the present time, then at the ideological crisis sociology and society now jointly face, and finally at how humanist sociology might well provide the paradigm for a new "normal" science in response to that crisis.

NORMAL SCIENCE AS A PARADIGM

Kuhn defines *normal science* as research activity "firmly based upon one or more past scientific achievements, achievements that some particular scientific community acknowledges for a time as supplying the foundation for its further practice." Those past achievements shape up a paradigm—that is, a guide as to how to do research, as to the kinds of data to use, and as to the major outlines of theory to be pursued and applied. More than a pattern or an example, a normal science is the body of accepted precedent within the scientific community or school of which it is the approximate consensus.

[1] T. S. Kuhn, *The Structure of Scientific Revolutions* (Chicago: University of Chicago Press, 1962).

At its outset a paradigm is "sufficiently unprecedented to attract an enduring group of adherents away from competing modes of scientific activity" and also "sufficiently open-ended to leave all sorts of problems for the redefined group of practitioners to resolve." Both the paradigm and the research springing from it are legitimate grist at any given time for the writers of elementary and advanced textbooks. "Normal" or consensus textbooks, to the extent that they exist in any given science, are thus efforts to define the current status of the prevailing paradigm.[2] As Kuhn adds: "No part of the aim of normal science is to call forth new sorts of phenomena; indeed those that will not fit the box are often not seen at all. Nor do scientists normally aim to invent new theories, and they are often intolerant of those invented by others. Instead, normal-scientific research is directed to the articulation of those phenomena and theories that the paradigm already supplies."[3] In terms of the discussion of four types of scientific activity within sociology in Chapter Five, Kuhn's "normal" science would be the sort exemplified by the bureaucrats and the technicians.

Paradigms achieve more sweeping influence in the somewhat crystallized scientific fields. Kuhn concludes that "it remains an open question what parts of social science have yet acquired such paradigms at all."[4] As yet, sociology has had no paradigm-dominated traditions comparable in acceptance to Ptolemaic or Copernican astronomy or Aristotelian, Newtonian, or Einsteinian dynamics. Even when the University of Chicago sociology department in the first decades of this century had a dominating role in United States sociology, it was merely the strongest among many schools of sociological thought and method. Its basic textbook, Robert E. Park's and Ernest W. Burgess's *Introduction to the Science of Sociology*,[5] first published in 1921, was the nearest approach yet in the United States sociological communities to a predominant paradigmatic statement.

SOCIOLOGY'S THREE ROUGH
PARADIGMS

That at least three significant paradigms have taken some form and currently have gained influence in sociological circles is due to a complication in the work of sociologists not present in that of physical

[2] *Ibid.*, p. 10.
[3] *Ibid.*, p. 24. Kuhn cites Bernard Barber, "Resistance by Scientists to Scientific Discovery," *Science*, CXXXIV (1961), 596–602.
[4] *Ibid.*, p. 15.
[5] R. E. Park and E. W. Burgess, *Introduction to the Science of Sociology*, 2nd ed. (Chicago: University of Chicago Press, 1924).

and biological scientists. The complication is that sociologists are men and women who study men and women in their groups and society under subsidies from men and women. This opens sociologists to ideological influences from which physicists, chemists, and biologists as such are relatively free. Thus ideologies based upon differences in social interest and concern have helped to form three rough and more or less "normal" sociologies, each with a somewhat different constituency both professionally and publicly. The three are (1) the managerial-bureaucratic, (2) the problematic-technical, and (3) the humanist-existential. Both the problematic-technical and the humanist-existential are perforce sufficiently open-ended and dynamic to provide only unstable "normal" sociologies. They are closely related to the cutting edges of sociological development. Thus they are difficult to "normalize" in terms of bureaucratic and technical criteria.

ORGANIZATION MAN'S SOCIOLOGY

The *managerial-bureaucratic paradigm* accepts the myth of an equilibrating social order, the "social system," as its basic conception of society. This systemic structure, with congeries of subsystems nested within it, is usually subjected to what is called functional analysis, a concern with how the system's parts satisfy the system's and its members' needs and maintain an adequate degree of integration and balance. This usually implies the indispensability of certain functions in the maintenance of the system as an ongoing enterprise. Alternative social structures or cultural forms may perform functions necessary for the persistence of subsystems or of "the system." In other words, functional needs are satisfied by alternative social structures, a range of possible structures. If "the system" is to persist, these needs "must" be satisfied.

The school of adherents enthralled by this paradigm exhibit a pretentious display of systematic theory based particularly upon the writings of Max Weber and Vilfredo Pareto and developed in this country by Talcott Parsons, Robert K. Merton, S. A. Stouffer, and George Homans, among others.[6] The dignity and possible autonomy of mass man does not appear to interest them; they are preoccupied with how he can be man-

[6] See Talcott Parsons, *The Structure of Social Action* (New York: McGraw-Hill, 1937), and *The Social System* (Glencoe, Ill.: Free Press, 1951); Parsons and E. A. Shils, eds., *Toward a General Theory of Action* (Cambridge: Harvard University Press, 1951); R. K. Merton, *Social Theory and Social Structure*, rev. ed. (Glencoe, Ill.: Free Press, 1957); S. A. Stouffer, *Communism, Conformity, and Civil Liberties* (New York: Doubleday, 1955); George Homans, *The Human Group, Social Behavior*, and *The Nature of Social Science* (New York: Harcourt, Brace and World, 1950, 1961, 1967).

aged, led to preconceived goals, and with how the bureaucratized "system" can be maintained and flourish. This bias is taken by the school to support, not undermine, their contention of being "value free," of assuming strict value neutrality in their scientific investigations.[7]

This ahistorical paradigm has gained academic as well as industrial prestige through the dedication of Parsons to what he calls the convergence of all manner of social-psychological and sociological theories within his own evolving theoretical octopus, a highly abstract and (at any point in its life history) dogmatic organon.[8] The paradigm has also gained through its adherents' use of highly "sophisticated" (read "impressive even when not relevant") and "unmanipulable" or "highly objective" (read "quantitative and conservatively oriented") methodologies. With the aid of cybernetics and of the digital computer, this group has been able to interpret their systematic functionalism for the powerful through such schematic gadgetry as model-building (the construction of simplifications of the "social system," an aspect of it, or a "subsystem" with little attention to the human constituents) and games-playing (a caricature that reduces a somewhat repetitious aspect of human interaction to the proportions and to the relative importance of a chess or a bridge contest).[9]

The most convincing signal of the acceptance of this paradigm by substantial power manipulators was the setting up during World War II of a four-year study by the Research Branch, Information and Education Division, United States Army, cosponsored by the Social Science Research Council. Some 134 civilian and military specialists labeled social scientists were listed as having participated in this project. The Carnegie Corporation of New York provided the funds for the publication of the

---

[7] A. W. Gouldner, "Anti-Minotaur: The Myth of a Value-Free Sociology" and other papers in Maurice Stein and Arthur Vidich, eds., *Sociology on Trial* (Englewood Cliffs, N.J.: Prentice-Hall, 1963).

[8] Many allege or anticipate the demise of Parson's influence. What is currently called "Parsonian" in a general way has had other labels in the past. It will probably be replaced only by something different in name and style, not in basic intent and character. Some tied intellectually to the managerial-bureaucratic paradigm are now playing with Goffman's dramaturgy and Garfinkel's ethnomethodology. See J. F. Scott, "The Changing Foundations of the Parsonian Action Scheme," in W. L. Wallace, ed., *Sociological Theory* (Chicago: Aldine, 1969), pp. 246–67; A. W. Gouldner, *The Coming Crisis of Western Sociology* (New York: Basic Books, 1970); Erving Goffman, *Interaction Ritual* (Garden City, N.Y.: Doubleday, 1967), and other books; Harold Garfinkel, *Studies in Ethnomethodology* (Englewood Cliffs, N.J.: Prentice-Hall, 1967).

[9] Anatol Rapoport, "Uses and Limitations of Mathematical Models in Social Science," in Llewellyn Gross, ed., *Symposium on Sociological Theory* (Chicago: Row, Peterson, 1959); H. Solomon, ed., *Mathematical Thinking in the Measurement of Behavior* (New York: Free Press, 1960); J. G. Kemeny and J. L. Snell, *Mathematical Models in the Social Sciences* (Boston: Ginn, 1962); J. Berger *et al.*, *Types of Formalization in Small-Group Research* (Boston: Houghton Mifflin, 1962); J. S. Coleman, *Introduction to Mathematical Sociology* (New York: Free Press, 1964).

resulting four volumes: S. A. Stouffer and others, *The American Soldier, Adjustment During Army Life* (I) and *Combat and Its Aftermath* (II); C. I. Hovland and others, *Experiments on Mass Communication* (III), and S. A. Stouffer and others, *Measurement and Prediction* (IV), all issued by Princeton University Press in 1949–1950.[10] "Sociology" of that kind had arrived. Given the goals or problems set by management, such studies offer promise of "enlightened" policy recommendations, but it is a promise inevitably damaged by the nature of the assignment and its funding and by the commitment of researchers to the managerial-bureaucratic paradigm.

Above all, the adherents of the managerial-bureaucratic or functional-systemic paradigm have been able to develop an inclusive, impressive, and thus vendable body of theory and method. They gain for themselves significant roles in government, business, and voluntary organizations as the dispensers of a new magic. They also help graduate students to become useful to the entrepreneurs of power rather than merely to liberal-arts college students and the pursuit of knowledge. In return, the graduate students help with the details of managerial-bureaucratic assignments; thus they often "work out their doctoral dissertation" as a spinoff from a major project in a manner not at all conducive to training in autonomous scientific research.

THE TECHNICIAN'S SOCIOLOGY

The *problematic-technical paradigm* gained strength in American sociology earlier than the managerial-bureaucratic one, and it continues to flourish. It has not achieved the degree of stability of definition, and it especially has not developed the enticing conservative promise of the latter. Stimulated in particular by leaders of the University of Chicago sociology department—Albion W. Small, Robert E. Park, W. F. Ogburn, E. W. Burgess, Louis Wirth, and Herbert Blumer—in a sense its adherents can be praised for being exceptionally fine journalists and more. Theirs is not the journalism of the daily newspaper, radio, or television, even though it often deals in part with the same issues and facts, because it is not so ephemeral. They seek to be less passingly topical than careful magazine writers by probing even more deeply than would a competent reporter-analyst. They do this by using more time and by borrowing and

---

[10] See the efforts to play down, distort, and "answer" reviews by humanist critics and to brag about praise from the bureaucratic and technique-oriented in Daniel Lerner, " 'The American Soldier' and the Public," in R. K. Merton and P. F. Lazarsfeld, eds., *Continuities in Social Research: Studies in the Scope and Method of "The American Soldier"* (Glencoe, Ill.: Free Press, 1950), pp. 212–51.

developing a body of communicable technique and theory related to their study of social-problem situations. Park's and Burgess's *Introduction to the Science of Sociology,* mentioned above, serves even now as one of the principal texts for this broad and loosely integrated sociological community. At the same time, it must be added that the Park and Burgess book also stimulated the existential humanists.

Unlike devout adherents of the managerial-bureaucratic paradigm, the problematic-technical-oriented are not necessarily elitist and manipulative in their value adhesions. In terms of those adhesions, they range between extremes of elitist-mechanist-manipulative and democratic-humanist—in other words, between being subservient to an elite as depersonalized manipulators and being relatively autonomous workers for popular objectives. A great many studies reflect research from this viewpoint. They include such stimulating works as Frederick Thrasher's *The Gang* (1927), Louis Wirth's *The Ghetto* (1928), Harvey Zorbaugh's *The Gold Coast and the Slum* (1929), R. S. and H. M. Lynd's *Middletown* (1929) and *Middletown in Transition* (1937), C. R. Shaw and others' *Delinquency Areas* (1929) and Shaw's *The Jackroller* (1930), John Dollard's *Caste and Class in a Southern Town* (1937), E. V. Stonequist's *The Marginal Man* (1937), R. E. L. Faris and H. W. Dunham's *Mental Disorders in Urban Areas* (1939), W. L. Warner and others' *The Social Life of a Modern Community* (1941) and *The Social System of American Ethnic Groups* (1945), and many other works.[11]

Those who share the problematic-technical orientation are often influenced by the symbolic-interactionist tradition of C. H. Cooley, G. H. Mead, and R. E. Park, to which Herbert Blumer [12] gave the name, but they also include sociologists more institutionally or culturally oriented.[13] They typically push quantification as far as appears practical for the purposes of reporting and analyzing data concerning actual problem situations, but statistical virtuosity seldom becomes for them an end in itself. What they have in common is chiefly a concern with using their research techniques and theories to shed understanding or to help people cope with social problems as those problems are defined by constituted authorities or by responsible voluntary group leaders. In terms of the status-ladder typology described in Chapter Five,[14] they are technicians rather than bureaucrats.

[11] This list is meant to be suggestive. It is drawn from studies widely known in educated circles, and a great many more references might be added.

[12] Herbert Blumer, "Social Psychology," in E. P. Schmidt, ed., *Man and Society* (New York: Prentice-Hall, 1938), pp. 171–72.

[13] For example, A. G. Keller, *Societal Evolution,* rev. ed. (New York: Macmillan, 1931), as a basis for rationalizing a reformist-problematic-technical orientation.

[14] More broadly treated in Lee, *Multivalent Man,* Part 3.

SOCIOLOGY FOR PEOPLE

The third and roughest of our paradigms, but the most important, is the *humanist-existential* one. It characterizes the high road of social thought in our society. It is not the exclusive possession of sociologists. In relating themselves to it, sociologists come to terms with social philosophers, historians, and belletrists, as well as other humanist social scientists. In connection with this paradigm, all relevant contributions demand attention regardless of the label on the contributor.[15]

The rough humanist-existential paradigm calls for a man-centered sociology in the service of human needs and goals as they are popularly defined. Thus it is democratically oriented by its very nature. Since it is not elitist and manipulative in its value adhesions, it is not attractive as an instrument to power seekers and their eager assistants. Its support comes from a popularly held ideology justifying and rewarding sociological research activity as an important allocation of energies for the guidance and enrichment of life in society. Its adherents find their rewards in the contributions they can make to formal and informal education rather than as technicians in the service of special interest groups or as aids to managers and entrepreneurs.

Some of the sociologists whose work served to develop the problematic-technical paradigm did even more to nurture the humanist paradigm, especially C. H. Cooley, W. G. Sumner, W. I. Thomas, and R. E. Park. There were many more,[16] and nonsociologists, such as the philosopher John Dewey, the psychologist William James, and a variety of cultural anthropologists also aided.[17] Monumental contributions to this tradition, to name but a few, have come from as varied a range as Cooley's *Human Nature and the Social Order* (1902), Sumner's *Folkways* (1906), W. I. Thomas and Florian Znaniecki's *The Polish Peasant in Europe and America* (1918–1921), and Pitirim A. Sorokin's *Social Mo-*

[15] Note the admitted debt for ideas on "manifest" and "latent" functions to Lincoln Steffens, *Autobiography* (New York: Harcourt, Brace, 1931), esp. pp. 46–47, on the part of F. S. Chapin, *Contemporary American Institutions* (New York: Harper & Bros., 1934), pp. 40–54. For similar debts to Steffens, see W. F. Whyte, *Street Corner Society*, 2nd ed. (Chicago: University of Chicago Press, 1955), pp. 282–83, and R. K. Merton, *Social Theory and Social Structure*, rev. ed. (Glencoe, Ill.: Free Press, 1957), pp. 75–76.

[16] An exhaustive list would be very long but would include the following: H. E. Barnes, Howard Becker, C. M. Case, M. R. Davie, Jerome Davis, C. A. Dawson, Émile Durkheim, W. E. Gettys, Ludwig Gumplowicz, C. W. Mills, H. A. Phelps, Georg Simmel, P. A. Sorokin, Herbert Spencer, Willard Waller, and Florian Znaniecki.

[17] Some of the many cultural anthropologists are Ruth Benedict, Franz Boas, E. H. Erikson (also a psychologist of note), A. I. Hallowell, Abram Kardiner, A. L. Kroeber, Margaret Mead, Edward Sapir, W. L. Warner, and J. W. M. Whiting.

bility (1927). Like the earlier humanist sociologists, their recent and contemporary successors tend to be relatively individualistic investigators and writers rather than organizers of large research projects or consultants. They include the authors of a number of successful student-oriented textbooks. A few random but outstanding examples of the latter are C. Wright Mills, Willard Waller, Peter L. Berger, Maurice Rea Davie, and Robert Bierstedt.[18]

This exuberant writing about certain promulgators of a humanist-existential viewpoint must carry with it a caveat: Like all other terms in social science, *humanist* and *existential* are subject to a variety of definitions, some of them far from the intent of the present usage. Just calling some methodological mumbo jumbo *humanist* does not make it relevant to human concerns. Just labeling some philosophical gamesmanship *existential* does not make it an acceptable interpretation of events. Hopefully the characterizations and illustrations of the humanist-existential paradigm offered here accurately communicate the conception as it is used in this work.

When confronted by embarrassing data involving the concerns of important vested interests, bureaucratic-managerial sociologists can retreat into lofty and abstract systems theory. Problematic-technical sociologists at a similar juncture can conveniently change their focus by referring to considerations of relevance and research technique. But the humanist-existential community among sociologists expects its members to face as fully as they are able the relevant implications—wherever they may be found—of social control, conflict, and exploitation, of degradation, degeneracy, creativity, and nobility, and of individual, group, and societal multivalence (related as they are to hypocrisy, the generation gap, the credibility gap in public affairs, and mature adjustment). Social pressures to meet such challenges arise for perceptive sociologists who are existential humanists from our society's idealistic definition of the moral behavior expected of our scholars, scientists, and belletrists. Sociologists who do not meet such expectations are assumed by the community of existential humanists to be technicians or bureaucrats whose products are biased by their working conditions and value commitments.

---

[18] See C. W. Mills, *The Sociological Imagination* (New York: Oxford University Press, 1959), and *Images of Man: The Classic Tradition in Sociological Thinking*, ed. with an intro. by Mills (New York: George Braziller, 1960); Willard Waller, *The Sociology of Teaching* (New York: John Wiley, 1932), and *The Family* (New York: Cordon, 1938); P. L. Berger, *Invitation to Sociology* (Garden City, N.Y.: Anchor Books, Doubleday, 1963); M. R. Davie, *Problems of City Life* (New York: John Wiley, 1932), and *World Immigration* (New York: Macmillan, 1936); and Robert Bierstedt, ed., *The Making of Society*, rev. ed. (New York: Modern Library, 1959), and *The Social Order*, 3rd ed. (New York: McGraw-Hill, 1970). This list is much too short, but hopefully it suggests the range of this type of textbook.

THE CRISIS IN BOTH SOCIETY
AND SOCIOLOGY

The differences among the ways these three rough communities obligate their members point to the emerging ideological crisis both in American society and in sociology. They also suggest a possible resolution. The cynicism and abstractness of the bureaucratic-managerial schools are stimulated by, and help to reenforce, the cynicism and lack of effective concern with mass-human problems common to the leadership of our loosely federated military-industrial complex, both in government and in corporations. The revolts of the young, the black, and the women against the status quo are triggered by awareness of that cynicism and lack of effective concern.

This ideological crisis of intellectualism and society has been more than a century in coming. Rising plutocratic entrepreneurs and their managers and technicians permeated all facets of American life during the half century following the Civil War. It was a development parallel to an earlier one in Europe. The plutocratic have continued since then to permeate and manipulate our social life ever more extensively and intensively.

Reacting against this biasing influence, against this successor to royal, ecclesiastical, manorial, and mercantile biases, liberal intellectualism did not crumple and disappear. Its adherents were accustomed to withstanding entrenched political and financial controls, but now they found themselves having to cope with more and more effective hirelings of vested interests. They had to confront increasing cynicism concerning traditional humanistic and democratic values of liberal scholarship and of social science. At first they appeared to believe that manipulators for the newly evolving status quo would be no more difficult to contend with than their predecessors. In this, autonomous intellectuals "underestimated the strength of the enemies of democracy. They did not realize what legions of Swiss Guards property can summon to its defense." [19]

PLUTOCRAT DEFINED. The hard realism with which W. G. Sumner [20]

---

[19] V. L. Parrington, *Main Currents in American Thought* (New York: Harcourt, Brace, 1930), III, 409. See also Andrew Hacker, ed., *The Corporation Take-Over* (New York: Doubleday, 1965), esp. the papers by A. A. Berle, Jr., and W. H. Ferry; Walter LaFeber, *The New Empire* (Ithaca: Cornell University Press, 1963); Gar Alpervitz, *Atomic Diplomacy* (New York: Simon & Schuster, 1965); W. A. Williams, *The Tragedy of American Diplomacy* (New York: Delta Books, 1962); Morton Mintz and J. S. Cohen, *America, Inc.* (New York: Dial, 1971).

[20] See esp. W. G. Sumner's *War and Other Essays*, ed. by A. G. Keller (New Haven: Yale University Press, 1911), esp. pp. 160, 204–207, 261–62, 325–26, and *Earth Hunger and Other Essays*, ed. by Keller (New Haven: Yale University Press, 1913), esp. pp. 283-300, 310-11, 316-17, 328-30.

in the late 1880s assessed the ravages of plutocracy in our society and in our intellectual worlds repelled and still repels many academicians. As Sumner said, "A plutocrat is a man who, having the possession of capital, and having the power of it at his disposal, uses it, not industrially, but politically; instead of employing laborers, he enlists lobbyists. Instead of applying capital to land, he operates upon the market by legislation, by artificial monopoly, by legislative privileges; he creates jobs, and erects combinations, which are half political and half industrial; he practices upon the industrial vices, makes an engine of venality, expends his ingenuity, not on processes of production, but on 'knowledge of men,' and on the tactics of the lobby. The modern industrial system gives him a magnificent field, one far more profitable, very often, than that of legitimate industry." [21]

PLUTOCRACY VERSUS HUMANISTIC DEMOCRACY. Similarly, the social historian Charles A. Beard worried with the same problem at various stages in American history in such profound contributions towards realism as his shocking *Economic Interpretation of the Constitution* (1913) and other critical revisions of American historical mythology, still bitter pills to Swiss Guards.[22] As he pointed out, "For years the possessors of great fortunes and the members of the 'middle class,' so-called, had largely dominated, while they directed, the transactions of politics and the currents of thought; but they had often been in antagonism themselves, concealed or above board. . . . Whether the struggle between the plutocracy and the middle class could be narrowly delimited and carried on indefinitely [from the 1930s] with the weapons and arguments evolved during the past fifty years became a question of social philosophy, historical interpretation, and time. If it could not be so delimited and continued endlessly without resolution, what forms were the future relations of the two groups to assume, especially in the presence of labor pressures in town and country?" [23]

Beard idealized what he called humanistic democracy, but he conceded in the 1930s, as he probably would have today, that "Critical leaders of this [humanistic] democracy had no illusions about the peril of sheer force and cruelty, exalting the irrational, despising justice and mercy—despite noble professions on all sides. . . . [The] humanistic wing of American democracy sought to provide the economic and cultural foundations indispensable to a free society, by rational methods of examination, discussion, legislation, administration, and cooperation, employing the sciences, letters, and arts in efforts to fulfill the promises

[21] Sumner, *Earth Hunger*, p. 298.
[22] He continued to worry with this problem. See C. A. Beard, *The Idea of National Interest* (New York: Macmillan, 1934), and with M. R. Beard, *America in Midpassage* (New York: Macmillan, 1939), I–II.
[23] Beard and Beard, *America in Midpassage*, II, 554–55.

of its heritage and aspirations."[24] In these struggles such middle-class ideals did not remain unadapting. They absorbed the dynamism of a more participatory and less legalistic sense of democratic process, but they retained their central emphasis upon the dignity of the individual and the necessary autonomy of the intellectual in a free marketplace for ideas.

In speaking thus of the plutocratization of American society, one need not attribute in the process such a conspiratorial role to "the power élite" as did C. Wright Mills and doctrinaire critics with communist, socialist, and anarchist frames of reference.[25] What unity of propaganda "line" those in power exhibit in American society exists among a shifting aggregate with sharp interpersonal and intergroup rivalries and conflicts. Their *modus operandi* in relatively open society is such that any dependable social cohesion among them beyond temporary expediencies is not only unlikely, it is impossible. Whatever apparent or actual agreement exists among them at times on points of ideology arises from common acceptance of plausible ideas and from similarities among their problems and orientations to society. Only under the brittle and transient conditions of a fascist dictatorship can such an élite temporarily appear to form a cohesive organization.

REACTIONS AGAINST PLUTOCRACY. In this struggle so briefly characterized, Sumner and Beard were joined by many others dedicated to an autonomous intellectualism in the service of man. With the aid of muckraking journalists[26] and such disenchanted novelists and essayists as James Branch Cabell, Theodore Dreiser, Upton Sinclair, Sinclair Lewis, and Henry L. Mencken,[27] many existential humanists in all the social

---

[24] *Ibid.*, p. 949.

[25] C. W. Mills, *The Power Elite* (New York: Oxford University Press, 1956), and Mills, ed., *The Marxists* (New York: Dell, 1962); Daniel Guérin, *Anarchism*, intro. by Noam Chomsky, trans. by Mary Klopper (New York: Monthly Review Press, 1970); I. L. Horowitz, *Three Worlds of Development* (New York: Oxford University Press, 1966); Richard Rovere, *The American Establishment* (New York: Harcourt, Brace & World, 1962); G. W. Domhoff, *Who Rules America?* (Englewood Cliffs, N.J.: Prentice-Hall, 1967).

[26] See C. C. Regier, *The Era of the Muckrakers* (Chapel Hill: University of North Carolina Press, 1932); Louis Filler, *Crusaders for American Liberalism* (New York: Harcourt, Brace, 1939); I. M. Tarbell, *All in the Day's Work* (New York: W. W. Norton, 1939).

[27] See J. B. Cabell's ironic novels, *The Cream of the Jest* (1917), *Jurgen* (1919), and *Figures of Earth* (1921), and his essay *Beyond Life* (1919); Theodore Dreiser, *The Financier* (1912), *The Titan* (1914), *An American Tragedy* (1925), and *The Stoic* (1947); Upton Sinclair, *The Jungle* (1906), *King Coal* (1917), *The Brass Check* (1919), *Oil* (1927), and others; Sinclair Lewis, *Main Street* (1920), *Babbitt* (1922), *Arrowsmith* (1925), *It Can't Happen Here* (1935), *Kingsblood Royal* (1947), and others; and H. L. Mencken, *In Defense of Women* (1917), *The American Language* (1918 and later revs.), *Prejudices* (six series, 1919–1927), and others. See also Maxwell Geismar, *Rebels and Ancestors* (New York: Hill & Wang, 1961), and *American Moderns* (New York: Hill & Wang, 1958), esp. pp. 49–53.

sciences gradually came to some realization of the seriousness of the maturing crisis. If they were to continue to accomplish anything substantial, if they were to avoid taking on some special interest's livery themselves, they had to approach social issues "recognizing the masterful ambitions of property, recruiting democratic forces to overmaster the Swiss Guards, leveling the strongholds that property erected within the organic law, and taking care that no new strongholds should rise." They saw their principal problem, in the words of the literary critic-historian Vernon L. Parrington, to be what it had for so long really been, "the subjection of property [as the chief reservoir of social power] to social justice" [28] in the new plutocratic American and world context of the twentieth century.

SOME SOCIOLOGISTS STRUGGLE; MANY JOIN UP

Some of the rising aggregation of sociologists—like their fellows in the other social sciences—have tried to continue traditions of autonomous liberal-arts education democratized to meet the needs of modern industrial mass society. They do so in terms of the rough humanist-existential paradigm as described and illustrated in the foregoing.

Other social scientists, more "realistic," try to work out one of the two principal Faustian compromises with the surprisingly like-minded leaders of the loosely federated military-industrial complex. Some select the alternative of becoming reformist technicians for hire, problem-solving mercenaries for available clients. Others decide that they can best serve themselves and humanity by attempting to become influential more directly with the powerful as their consultants, to become courtiers of the plutocrats.[29]

Those who are adherents of the problematic-technical paradigm rationalize their mercenary course of life by saying that our society is sound and that all it needs really is an updating for it to have its maladjustments eliminated or mitigated. Involved as they are in minor efforts at reform or adaptation, they may even perceive themselves, and be perceived, as daring innovators and critics of the status quo. Often with little thanks except from those whom they directly serve, they actually perform roles supportive of the entrenched establishments through help-

---

[28] Parrington, *Main Currents in American Thought*, p. 409.

[29] On the influence on sociologists' work of their conceptions of their "market," see L. A. Coser, *The Functions of Social Conflict* (New York: Free Press, 1956), esp. Chap. 1. On the frustrations of fashionable Western sociologists, see H. R. Lantz, "Foreword" to J. J. Wiatr, ed., *The State of Sociology in Eastern Europe Today* (Carbondale, Ill.: Southern Illinois University Press, 1971).

ing to create an illusion that society is somehow adapting to meet new needs and to eliminate old abuses. They do this by providing evidence of efforts to cope with selected peripheral social problems and evidence of some successes, or at least "good tries."

Those courtiers who are adherents of the now flourishing bureau-cratic-managerial paradigm in sociology, the would-be and actual "policy scientists," accept the view of most managers that the principal focus of concern should not be the obtaining of new, and thus unsettling, social knowledge. It need not be the updating or adjustment of their organiza-tion. As they see it, the focus of their efforts should be upon the develop-ment of better techniques and materials for "communication"—in other words, upon discovering more and more effective ways to convince their publics that their organization is, and their society can be, completely acceptable to all. All we need, they contend, is better popular under-standing and support for what those in control are doing or may want to do.

REVOLTS AGAINST DEHUMANIZED
SOCIAL SCIENCE

We have mentioned individuals who revolted against growing bureaucratic-managerial control of social science. The efforts of such individuals are useful, but they have limited influence in significant policymaking circles (controlling research grants, book publishing, peri-odicals, and academic jobs) until they are able to obtain an organiza-tional medium through which to indicate in a more concerted manner their professional and popular strength. To outsiders, professional social science societies may appear fusty and irrelevant, but they are crucial market places for ideas and personnel in each discipline.

By the 1940s bureaucratic-managerial control of the principal profes-sional society in sociology had become oppressive in the view of many of the problematic-technically oriented, as well as in the eyes of the humanist existentialists. Regional societies had remained somewhat open and flexible, but the American Sociological Society (ASS) glorified ab-stractions and methodological complications.

The first extensive organizational revolt in sociology against this rigidification and dehumanization took the form of the Society for the Study of Social Problems (SSSP). Its consequences modified sociologi-cal research, theorizing, and writing and penetrated—sometimes posi-tively and sometimes negatively—all sociological teaching. The society was an effort to bring sociological research and theorizing closer to press-ing human concerns of the day and to broaden opportunities for expres-sion by the younger and the more nonconformist sociologists.

During the 1940s my wife and fellow sociologist Elizabeth Briant Lee and I had often discussed with other sociologists the relative lack of attention in our discipline to our pyramiding social problems. At best, with notable exceptions, the attention had been spotty, imperceptive, and superficial. The possibility of being labeled a radical or being identified with the numerous so-called soft-headed clergymen and bleeding-heart reformers who had often been associated with sociology bothered many proper careerists who yearned for an impeccable label as scientist. Abstract theory and scientistic methodology attracted the bulk of attention not devoted to social engineering and narrow problem-solving assignments in behalf of respectable (conservative) clients.

Many of us then, as now, regard social problems as being necessarily the central concern of sociologists as social scientists. We look upon what dependably accurate and relevant sociology we have as the composite product of many thorough-going social-problem studies. As we pointed out in *Social Problems in America* in 1949, "Only through seeing and understanding actual instances of white-collar criminality, unemployment, despair, poverty, panic, and riot can the sociologist bring his theories into some degree of correspondence with social realities. Only by studying the accumulated generalizations of other investigators can the specific instance of crime, poverty, or panic come into some more adequate perspective." [30]

MODELS FOR REVOLT. In the early 1940s, groups dissatisfied with the crystallizing abstractions, methods, and goals of their disciplines had appeared in anthropology and social psychology. They formed the Society for Applied Anthropology (SAA) and the Society for the Psychological Study of Social Issues (SPSSI). The SAA's "primary object is scientific investigation of 'the principles controlling the relations of human beings to one another . . . and the wide application of these principles to practical problems.'" [31] SPSSI members "share a concern with research on the psychological aspects of important social issues. SPSSI is governed by Kurt Lewin's dictum that 'there is nothing so practical as a good theory.'" [32]

The SAA and the SPSSI supplemented the more theoretical and methodological emphases of their major disciplinary associations with committee projects, conferences, periodicals, and books devoted to action-related research on urgent human problems. Both were also planned to have less formal, more participant procedures than had been common in

[30] A. McC. and E. B. Lee, *Social Problems in America* (New York: Henry Holt, 1949), p. vi.

[31] *Human Organization* (official quarterly, Society for Applied Anthropology), from the standing statement of purpose printed in each number.

[32] *Journal of Social Issues* (official quarterly, Society for the Psychological Study of Social Issues), from the standing statement of purpose printed in each number.

the major societies, and they were not to boggle at launching into social-action-related programs. Both have been (and continue to be) quite successful in providing opportunities for expression to the young and the youthful in viewpoint. Since both fields had major societies receptive to organizational experimentation, these new societies readily gained acceptance.[33]

To MAKE A REVOLT ACCEPTABLE. The American Sociological Society (called Association or ASA since 1958 in order to avoid the acronym ASS) had long had more or less continuing "sections," but they afforded little opportunity for experimentation and innovation. The sections were unstable and lacked autonomy. In addition, the ASS officers and council members typically reacted negatively to ·proposals for liberalizing the organization's structure.

The Society for the Study of Social Problems was obviously a revolt against the major society's rigidities, but a number of us tried to bring it into being in such a way that it would gain acceptance as an organizational supplement to the ASS, not as an effort to weaken or supplant it. We sought to make it comparable to the Rural Sociological Society (RSS), a society affiliated with the ASS and represented on the ASS council but otherwise an independent entity. This model would hopefully permit the autonomy and democratic ferment characteristic of SPSSI and SAA and still not be as subject to the whims of ASS control as would be a continuing "section" within the ASS.[34]

A PUSH TOWARD A MORE
INVOLVED SOCIOLOGY

To be organized, SSSP needed these requisites in addition to the important leverage (SPSSI and SAA competition) and models (SPSSI and RSS) available to us: (1) sponsoring committee members who saw similar needs and recourses and who would bring in a wide range of participants,[35] (2) financial resources for both short-term and longer-

[33] SPSSI became a permanent section of the American Psychological Association (APA), shares in the APA's convention program, enjoys semiautonomous status, attracts members who do not belong to APA, and even has established its own local units in some areas.

[34] My experiences as a member of two working committees of SPSSI and my study of that society's highly democratic methods of operation stimulated me to work for the formation of the Society for the Study of Social Problems (SSSP). For a sociologist, SPSSI's orientation was too psychological, but the intimacy, inclusiveness, and fearlessness with which committee colleagues approached their fact-gathering and their analyses of social issues were impressive.

[35] E. W. Burgess of the University of Chicago and A. M. Rose of the University of Minnesota joined with me as the organizing committee. Of the elder statesmen of sociology at the time, Burgess appeared to be the one most sympathetic to what

term projects, (3) visible evidence of activity, involvement, and strength in the form of conferences and publications,[36] and (4) more and more members.[37]

The formal organization meeting of SSSP took place on September 6, 1951 in the faculty lounge of Roosevelt College, Chicago.[38] It came into being to fill a serious gap in sociology's organizational structure, one that could not be filled as well in any other way. Through its considerable influence upon ASS programs and policies, it also made substantial contributions to the preparation of the profession and of the regional and national professional societies for the strenuous tests and tensions of succeeding decades.

During 1951–1954, the first three years of SSSP's formal organization, there were many occasions when the whole enterprise appeared perilously shaky—even at the point of collapse. Some who took office in SSSP had little interest in its success, but there were always others who "covered" for such, and the "show went on."[39]

---

we were trying to accomplish. Burgess agreed to take on the job of acting chairman for 1950–1951 and then of president for 1951–1953 on condition that he would not have to "do the work," as he put it. As acting secretary in 1950–1951, vice-president in 1951–1952, president-elect in 1952–1953, and president in 1953–1954, I joined with many others to "do the work."

Many of us used the 1951 and 1952 spring meetings of the regional sociological societies as vehicles for developing interest in SSSP. Unfortunately, as far as SSSP work was concerned, Rose spent the academic year 1951–1952 in France. Prior to his departure, he was of some assistance in enlisting midwestern support.

[36] In order to keep SSSP dues low for regular members and even lower for student members, we sought to establish a journal that would be largely self-supporting. The financing of the quarterly journal *Social Problems* required legerdemain by its organizers too complicated and extensive to recount here, but it was launched in June 1953 and continues to thrive. The principal organizers of it were Jerome Himelhoch, S. F. Fava, and S. H. Aronson.

SSSP also emulated SPSSI's success in getting committees to develop sponsored books—in other words, symposia on specific social problems from which royalties went to the society. The first two books sponsored by SSSP assured the society of a more secure margin of funds from 1956 onward. They were: Jerome Himelhoch and S. F. Fava, eds., *Sexual Behavior in American Society: An Appraisal of the First Two Kinsey Reports* (New York: W. W. Norton, 1955); A. M. Rose *et al.*, eds., *Mental Health and Mental Disorder* (New York: W. W. Norton, 1955).

[37] S. H. Chapman chaired the first membership committee, and his vigorous direct-mail campaign helped quadruple our membership by the time of our second annual meeting.

[38] A. McC. Lee, "To the Editor," *Social Problems*, IX (1961–1962), 386–89. (Some basic documents on the organization of SSSP.)

[39] Perhaps our most difficult annual meeting was our second one. Some of those entrusted with arrangements did not take the society's existence seriously, but George Simpson of The City College of New York handled program arrangements for the convention, and E. B. Lee organized on the spot a functioning secretariat. Several of us quietly paid in our life-membership fees to guarantee the society's financial solvency. What could have been—and nearly was—a catastrophe was turned into a highly successful convention.

THE REVOLTS CONTINUE

Fortunately for the health of sociology as a viable scientific and academic discipline and as a useful social instrument, revolts against organizational inadequacy did not stop with the formation and success of SSSP. In the 1960s and 1970s the young, the blacks, and the women have sought and found new means of organizing themselves to influence sociological concerns, employment, and recognition. SSSP's influence in making the whole sociological professional structure more flexible did much to pave the way for the more intelligent reception of such insurgent contributions.

THE SOCIAL CRISIS CANNOT
BE DISGUISED

The ideological and social-scientific crisis of our time is no longer disguised by reformist palliatives and soothing propagandas. The disillusioned and rebellious blacks, youth, and women are demanding fundamental reconsiderations of how our society operates and of how it can come to operate. If they can learn to understand how a thoroughly scientific approach might yield adequate insights and thus facilitate reorganization, they might well come to support a humanist-existential approach to their problems. It offers no panaceas. It can yield sane critiques of the efforts of Swiss Guards and sound bases for social planning. The vertically invading masses, with their increasing literacy, social sophistication, and sense of urgency, may play with many panaceas, but they make broad acceptance of a humanist-existential approach increasingly likely.

Meanwhile, existential-humanist social scientists will continue to develop understandings of society and of ideas for its reorientation and reorganization that will be useful in group and societal guidance. Those ideas will gain acceptance as educated groups use them to modify group cultures and societal culture and as educated groups are broadened to become more inclusive. The existential-humanist paradigm will thus come to furnish a frame of reference popularly influential in the formation of policy decisions. Linked as it is to human growth and change, it offers constant human invigoration.

CHAPTER 8

Defenses Against Manipulation

Social actionists take propaganda to be one of their key instruments. In our competitive society, they make tides of propaganda beat against our eyes and ears. Buy this! Join that! Fight for/against this! Vote for/against that! The messages are confusing. The volume is overwhelming. Hopefully, we are thought by some to develop a certain immunity to these efforts or to learn how to balance one appeal against others. But do we?

What can we, as the objects of the propagandists, do about their efforts? What can we do about other techniques of the social actionists? To what extent can we wisely select the winners in the struggle for our mind? Into how many aspects of our lives do such pleadings and other manipulations for special interests penetrate?

IDEOLOGY IN ACTION

As we saw in the previous chapters, propaganda is ideology in action, given application. Propaganda is an ideology being expressed; it is current events being interpreted in terms of an ideology or associated with an ideology in a manipulative effort.

The root sense of *propaganda* is suggested by its Latin etymology. It directly translates as *propagating*. As introduced into general English usage by the Roman Catholic Church, it referred at first just to the missionary program of the Sacred Congregation for Propagating the

Faith (*de Propaganda Fide*) in seeking converts to that church.[1] A recent American dictionary reflects our broadening of the word's definition to "information or ideas methodically spread to promote or injure a cause, group, nation." [2]

Propaganda is a term that suggests similarities among phenomena associated with sharply contrasting values. Some such comparisons are shocking. Therefore many who find security in the assertion of a value insist that their opposition's utterances are "biased propaganda." [3] Their own utterances, they contend, are not *propaganda* at all, but something that should be given such a favorable, or at least colorless, label as *education* or maybe *publicity*. This is one of the many ways in which the defensive application of values distorts social perception and analysis. Social techniques or instruments that serve a variety of conflicting or competing purposes are best understood first without reference to those who use them, and then in context. If *propaganda* were to be used only by the "evil," the "good" would be handicapped in the relatively democratic struggles for public support in our society.

PROPAGANDA DEFINED. To substitute *mass communications* as a colorless synonym for *propaganda* in a discussion may have the advantage of

---

[1] Umberto Benigni, "Propaganda, Sacred Congregation of," *Catholic Encyclopaedia*, XII (1913), 456–61, esp. 456.

[2] *The Random House Dictionary of the English Language,* coll. ed. (New York: Random House, 1968), p. 1060. See also such earlier treatises as Edgar Stern-Rubarth, *Die Propaganda als politisches Instrument* (Berlin: Trowitzsch, 1921); E. L. Bernays, *Crystallizing Public Opinion* (New York: Boni and Liveright, 1923), *Propaganda* (New York: Liveright, 1928), and *The Engineering of Consent* (Norman, Okla.: University of Oklahoma Press, 1955); Gerhard Schultze-Pfaelzer, *Propaganda, Agitation, Reklame* (Berlin: Stilke, 1923); Gustave Le Bon, *The World Unbalanced* (London: Unwin, 1924); H. D. Lasswell, *Propaganda Technique in the World War* (New York: Alfred A. Knopf, 1927), and, with Dorothy Blumenstock, *World Revolutionary Propaganda: A Chicago Study* (New York: Alfred A. Knopf, 1939); V. I. Lenin, *Agitation und Propaganda* (Vienna: Verlag für Literatur und Politik, 1929); Hans Thimme, *Weltkrieg ohne Waffen* (Stuttgart: Cotta, 1932); F. E. Lumley, *The Propaganda Menace* (New York: Century, 1933); L. W. Doob, *Propaganda* (New York: Henry Holt, 1935), and *Public Opinion and Propaganda*, 2nd ed., reissue (Hamden, Conn.: Shoe String Press, 1966); F. C. Bartlett, *Political Propaganda* (Cambridge, Eng.: Cambridge University Press, 1940); B. L. Smith, H. D. Lasswell, and R. D. Casey, *Propaganda, Communication, and Public Opinion: A Comprehensive Reference Guide* (Princeton: Princeton University Press, 1946); Daniel Lerner, ed., *Propaganda in War and Crisis* (New York: George W. Stewart, 1951); C. D. MacDougall, *Understanding Public Opinion* (New York: Macmillan, 1952); Daniel Katz, Dorwin Cartwright, S. J. Eldersveld, and A. McC. Lee, eds., *Public Opinion and Propaganda* (New York: Dryden Press, 1954); William Albig, *Modern Public Opinion* (New York: McGraw-Hill, 1956); V. O. Packard, *The Hidden Persuaders* (New York: David McKay, 1957); Jacques Ellul, *Propaganda* (New York: Alfred A. Knopf, 1965); Bernard Berelson and Morris Janowitz, eds., *Reader in Public Opinion and Communication*, 2nd ed. (New York: Free Press, 1966).

[3] See, for example, Karin Dovring, *Road to Propaganda: The Semantics of Biased Communication* (New York: Philosophical Library, 1959).

shelving a word often employed unthinkingly to classify some spokesman or cause or organization as suspect or repulsive. The substitution many times also has the disadvantage of shifting the attention away from communications in its social context and especially from how social manipulators utilize propaganda. Thus, as in many other social scientific works, the term *propaganda* is used here when appropriate. It has the realistic connotation of having a role in social struggle.

Thus, let us brush aside the propagandistic use of *progaganda* and look upon it as a way of disseminating ideas rapidly to many people. More formally, it is the expression of a contention overtly set forth or covertly implied in order to influence the attitudes, and through attitudes, the opinions and actions of a public.[4]

Since any propaganda effort can best be understood as part of social competition and conflict, let us look at what is typically involved in purposive social manipulations that go into such struggles. Then let us discuss defenses available to us against such mass manipulations and especially against misleading propaganda. After all, the promise of an education in the liberal arts and sciences has traditionally included, among other things, the learning of wise ways to select the people, movements, and ideas we may be able to trust and distrust, support and reject. Is our current conception of the liberal arts and sciences providing such wisdom for enough people?

Let us characterize the behavior of social actionists in our society in terms of the orientation they typically exemplify toward the "materiel" they manipulate. This will consist of generalizations from firsthand observations of successful actionist entrepreneurs in business, labor organization, politics, religion, art, civic affairs, and academia. Each case is a specific individual and quite human; he is therefore highly complex. Like most human beings, each is very much a "multivalent man." [5]

The following description of the social viewpoint and tactics of an ideal-typical social actionist does not dwell upon his human complications, even though they are most intriguing and significant. Rather, only the actionist orientation is set forth, the orientation they all appear to share and that each seems to regard as his basic *modus operandi*. If the portrayal of this orientation appears harsh and even brutal, stripped as it is of rationalizations in terms of human compassion and societal welfare, please bear in mind that it is not a view that is being advocated

---

[4] A. McC. Lee, *How to Understand Propaganda* (New York: Rinehart, 1952), pp. 2, 18.

[5] A. McC. Lee, *Multivalent Man* (New York: George Braziller, 1966). The term *multivalent man*, then labeling an undeveloped conception, was suggested by Willard Waller, *The Family: A Dynamic Interpretation* (New York: Cordon, 1938), p. 163. See also H. C. Warren, ed., *Dictionary of Psychology* (Boston: Houghton Mifflin, 1934), p. 173, for a similar but even more vague conception.

here. It is what appears to be overriding in the social actionists' actionist frame of reference. It is a cultural byproduct, nurtured and transmitted from generation to generation in certain nonsibling peer groups
in our society. It appears to be the most common basic policy guidance
to which actionists take recourse in their thinking about their work in
our society.

SOCIETY IS THE ACTIONIST'S
STOCKPILE

Regardless of how sacrosanct we may regard any aspect of society,
the social actionist *as actionist* looks upon *everything* in society as a
stockpile of materiel more or less available for his use or for that of his
competitors or opponents. The special qualities, adaptabilities, and difficulties of such constituents as implements or media are carefully and
objectively studied and assessed in relation to operational needs and possibilities. Depending upon commitments to values, to ideologies, and to
personal and social goals and relationships, the actionist looks upon
people, organizations, laws, constitutions, ideas, media, cultural elements,
and even commitments as employable, exploitable, and even expendable.
Such materiel, it needs to be insisted, may include any thing, any person,
any organization, any aspect of society's heritage or culture that might
conceivably be serviceable to him. Just as a military actionist expends
fifteen thousand men to gain a strategic position, so an industrial actionist readily consigns to the scrapheap a product, a factory, a town, or a
category of employees skilled in a labor routine or a professional specialty
when it no longer serves his purposes.

THE ACTIONIST'S GOALS. At the outset the social actionist focuses his
attention upon certain personal and social goals that he believes to be
attainable. Since to succeed he must often be what is called an oppor-
tunist, his social goals are characteristically subject to modification,
redefinition, or replacement, and his personal goals are best identified as
flexible. With these flexibilities in goal as a basis, the social actionist seeks
an ideology and a strategy that will forward his efforts to achieve his
current conception of his goals. Both of these searches could scarcely be
undertaken by a thoughtful and dedicated social scientist. The social
scientist would see the larger social setting, not just the next steps, and
would be aware of the value commitments often implicit in viable traditional ideological elements. He might well perceive contradictions between a traditional ideology's idealizations (the stuff that gains popular
support) and the opportunism of the actionist (the stuff that keeps him

from having to recognize and accept defeat). The actionist usually expects ideological contradictions to get lost in rhetoric. The social scientist might demand a much more substantial theoretical product than the actionist thinks he needs. The social scientist thus reveals his faith in his own intellectual product. The actionist betrays his fundamental belief in that to which his ideology must always be subservient—himself.

A PATCHWORK OF ENTICING IDEAS. Many times the ideological search results in a jerry-built, ill-defined, illogically stated rationale. It is couched in glittering generalities and name-calling terms that are interpreted to suit many different interests, the interests of diverse publics and power brokers, so long as those publics and power brokers remain uncritical. The "ideology" may be just a group of vague pleasantries and caveats surrounding a personality, an institution, a group of commercial products, or an urban reform program. A political-party program or the sales manual for many a commercial product illustrates well the end-product.

The successors to ancient tribal bards—the plausible journalists, clergymen, speech-writers, advertising copy specialists, and public-relations counselors of our day—all can do much to give such flimsy ideologies some appearance of coherence, consistency, and "sincerity." Bards similarly served their ancient tribal chieftains. Their products were sagas rather than TV spectaculars, but their purpose was much the same. The current minnesingers and counselors try to make the personalities and/or aspirations of our powerful ones and would-be powerful ones compel attention, attract support, and appear substantial wherever they are exposed.

A FLEXIBLE AND CHANGING STRATEGY. The results of the second search—that for a social actionist's strategies—are again frequently such as to arouse no confidence in a methodical lawyer or banker or social scientist, but they may still satisfy the actionist's principal criterion for their use: They appear to be what will achieve his goals.

The entrepreneur of social action has much in common in viewpoint with the old-fashioned military actionist. An analogy with strategists of contemporary six-day or even six-hour wars is a little too frightful to think about and too short to be useful for our purposes. Principally, the actionist constantly reconnoiters the terrain, as it were, in order to select or improvise strategies appropriate to changing conditions of competition, conflict, or unilateral aggression. Issues get used up. Personnel becomes outmoded. New issues, readaptations of old issues must constantly be planned and then related to the actionist's alleged ideology, then stated as simply as possible, maybe even as a slogan or a joke.

Strategy especially involves ways to use (1) personnel, (2) organizations, (3) propaganda, (4) media of communication, and (5) existing sentiment materiel in the light of (6) the changing social situation. Let us look briefly at each of these facets of a typical actionist's efforts in our society today:

TO EXPLOIT INDIVIDUAL
POTENTIALITIES

1. *Personnel* for social action might include any type or group of human beings, but they can be said to consist of eight principal types. These types are (a) leaders, (b) promoters, (c) manipulators, (d) sponsors, (e) bureaucrats, (f) rank-and-file volunteer workers, (g) "just members," and (h) "fellow travelers." These are not mutually exclusive categories. They are rough role types. Like other more or less specialized roles, they draw to their performance different emotional and intellectual personality types whose multivalence further complicates the situation.

The role of social actionist being discussed is further specialized, as the foregoing list suggests, into those of leader, promoter, and manipulator. The leader is the principal spokesman for a movement or organization or agitation. He may be a mere puppet of the manipulator. He usually is a person with a degree of charismatic quality who feels he has some special mission. He provides the personal symbolism that spearheads the zeal and the emotional drive of a campaign or program. Because successful social action involves many technical problems today, the professionally competent promoter furnishes the arts of speech-writing, influencing mass media, arranging public meetings, and infiltrating programs of other organizations. The promoter is usually specialized in one or more types of activity necessary to social action. He tends to bring an objectivity and workmanlike quality to an effort that helps to stabilize it and give it more consistent direction. The third type of actionist, the manipulator, is more often a prime maneuverer rather than a mere employee. He is a power broker, privy to sources of available funds and to the terms upon which funds and other support may be obtained. Often looked upon as a "necessary evil" in a social-action program, he is frequently an experienced lawyer, politician, or business entrepreneur who has quietly worked himself into a powerful control position.

The other five role types are instruments of the first three. Promoters and manipulators seek out sponsors, or fronts, upon whose status and influence their agitation can ride piggyback, as it were. Bureaucrats trail behind the leaders, promoters, and manipulators into any movement or organization. Their small talents and narrow aspirations make them helpful job-holders, parts of the "machine." Rank-and-file volunteers and "just members" furnish impressive bulk and a degree of substantiality to religious bodies, political organizations, and civic societies. Fellow travelers, the fifth of these types, are friends of any social action that carry its message to other groups without being identified with the action in a formal sense.

Leaders, promoters, and manipulators develop shrewd senses of the personality characteristics and motivations to be found most dependably among given groups of people. Through experience, they learn how to use them. The more experience they have, the less they have to depend upon loose formulas in order to exploit human potentialities.[6]

TO CONTROL SOCIAL STRUCTURES

2. *Organizations*, like so much else in society, derive what influence they have from popular support and acquiescence. Their leaders are prone to forget this as they find themselves more and more shored up in their positions through their control of organizational decision-making structures, finance, and physical assets. On the other hand, leaders under attack find it expedient to turn to mergers, interorganizational deals, and especially propaganda to build influence. Mergers and deals are ways to borrow or buy acquired influence; propaganda is a return to a direct approach of gaining popular support.

Social power appears to be based upon many things. It includes the control of money, physical resources, patents, know-how, contacts, communications media, and organizational structures. All such power and its control depend ultimately upon popular interest, acceptance, support, or acquiescence. Without morale, an army fails, and without a popular market, a commodity disappears. Without faith in the value of a currency, the credit structure based on it collapses. Without belief in the even-handedness of police surveillance, rioting and vigilante procedures become possibilities.

Those who control established organizations often have a power derived from myth and acquiescence that bears little relationship to the current mobilizable social strength of their actual supporters. As the noted journalist Heywood Broun asserted to illustrate this point, "There is not a single New York editor who does not live in mortal terror of the power of this group [officials of the Roman Catholic Church]. It is not a case of numbers but of organization. . . . If the church can bluff its way

[6] See A. McC. Lee, "Socialization of the Individual," in Lee, ed., *Principles of Sociology*, 3rd ed. (New York: Barnes & Noble, 1969), pp. 24–26, and *How to Understand Propaganda*, pp. 86–89. See also S. M. Cutlip, *A Public Relations Bibliography*, 2nd ed. (Madison: University of Wisconsin Press, 1965); Joe McGinniss, *The Selling of the President 1968* (New York: Trident Press, 1969).

into a preferred position, the fault lies not with the Catholics but with the editors." [7]

ORGANIZATIONAL TACTICS. The chief tactics for dealing with organizations that are available to promoters and manipulators are (a) controlling them through the employment, seduction, corruption, or capture of their trusted leadership, (b) gaining support of additional organizations by finding or successfully alleging common interests with organizations already controlled, (c) creation or capture and exploitation of "front organizations," and (d) boring from within uncommitted or even antagonistically committed organizations—in other words, placing agents in key spots within them.

The first of the above tactics is clear enough. Actionists first find it expedient to obtain a base of operations in one or more organizations that they control.

The second tactic includes joint lobbying, joint campaigns to control elections by citizens or by stockholders and to infiltrate committees, commissions, and bureaucracies, and joint money-raising schemes, such as community-chest drives and trade-association and joint trade-union war chests for politico-economic programs.

Public-relations specialists have created or captured a whole range of front organizations for trade associations and corporations of this and other countries.[8] These are organizations controlled by their clients but apparently operated under other, and perhaps "independent," auspices. They include university departments, institutes, and bureaus,[9] federal, state, and local governmental committees, commissions, and bureaus,[10] and a variety of societies, foundations, corporations, and even trade unions.

The boring-from-within tactic is most often discussed publicly in connection with the infiltration activities of disruptive left-wing groups, such as the communists, but it has long been a device for extending the power of established social entrepreneurs and groups. Thus large financial, utility, and manufacturing firms find it expedient to stimulate "good citizenship" and "civic leadership" on the part of their key employees so

---

[7] Heywood Broun, "The Piece That Got Me Fired," *The Nation*, reprinted in George Seldes, ed., *The Great Quotations* (New York: Lyle Stuart, 1960), p. 116.

[8] On this, see for example, E. L. Bernays, *Biography of an Idea: Memoirs* (New York: Simon & Schuster, 1965).

[9] J. L. Avorn and the staff of *Columbia Spectator, Up Against the Ivy Wall* (New York: Atheneum, 1969); Noam Chomsky, *American Power and the New Mandarins* (New York: Pantheon, 1969); I. L. Horowitz, *The Rise and Fall of Project Camelot* (Cambridge, Mass.: M.I.T. Press, 1967).

[10] J. W. Fulbright, *The Pentagon Propaganda Machine* (New York: Liveright, 1970); David Horowitz, *Empire and Revolution* (New York: Random House, 1969); M. J. Green *et al.*, *The Closed Enterprise System* (New York: Grossman, 1972).

that they can participate in a wide range of community, state, and national activities. Some such employees even do this on leaves of absence with pay from their regular employment. One need not be a cynic to note the control implications of such operations.

So much for an outline of how actionists control and manipulate the groups available and potentially useful to them. What are the characteristics of the groups to which actionists give special attention? Group characteristics are quite complex and have frequently been discussed, and they therefore need not be discussed again here at great length.[11] Some of the principal aspects, in addition to size (human resources) and physical resources, that concern actionists are groups' cohesiveness, staying power and continuity, visibility, adaptability, and intergroup relations. Organizational adaptability or flexibility involves the ability to shift from long-term educational efforts, for example, to high-pressure political maneuvers, from the sponsorship of an exhibit or a conference to the infiltration of other organizations, and from serious efforts for a cause to entertainment.

The keen social analyst Willard Waller made some very telling comments on the nature of organizations when discussing the institutionalization of ideas. As he said, "Something happens to ideas when they get themselves organized into social systems. The ethical ideas of Christ, flexible and universal, have nevertheless been smothered by churches. A social principle degenerates into a dogma when an institution is built about it. Yet an idea must be organized before it can be made into fact, and an idea wholly unorganized rarely lives long. Without mechanism it dies, but mechanism perverts it. This is part of the natural flow and recession—the life principle in society."[12]

TO CAST NETS OF SYMBOLS

3. *Propaganda* has a somewhat reciprocal relationship with organization. When a social actionist has adequate organizational support for his current purposes, his propaganda efforts can be routine. When he has problems with obtaining or maintaining organizational backing and control, he is wise to turn to propaganda in order to gain or regain impetus.

[11] Lee, *How to Understand Propaganda*, Chap. 6, and *Multivalent Man*, esp. Chaps. 9 and 10. See also Herbert Blumer, "Collective Behavior," Part 2 in Lee, ed., *Principles of Sociology;* and Stanley Milgram and Hans Toch, "Collective Behavior: Crowds and Social Movements," in Gardner Lindzey and Elliot Aronson, eds., *The Handbook of Social Psychology,* 2nd ed. (Reading, Mass.: Addison-Wesley, 1968), IV, Chap. 35.

[12] Willard Waller, *The Sociology of Teaching* (New York: John Wiley, 1932), p. 441. See also R. M. MacIver and C. H. Page, *Society* (New York: Rinehart, 1949), p. 15, and W. G. Sumner, *Folkways* (Boston: Ginn, 1906), p. 53.

The basic ingredients of propaganda are omnibus words and the A-B-C pattern. Omnibus words are vague and glittering. They are emotionally charged symbols, both negative and positive, that might be called propaganda building blocks. They carry much of the burden of a message. The A-B-C pattern consists of the appeal, bond, and commodity, the ideological bridge that is implicit or explicit in one or many intertwined forms in all successful propaganda. The appeal is the come-on, the part of the message that strikes into the probable interests of intended publics. The bond is the tie-in that links appeal and commodity. The commodity is the item, idea, service, personality, project, ideology, cause, institution, or country that the propagandist is pushing.

Name-calling and virtue words—negative and positive symbols—are used not only to construct A-B-C bridges, but also to put together a variety of other types of association. Thus, for example, a proposal may be associated with a revered or a detested institution (transfer technique) or personality (testimonial technique), with the masses, the "common man," the "silent majority" (plain-folks technique), or with what is the "going thing," the "in-idea," what "everyone" is or is not doing or avoiding, accepting or rejecting (band-wagon technique). To illustrate, one can constantly perceive efforts to transfer the prestige of religion, science, and democracy to special projects that may or may not have any legitimate relationship with those revered ideologies and their institutional settings. Similarly, individuals with wide reputations for any reason are in demand as endorsers of special projects, which is using the testimonial device. These four techniques are employed both fairly and accurately and also quite unfairly and inaccurately.

WHAT ABOUT LOGICAL FALLACIES? Students of formal logic sometimes contend that the propaganda devices just mentioned do not go far enough in the analysis of content. They advocate the use of classical logical fallacies. The difficulty with those fallacies, however, is that they focus upon violations of a canon of logic rather than the nature and the content of the communication and the communication process.

When logicians say that a propagandist is using an *argumentum ad hominem* (argument "to the man"), is discussing ideas in terms of the personality or personal relations of the spokesman rather than in terms of their accuracy and relevance, they tell us to reject the propagandist's message because of his lack of propriety in the use of logical procedures as they see them. They do not face up to the practice as a common aspect of human intercommunication and do not weigh its use in that light.

When logicians call the testimonial technique's application an *argumentum ad verecundiam* (argument to modesty) or appeal to accept a view on the basis of authority, they have chiefly substituted a more complicated conception labeled in Latin for one that is straightforward enough for anyone's understanding. They have also attached the notion of fallacy to a practice widely and sometimes dependably used in popular discourse.

Similar comments can also be made about such other logical "fallacies" as *argumentum ad invidiam* (appeal to hate or envy) and *argumentum ad ignorantiam* (appeal based upon an adversary's assumed ignorance of the matter in dispute). These "fallacies" are too absolute, too technical in an irrelevant sense, and too lacking in a recognition of moral and cultural relativity.

The techniques of identification or association mentioned do not exhaust the possibilities at all, and they are types, not categories, of techniques. They are really ideal types, and in practice they usually appear in more complex and mixed forms. One can reconsider the list given (transfer, testimonial, plain folks, and band wagon) and come up with more specialized procedures, such as guilt by association ("a bad lot," "a bad neighborhood," Joe-McCarthyism) and guilt by heredity (racism, ethnicism, sexism, "bad stock") and their opposites, virtue by association ("name dropping," "good connections," arbitrary accreditation procedures) and virtue by heredity (racism, ethnicism, sexism, "good stock").

With this fairly simple basic armament the propagandist constructs and reconstructs the content of his communications to implement his strategies. Such communications are especially keyed to his constant selection and definition, and reselection and redefinition, of his current issues, to his case-making, and to the end-product of his simplification of the issues and their cases, often in the form of a slogan.[13]

TO GAIN ACCESS TO AUDIENCES

4. *Media of communication* set the potential size of the audiences that propagandists can reach. Gaining access to the audience of a given medium requires that an actionist get his message past the medium's "gatekeepers," or better still, get his message adopted by the medium's own staff. This is often easier to do with advertising than with materials intended to be treated as news or entertainment. Often actionists employ both advertising (sometimes said to be used as a "medium sweetener")

[13] See also Lee, *How to Understand Propaganda*, Chap. 3; William Hummel and Keith Huntress, *The Analysis of Propaganda* (New York: William Sloane Associates, 1949), esp. Chap. 4, which deals with the rhetoric of propaganda. See also the scholarly treatment by O. R. Holsti, J. K. Loomba, and R. C. North, "Content Analysis," in Lindzey and Aronson, eds., *The Handbook of Social Psychology*, II, Chap. 16.

and efforts to infiltrate nonadvertising space and time. Even with access, a propagandist still has the problem of turning potential audiences into actual, receptive, and responsive readers, listeners, or lookers. Audience reaction depends largely upon the message itself, the manner in which it is "played" by medium functionaries (reporters, copywriters, columnists, commentators, comedians, programmers), and upon current social conditions, the general social context or climate of opinion. Statements or dramatizing events must have a character that demands attention. Proposals must be a kind likely to be viewed with positive or negative seriousness.

THE WAYS TO REACH AUDIENCES. The principal propaganda media can usefully be typed in a few simple ways. They can be distinguished as formal or informal, and in terms of their relation to an actionist organization or movement, as internal, controlled-direct, uncontrolled-direct, and indirect media. In addition, during World War II it became customary in the Federal Office of War Information to talk about "white," "gray," and "black" propaganda media, types that may be found elsewhere than in international struggles. Let us illustrate these three sets of types quite briefly.

Formal media may more often occur to us than the informal ones in our thinking about the activities of social actionists. In addition to established newspapers, radio and television stations, advertising agencies, publicity firms, magazines, trade journals, book publishers, speakers, agencies, motion-picture studios, and other formal media, there are many informal or less formal ones that can play powerful roles in organizing public response. These are rumor and gossip, direct mail, leaflets, pamphlets, marginal book publishers, placards and small posters, printed and mimeographed handbills, speakers, pickets, and many more. Such a pamphlet-publishing organization as the nonprofit Public Affairs Committee becomes a rather formal medium when it issues 53 million pamphlets on 460 topics in 36 years, but pamphlets are ordinarily casual and separate publications rather than parts of a series-and-distribution arrangement such as the Public Affairs Committee has developed.

The institutionalized and "responsible" character of formal media makes them routinely available only to publicists for established and "responsible" organizations. But agitators for radical and innovative programs can gain attention in almost any medium by exploiting the potentialities of the "news" concept. As Louis Adamic summarized the extreme expression of that agitational opportunity, newspapers do "print the riots." [14] In addition, in periods of tension when formal media become

---

[14] Louis Adamic, "The Papers Print the Riots," *Scribner's Magazine*, XCI (1932), 110–11.

even more fully the vehicles of orthodox social rituals (sports, sensational crimes, the waywardness of our youth, "soap-opera" and "comic" types of entertainment), informal media take on power out of all proportion to their unpretentious character. The informal media even force their concerns into the news of the formal media. For example, they prevent the formal media from ignoring or burying such a disturbing event as a strike or riot.

The formal-informal relationship is best seen as a continuum. At the more formal end are the relatively rigid and institutionalized media: the daily newspapers, block-booked motion pictures, mass magazines, and radio and television networks. Their tremendous financial commitments are largely met by advertising, although they must also have popular adherence in order to get that advertising. Thus they are highly vulnerable to discordant pressures, both financial and popular. Their operators attempt to anticipate or avoid controversial issues and other hazards. They follow a nonspeculative, conservative course. Only in that manner do they ordinarily assume that they can maintain or better their existing competitive or monopolistic situation. At the other end are such "irresponsible" and unorganized media as gossip, stump speakers, volunteer pickets, and mimeographed handbills which are here today and perhaps untraceable tomorrow, all of which can be somewhat organized. At least they can be stimulated and even created, given aid, and motivated. They cannot be made into highly controlled or monopolistic instruments in our society as it is now organized. The student, black, and female agitators of the 1960s and 1970s are again demonstrating that our less formal media provide powerful recourses for democratic discussions and adjustments in our society.

SCHOOLS AND TEACHERS AS ILLUSTRATIONS. Internal, direct, and indirect types of media are well-illustrated by the propaganda roles of teachers and their organizations. Schools' and teachers' associations and unions use internal media to give directives and solicit reactions. Such media include convocations and institutes, as well as bulletins and newsletters. When "outside" interests can gain access to such media, they have a captive audience that may or may not be responsive. Critics of teachers and educational budgets keep careful watch over such media to spot unguarded statements and events that can be used for their purposes. Direct media are those through which messages are transmitted with admitted sponsorship to outside publics. In education these are textbooks, teachers' lectures, public statements and writings, and pronouncements by administrators and teacher organizations. Indirect media are legion. They carry endorsements or rejections of a program without the source of influence being indicated or obvious. In this area the compulsions toward cooperation range from news, facts, logic, services, and friendship to retainer fees, bribes, and coercion.

Broad changes in the relations of university teachers to social action during the nineteenth and twentieth centuries have altered their propaganda roles. At the outset of this period our colleges and universities were training schools for clergymen, lawyers, and other "gentlemen." Their professors were assimilated members of a social structure in which the vested interests of those roles were to be accepted and defended. Sharp criticisms of theology, the church, law, and judicial process came chiefly from "radicals" outside the academic halls. Then with the addition of more and more educational assignments to the college's program, professors with traditions other than those of the "old professionals" became increasingly numerous. They were professors informed about the practical worlds of engineering, physical and biological science, business, large-scale government, mass communications, social work, and all the rest.

During the transition from colleges controlled by those defensive of "old" professionalisms to those trained to produce technicians and "professionals" for an integrating technological society, the descendants of the former fought a losing battle against the "profanation of the temple" by the latter. To illustrate, the American Civil Liberties Union noted that during the 1920s "thousands of dollars were spent in universities for subsidies to schools of commerce, fees to professors and promotion work for text-books favorable to utilities. That there was 'a close connection between public utilities and the academic profession' was confirmed by the American Association of University Professors which undertook an investigation of the charges against members of the profession in 1930." Then what happened? "It is significant," the Union adds, "that after this exposure of the prostitution of the schools and colleges to the Power Trust no teacher was dismissed or disciplined. Some of them may have severed their connections, . . . but nothing happened remotely akin to the prompt dismissal of teachers or professors guilty of 'radical' utterances. The public furore aroused by the exposure of this propaganda has resulted in dissolving the [open] alliance between schools and utilities." [15] The word *open* is inserted because bribes in the form of fees for speeches, consultations, and grants for "research" persisted, became more routine, and continue to expand in frequency. In other words, what was an indirect propaganda medium now is often a direct one, albeit still often clothed in an academic disguise.

Why is it worthwhile for business and financial interests to subsidize

[15] A.C.L.U., *The Gag on Teaching*, 3rd ed. (New York: American Civil Liberties Union, 1940), p. 30. See also Richard Hofstadter and W. P. Metzger, *The Development of Academic Freedom in the United States* (New York: Columbia University Press, 1955); R. M. MacIver, *Academic Freedom in Our Time* (New York: Columbia University Press, 1955); and S. M. Lipset and S. S. Wolin, eds., *The Berkeley Student Revolt* (Garden City, N.Y.: Doubleday, 1965), esp. Chap. 5.

and control very expensive, prestigious, and privately financed universities? Because of the sentimental hold of the "old school tie"? Because it is healthy for our society to have a variety of interests represented in the control of higher education? Those appeals yield some funds, but far from enough. The private university provides a less complicated medium than the public one for obtaining research, development, and advocacy services on a tax-free basis. It is also thought to be somewhat safe to assume that a "name" professorship endowed in a private school for some noncontroversial and ornamental subject such as art history will not be given to some "bolshevik" or "mad man." Few doubt that the professor of a prestigious private institution is an independent expert, even though he may have been selected most carefully with the assurance that his public utterances will be happily and accurately congruent with the biases or interests of the donor of his chair or the grantor to his bureau.

As in England and elsewhere, the control situation in our "private" universities is changing as well. Even the lordly Harvard, with its endowment of more than $1 billion, has at times derived some two-thirds of its current operating budget from federal funds. For some time both secular and religious universities have more and more successfully been pressuring governmental units for subsidies in this country, often at the expense of needy public institutions. Where subsidy goes, as administrators of private schools are already learning, controls cannot be far behind. The acceptance of governmental support grants also begets a greater need for such grants.

Graduate academic departments now quite commonly sponsor bureaus and institutes that undertake subsidized research for branches of government, specific companies, industries, interested individuals, and trade unions. Professors and their undergraduate and graduate students thus get "fieldwork experience" and "laboratory research training" on what must of necessity be in most cases biased or narrowly technical projects and scarcely the greatly needed basic research to which academic institutions presumably should dedicate themselves. This relationship of academician to sponsor is accepted so uncritically and has become so "natural" that in many cases the biasing influence is not apparent to either, nor is the social and professional damage.

This situation is now rarely exposed or discussed. There is no "public furore" about it. In some cases, liberal graduate schools have thus become direct mediums of propaganda among their own students and also, through influence, among undergraduate and high-school students. In other cases, veiling is provided in one way or another—for example, by having funds transmitted "for basic research" either directly or by a foundation. One caustic critic of such practices has coined for them the expressions *sponsor pandering* and *foundation panhandling*.

WHITE, GRAY, AND BLACK. The white, gray, and black media differ somewhat as types from the internal, direct, and indirect ones. In terms of the latter labels, they are direct (white), undisguised indirect (gray), and disguised indirect (black). The use and the analysis of disguised indirect propagandas is slippery business. For example, the overzealous, super-duper American "patriot" frequently assumes that a traditionally Jeffersonian democratic position is "radical," disturbing, and hence, "of course," communist! On the other hand, passages from Jefferson's writings have been torn out of context and used for quite non-Jeffersonian purposes.

As in the case of personnel, the social actionist does not accept traditional assumptions or allegations about media. As nearly as possible, he must know the details of their manner of operation if he is to penetrate them effectively and accurately to influence their audiences.[16]

TO FIND COMPELLING APPEALS

5. *Existing sentiment materiel* provides the basis for selecting the "A" appeal to be used in the A-B-C pattern of propaganda construction. With an appeal, a propagandist can only attempt to manipulate what already exists in the minds of the groups of people he is trying to influence.

Simplifiers have worked out list after list of appeals and motives as ways to tap existing sentiment materiel, but such lists are merely caricatures, or at best, crude steps toward an understanding of this social-psychological complexity. To synthesize the mental equipment of a person from another culture requires a degree of preparation, study, and care that emphasizes the complexity and inclusiveness of a society's, and even of a group's, natural cultural patterns. In international psychological warfare, therefore, it has usually been more effective to employ a person who grew up in the enemy's culture than to attempt such synthesis. Even in intergroup communication, publicists and advertising men have found it expedient to obtain blacks to speak to blacks and similarly to depend upon other authentic ethnic and class specialists rather than upon formulas.

To say that opinions are patterned individually by sentiments, in groups by the predominant group mores, and in society by societal morality, gives the actionist some approach to the opinion problem. An

---

[16] Lee, *How to Understand Propaganda*, Chap. 5. See also Herbert Blumer, *Movies and Conduct* (New York: Macmillan, 1933); R. K. Merton, *Mass Persuasion* (New York: Harper & Bros., 1946); Katz *et al.*, eds., *Public Opinion and Propaganda*, esp. Chaps. 5 and 9; and Walter Weiss, "Effects of the Mass Media of Communication," in Lindzey and Aronson, eds., *The Handbook of Social Psychology*, V, Chap. 38.

opinion becomes public rather than personal not because of any group spirit or any necessary group decision, but rather, because common culture and common access to facts and ideas result in the emergence of similar opinions on a given subject in a given public. A public opinion differs from a common attitude or a more deeply held common sentiment in that a public opinion is expressed. An attitude or a sentiment is a mental pattern that may or may not resemble the expressed opinion.

MOTIVES ARE MULTIVALENT. The problem naturally arises as to how one person can express a personal opinion, an opinion of one of several different limited groups or publics, and an opinion of *the* public, all of which may differ in detail or even in entirety. But this common social phenomenon, called multivalence, finds ready illustration in popular experience, even though it is not often consciously recognized as such.

This matter of multivalence presents the actionist with his principal problem when he uses the reports of public-opinion pollsters. The type of opinion a person expresses, like his other behavior, depends upon the conditions under which his reaction (the interview response) takes place. An interviewer or listener ordinarily receives an expression of opinion typical or representative of *the* public (society) when he has not achieved any but a very general type of rapport with the other person. This is especially so if the interviewer fits into the stereotype of a schoolteacher, parson, or some other official representative of societal morals. If the person interviewed feels some group identification with the interviewer, then the person interviewed may express an opinion typical of that more limited public. "Now that I know you are a fellow grocer, I can talk more freely!" or "Why didn't you tell me that you fought in Viet Nam?"

SENTIMENTS ARE BASIC. Actionists can learn about the opinions of certain publics and of the general public, but these are surface matters. Opinions change. They may appear quite vacillating. To guide a propagandist, a knowledge of common sentiments is much more useful than reports on opinions. Sentiments are basic patterns of emotion and thought underlying how people behave. They are deep and largely unverbalized. Although powerful in the determination of opinion and behavior, we can learn about sentiments only by analyzing what people say and do. We cannot approach them more directly.

Through analysis of the spontaneous statements and actions of leaders and members of publics as gathered by "political scouts" and by "scientific pollsters," propagandists can gradually build up dependable "clinical knowledge" [17] of the sentiment materiel with which they have to

---

[17] Lee, *Multivalent Man*, Chap. 22. See also the therapeutic rather than scientific research definition of the expression by Louis Wirth, "Clinical Sociology," *American Journal of Sociology*, XXXVII (1931–1932), 49–66. See also W. W. Argow, "The Practical Application of Sociology," *American Sociological Review*, VI (1941), 37–40, esp. 38.

work. The political scouts may work for a political actionist, or they may be salesmen of a corporation, union representatives, social workers, media reporters, or whatnot. As political scouts, they report what people are spontaneously saying and doing—what might be called background material behind systematic opinion surveys. When compared and analyzed in the light of repeated polls and other data having to do with ethnic, occupational, and class patternings and behaviors, shrewd analysts find few surprises in changed opinion reports, votes, sales records, or lists of voluntary contributors.[18]

TO UTILIZE THE CURRENT CLIMATE OF OPINION

6. *The changing social situation,* often called the changing climate of opinion, is ever-present in the thoughts of the successful social actionist. What was impossible yesterday may become easy today with a change in the overall situation. War, depression, inflation, urban tensions, student unrest, growing evidence of environmental pollution, population pressures, black dissatisfaction and upward mobility, female agitation against male sexism, relaxed bans against pornography, and more can all figure strongly in what is currently possible to the actionist. Particularly in a country with such powerful, interrelated, and quasi-monopolistic mass media as ours, at any given time there appears to be a pall of orthodoxy somewhat shrouding all popular thought and discussion—except for the "queer," the "radical," and the "dangerous." A great many people find it most comfortable to adapt themselves to that climate of opinion, and social actionists exploit this tendency toward conformity.

Propaganda grows out of and plays a part in social cleavages and tensions, struggles, and competitions. Its effectiveness in an overall sense is controlled by the trend of popular sentiments and by the limits to social change set by human and physical environmental conditions. Both social actionists and scientific students of social manipulation and propaganda share the conclusion, therefore, that social forces, social structures, and their changes, and major human and other events, outweigh special efforts time and again in determining the outcome of a struggle.

CLEVERNESS PLUS LUCK. The success of a social actionist is admittedly

---

[18] Lee, *How to Understand Propaganda,* Chap. 7. See also Herbert Blumer, "Public Opinion and Public Opinion Polling," *American Sociological Review,* XIII (1948), 542–54; Katz *et al.,* eds., *Public Opinion and Propaganda,* Chaps. 1–3, 6–7, 10–12; Berelson and Janowitz, eds., *Reader in Public Opinion and Communication,* Chaps. 1–3, 9–11; N. R. Luttbeg, ed., *Public Opinion and Public Policy* (Homewood, Ill.: Dorsey Press, 1968), Secs. 4–7.

a combination of cleverness and luck. The capable use of techniques and controls counts, even though the social factors involved in any given situation are much too uncontrollable and complex for an actionist to be said to have achieved a goal through sheer cleverness alone. The intelligent and experienced propagandist or other actionist can serve as a catalyst of social change or as a temporary stumbling block to delay it. Reference is not made here to propaganda struggles between relatively similar brands of cigarettes, perfumes, or automobiles, but to the overall effort concerning cigarettes or perfumes or automobiles—or collectivism or private enterprise or state socialism. For either catalyzing or blocking, or for combinations of the two. many techniques and media are available. Those we have examined have largely been partial ones. They deal with the content of messages, personnel, propaganda media, organizations, and popular sentiments. Let us now look at some of the more inclusive strategic techniques.

The endless variety of overall strategic techniques is all closely related to the issue selected for a given phase of a struggle. Here are fifteen commonly used strategies of this sort: *hot potato, stalling, least-of-evils, scapegoating, shift of scene, change of pace, big tent, conflict, appeasement, confusion, big lie, censorship, person to person, program of deeds,* and *leadership.* Most of these are almost self-defining or have been discussed at length elsewhere. Here are brief comments on each of them:

Hot potato springs an event, a trap, a situation upon an opponent that will force the opponent to compromise himself, to handle something in an embarrassed or guilty manner. Hot potatoes are often statements torn out of context, made in a different climate of opinion.

Stalling, the use of plausible delaying tactics, sometimes causes the opposition to lose vigor, interest, and support before a decision can be reached. Many "investigations" have this purpose rather than fact-finding.

Hitler's favorite was the *least-of-evils.* He asserted that his program's alternative would be a bloody Communist terror. Efforts to legalize traffic in marijuana and to institute state gambling systems are regularly based upon the least-of-evils argument. Whether a given use of least-of-evils is delusory or a sound judgment of the available alternatives depends upon one's conception of one's own interests and those of one's associates.

Scapegoating is often a strategy of disaster. It may be used to picture a group or a person (such as the Jews and Poles in Nazi Germany, the capitalists in communist ideology, a given city boss in reformist political propaganda) as the focal point of blame and dissatisfaction for selected or general social woes. The allegation is at best an oversimplification and at worst, as in Nazi propaganda against Jews and Poles, cruelly delusory. Our mass media continually parade an assortment of scapegoats—the whiskey interests, Wall Street, the labor bosses, machine politicians, the Communist menace, the yellow peril, the Black Panthers, the peaceniks or doves, the hawks, and the military-industrial establishment.

In some cases it is not clear whether scapegoating is a deliberate strategy or merely develops as a useful happenstance. For example, with popular American revulsion mounting in the early 1970s against the human wastage and the brutalizing influences of the undeclared Indochinese War, First Lieutenant William Calley of the frightful My Lai massacre of noncombatants appears to have been seized as an army scapegoat once a photojournalist had forced it to the nation's attention. By finding him guilty of multiple murders after a long and spectacular military trial, perhaps army commanders hoped to establish publicly their abhorrence of the wanton destruction of noncombatants. If that was the strategy, it was poorly calculated. "For reasons that seemed to spring from the natural human tendency to translate moral dilemmas into personal terms, the Calley case was turned overnight into a symbol of the entire American tragedy in Vietnam." [19] Instead of serving as a scapegoat's trial, the trial triggered vivid public reviews of war's inevitable degradation and brutalization of its participants.

Shift of scene often disorganizes the opposition by moving to a more favorable arena. In politics it may be a shift from election fights to lobbying in administrative halls or a legislature, to litigation in connection with a relevant issue through the courts, to appealing more directly to constituencies between elections in a propaganda campaign in the mass media. Parades, petitions, delegations, mass meetings, TV programs, study commissions, investigations—each helps to shift the scene, and perhaps to catch the opposition off guard.

Change of pace can be equally useful to a strategist, and sometimes it is employed with shift of scene. Commercial advertising illustrates this strategy with its shifts from emotional to factual appeals, from lottery-type inducements to ones stressing economy, from sex appeal to mystery to mechanical know-how.

Big-tent strategies of their own are available to large organizations with extensive and varied constituencies. This is partly a matter of diverse appeals and partly one of contrasting organizational opportunities and instrumentalities. Like a large circus's many rings, big-tent strategies offer many attractions, many things to see and do simultaneously. They can appeal to a great many different groups on their own terms and at the same time. Thus a corporation such as "Ma Bell," the telephone company, can attempt to appear as a benevolent employer, a sponsor of

[19] Kenneth Auchincloss, "Who Else Is Guilty?" *Newsweek*, April 12, 1971, p. 30.

scientific research, a friend of education, a family servant, a part of the community health and safety protection network, a gilt-edged investment. A social movement such as that for black rights gains from the efforts of unrelated organizations with a variety of contrasting strategies: court action, legislative modification, governmental and private administrative recourse, education, agitation, and conflict.

Viewed in a slightly different manner, big-tent can be a strategy of developing a more general social movement in such a way that a great many organizations will attempt to tie in with it. Instances have been Prohibition, our various wars, antiwar programs, and ecology and anti-pollution efforts.

Conflict, appeasement, and *confusion* are sometimes phases through which change of pace may go. Conflict refers to the actionist services of strikes, lockouts, boycotts, picketings, shows of official force, defiances of soldiers or police, riots, and wars. While the more violent types of conflict demand attention in the media and shock people into a consciousness of a confrontation, they are typically more costly than advantageous. Hence nonviolent confrontations—actually nonviolent conflicts—have often demonstrated greater utility in the accomplishment of social goals than recourse to violence.

A more acceptable synonym for appeasement is compromise (horse-trading, or give-and-take). Confusion may serve extremists of the left or right or those who merely muddle along. Alleged or actual confusion is often the smokescreen behind which actionists can affect a *fait accompli.* "After all," they assert, "someone just had to do something!"

Big lie and *censorship,* although frequently used, are self-defeating tactics in all but a short-run sense. In recent decades our media's critical rhetoric has substituted *credibility gap* or *communications gap* for the *big lie* in referring to differences in verity among our public officials and media commentators. American official or commercial censorship has customarily been something other than bringing pressure to bear upon a medium at the point of publication. In the United States, even in war-time, censorship's goals are usually obtained by controlling access to facts, by timing the release of news materials, by "gentlemen's agreements" with media representatives concerning news treatment, and by trusting the "good judgment" of those who own or control mass media.

Censorship—even by gentlemen's agreement or by good judgment—breeds rumor, barbed antiestablishment humor, and disrespect for, and lack of confidence in, formal announcements and policy statements. The more effectively a country's public discussions are censored or controlled, the greater the extent to which people come to regard them as empty rituals divorced from the reality of flesh-and-blood situations. The big lie is a byproduct of censorship. The term tends to become a catch-all name-calling label, a way of denigrating opposition propaganda indiscriminately.

In the high-pressure struggle for control of our minds, the apparent sincerity of *person-to-person* utterances often undercuts our resistance to tired symbols and rituals of communication. This has been the power of the empathetic actor-turned-politician-or-salesman on television. The mystic quality of a friendly and "sincere" person "directly" in communication with us convinces many, at least until the processes of comparison and discussion shatter the spell.

What makes the account of an event believable? The realism of person-to-person communication can be one factor. Others are acceptance of the *leadership* of a spokesman or a medium, verification through comparison with other information and experience, including the prejudices a person has accumulated, and cross-checks with reports in other media. Thus stratagems based upon dramatic events, a *program of deeds,* and upon the development and maintenance of a leadership image, can create impressive degrees of conviction. Deeds can be faked or overrated, but deeds that bear an aura of genuineness have a spontaneity and uncontrollable character that is hard to stage in a phony manner. Fortunately, too, despite the abuses of leadership roles, such a democratic framework as we have in the United States tends to make the threats implicit in every successful leadership self-limiting.

THE STRUGGLE AGAINST BEING MANIPULATED

So much for an outline of a social actionist's typical orientation, methods of operating, and facilities available to him. How can we, as members of a mass society, free ourselves enough of the manipulators' spells to think some thoughts of our own about the passing propaganda struggles? How can we separate ourselves enough from the growing pall of orthodoxy to gain some understanding of that orthodoxy? How can we be less puppets and more the rational human beings the traditions of democracy idealize? Is it worth it? Why not just drift with the stream of humanity through time and space and take what comes during our brief stay on earth?

Those who believe that we need not be puppets know that human beings with a glimpse of human potentiality cannot just drift. We need not be discouraged by the intricacies of modern mass society. Panzer divisions, rocket planes, hydrogen bombs, huge engines of propaganda, and inclusive webs of interpretation and organization impress us as regimentations of man's ingenuity. But humanity could live happily if it were to lose all of these. Society and human life require much more than mechanisms to continue and to have significance.

TWO TYPES OF DEFENSES. Defenses against being manipulated for interests other than our own and against our will are chiefly of two types. On the one hand, we need to know as accurately as possible how social actionists do their work, for what goals, and with what success. The more we know and understand how actionists operate, the more we can be aware of how our interests are or are not served by their manipulations. On the other hand, we must give up one common human aspiration: We must sacrifice any faith we might have in certainty and realize that in life wisdom lies in probabilities. In a world in which all is relative to all else and in which all is constantly changing, there is no certainty, no valid absolute or dogma. For many this is a horrible thought, a nightmarish speculation to be rejected as quickly as possible. To a growing multitude of others who can face life without mental crutches, it presents a breathtaking challenge to human intellectual enterprise and endless opportunities for human growth and welfare.

As John Dewey notes, "men cultivated all sorts of things that would give them the *feeling* of certainty. And it is possible that, when not carried to an illusory point, the cultivation of the feeling gave man courage and confidence and enabled him to carry the burdens of life more successfully. But one could hardly seriously contend that this fact, if it be such, is one upon which to found a reasoned philosophy." [20] Dewey identified the "quest for certainty by means of exact possession in mind of immutable reality" with "the old spectator theory of knowledge." [21] He pointed out that a notion of "immutable reality" could only be a fantasy or an inculcated dogma. He sought to replace it with a knowing through participating that he related to a more durable and useful principle of indeterminacy such as was formulated by the physicist Werner Heisenberg.[22] More commendable and more relevant here is the comprehensive principle or theory of societal and cultural (including cognitive) relativity developed by such social scientists as Julius Lippert and Her-

[20] John Dewey, *The Quest for Certainty* (1929; New York: Capricorn Books, 1960), p. 33.

[21] *Ibid.*, p. 204.

[22] *Ibid.*, pp. 201–4. Dewey seized upon a principle enunciated by Heisenberg in 1927, dealing with subatomic phenomena, and then assumed it "to be a 'governing' framework of nature to which all particular phenomena conform [p. 201]." See Werner Heisenberg, *Philosophic Problems of Nuclear Science* (New York: Pantheon, 1952). The theory of cultural relativity, based upon human behavioral data, is much more relevant to Dewey's and our data.

bert Spencer, modified and refined since.[23] As Dewey said, "Intelligence in operation, another name for method, becomes the thing most worth winning." [24] This is intelligence as equipment and ability to cope with, and to participate in, reality. Only upon this type of intelligence can the emerging participatory democracy—a more broadly participatory and egalitarian society—be built.

The human being who gives up absolute, pat explanations, and stereotyped notions can learn to see what is going on in society. But what can he do about what he sees? He can realize that society frequently finds expression in the utterances of an indiviual or a small group. Such an individual or group of persons, if they wisely represent interests vital to their fellows, can have influence out of all proportion to their number or prominence. Even an individual can start a tear in the mantle of social orthodoxy.

Thus when we accept available lessons of modern science, history, and personal experience, we can gain an understanding of propaganda and propaganda analysis. These matters then should become focal points for our general liberal education or reeducation around which we can organize or reorganize our reading and social experiences. We can then reach tentative decisions in our own minds about important issues on the merits of facts stripped as much as possible of propaganda shortcuts, gadgets, and distortions. These decisions we should hold subject to revision in the light of new developments and added evidence. In short, we can refuse to be stampeded by anyone and by any cause. After reaching this point, to the extent possible in the light of our talents and opportunities, we can seek, act, and urge others to act as intelligently as they can in view of available facts.[25]

[23] Reference here is not to the more doctrinaire type of cultural relativity. Clyde Kluckhohn defines the term quite well: *"Cultural relativity* designates the idea that any item of behaviour must be judged *first* in relation to its place in the unique structure of the culture in which it occurs and in terms of the particular value system of that culture. Thus it embodies a *principle of contextuality*. The term has, on occasion, been used to suggest that cultural items (such as ethical norms) may only be judged within their context or are so unique that comparative appraisals are ruled out; but this need not be the case." (Julius Gould and W. L. Kolb, eds., A *Dictionary of the Social Sciences* [New York: Free Press of Glencoe, 1964], pp. 160–61). Its broader cross-cultural sense owes much to Julius Lippert, *The Evolution of Culture*, trans. and ed. by G. P. Murdock (1886–1887; New York: Macmillan, 1931), Herbert Spencer, *The Principles of Sociology*, 3rd ed. (New York: D. Appleton, 1898), and esp. W. G. Sumner, *Folkways* (Boston: Ginn, 1906).

[24] Dewey, *The Quest for Certainty*, p. 204.

[25] Lee, *How to Understand Propaganda*, Chap. 10. See Gustavus Myers, *History of Bigotry in the United States*, ed. and rev. by H. M. Christman (New York: Capricorn Books, 1960); H. L. Nieburg, *In the Name of Science*, rev. ed. (Chicago: Quadrangle Books, 1970); and M. E. Olsen, ed., *Power in Societies* (New York: Macmillan, 1970).

If we should dare to teach this kind of propaganda analysis in our high schools and colleges, and if we dared to live up to its implications, we would be implementing in our society a basic promise of a liberal arts education. We would also be dealing with a significant factor making for the generation gap. This factor is sometimes inaccurately called "hypocrisy." It might better be labeled "entrenched myth" or "delusion." Without being subjected to such delusion, our students would have greater faith in their parents, their schools, their society, and especially, in themselves.

CHAPTER 9

Perplexities of
Social Perception

Social science attracts people who hope to find in it some sort of answer or aid. What is the matter with society that I cannot fit it to me, or myself to it? Can anything be done about man's inhumanity to man? Why do we have wars and authoritarianism? What can be done about degradation in our slums and social isolation in our suburbs? Is there some effective manner in which we can cope with the rising tide of drug abuse? How is it that we have failed to deal adequately with organized crime? Can anything be done about the pollution of our soil, our water, our atmosphere, and even our media of mass communication?

These and other questions about social problems are easy to state, but to shed light on them requires careful and determined probing. In addition, to try to expand our knowledge concerning any social problem quickly ceases to be merely a desk-centered task, an intellectual exercise carried out in a calm atmosphere. When one really digs into any social problem, it becomes controversial. The relevant facts are likely to be contradictory and infected with special interests, special pleadings, and emotional attachments. Socially entrenched prejudices and influences point to expedient conclusions that may be called imperative. In other words, they may prescribe currently "respectable" conclusions about the nature of a social problem. These conclusions may not be at all accurate and may have long since lost whatever usefulness they might have had, if any.

If the currently acceptable explanations of a social problem were providing an adequate basis for coping with it, there would be no need for fresh investigation into its nature. As long as a social problem persists as a troublesome aspect of social behavior, such fresh investigation will be needed. Its results are likely to be unsettling to the vested interests who help to maintain the social problem and who may benefit from the problem's existence.

THE INVESTIGATOR'S INTIMATE OBSTACLE

Curiously enough, the chief obstacle any investigator confronts when he digs deeply into a social problem is not vested interests or social pressures, as great and powerful as these may be. It is not social resistance to new perceptions of society's character, as deep-set as this resistance surely is. After all, there are frequently dissatisfied groups or influential individuals who will support any given investigation or innovation.

The investigator's chief obstacle is his lifelong social conditioning. If he is to gain a fresh and useful conception of any important social problem and its social setting, he has to find ways to overcome that obstacle.

Many a social scientist has turned away from the rocky path of creative individualistic investigation because he cannot endure the travail —the "cultural shock" [1]—of modifying his own intellectual equipment. In turning away from that rocky path, he often finds himself embraced in the lush appreciation and support given to those who are called positive or constructive. *Positive* and *constructive* are double-talk words; they refer to being traditional or protective of vested interest or the status quo—in other words, subservient to established "truth" and authority.

Our society seriously needs to have its problems studied ever more fundamentally, freely, and accurately. Reference is made to the study of society's problems rather than the study of society because our need for information on problems is most pressing. With the attack made on problems, we will learn more and more about the nature of society.

Enthusiastic and dedicated social scientists are finding ways to learn more about social problems. Even if you may not wish to join them in their absorbing and highly important work, it is imperative that as many people as possible understand what they are trying to do and why they should be encouraged, or at least not unduly impeded. Their pas-

---

[1] C. M. Arensberg and A. H. Niehoff, *Introducing Social Change* (Chicago: Aldine, 1964), pp. 185–89. See also W. F. Whyte, *Street Corner Society*, 2nd ed. (Chicago: University of Chicago Press, 1955), pp. 279–358, and the appendix, "On the Evolution of *Street Corner Society*," esp. pp. 299–309. A less adequate approach is given in P. K. Bock, "Forword: On 'Culture Shock,'" in Bock, ed., *Culture Shock: A Reader* (New York: Alfred A. Knopf, 1970), pp. ix–xii.

sionate distrust of "final truth," no matter how "moral," needs to be seen as a valuable social instrument, even though in a particular instance it may appear socially irresponsible. What we object to in pollution, germ and nuclear warfare, and overmechanization are not the findings of scientists, but the socially destructive uses of their findings.[2]

OBSTACLES AND PATHWAYS TO
PERCEPTION

The three preceding chapters discuss social roles of ideologies and their associated rhetoric or propaganda, their relations with social competition and conflict. This chapter turns again to the social roles of the social scientist and focuses on him as a social instrument. Here we shift from discussing the kind of instruments ideologies and propagandas are to a more specific treatment of the kind of instrument a social scientist is. Thus we hope to help clarify what he can be expected to do for us. The next chapter examines how this human instrument is functioning in society. The final chapter offers an agenda of things to which the social scientist might well devote himself.

Here, then, the focus is on how the lifelong social conditioning of the investigator provides him with obstacles, as well as advantages and strengths, in his attempts to do original and useful research into social problems. Included are brief suggestions of some of the unorthodox intellectual pathways such an investigator may find he has to follow in order to overcome his built-in obstacles. This outline of the nature of some of those obstacles and of suggested pathways through or around them may help to make more evident the general character of the social problems that are a researcher's tasks.

DIFFICULT PERPLEXITIES. Intellectual obstacles and pathways associated with creative social perception and thought include: (1) criticism, (2) innovation, (3) mental abnormality, (4) criminality, (5) violence and war, (6) social power, control, and manipulation, (7) social legitimacy, (8) relevance or social setting, and (9) culture shock.

The above are really nine difficult perplexities in the sense that the traditional conception associated with each of those terms is easy and popular, but it is destructive of scientific inquiry. A scientifically useful pathway past such a conception is unorthodox and controversial, and it may require real courage to take it. Nonetheless, each of these nine confusing situations, and many others not mentioned here, may well have to be resolved by the scientifically productive social scientist in an unconventional or nonconforming manner. Only thus can he find his

---

[2] See J. F. Glass and J. R. Staude, eds., *Humanistic Society: Today's Challenge to Sociology* (Pacific Palisades, Calif.: Goodyear, 1972), Part 3.

way past his own emotionally charged intellectual blocks in order to perceive novel, exploratory, and perhaps more tenable social knowledge.

TO "TELL THINGS LIKE THEY ARE"

1. *Criticism* is both sweet and sour. The social scientist as critic makes judgments or evaluations about the merits or shortcomings of widely held theories in the light of the facts he collects. When he is diplomatic and takes what is called a constructive viewpoint, he is praised; he is saying what people want to hear. But the grubbing for significant and more accurate observations and conceptions does not mix with diplomacy. A person *working as a social scientist* who investigates ethnic segregation or the pollution of mass-communications media cannot be concerned about the feelings or vested interests of segregating real-estate salesmen or ethnic leaders, or of propagandizing television or newspaper operators. As young people like to say now, the social scientist has to "tell things like they are." That is his job as social scientist. Only in that way can he give us more accurate, less prejudiced conceptions of reality.

When a social scientist discovers how mass-communications media become polluted, when he reveals whose interests such pollution serves, or when he specifically indicates many who have vested interests in exploiting the slums as they now are, he is often called a destructive or a negative critic, especially by those he places in an unfavorable but more accurate light.

Most of us have grown up being taught the virtues of diplomacy, of being "constructive" and "positive," of not being offensive to others, especially to those in authority. Such teachings make for pleasant, non-controversial relations with other people.

A person as social scientist certainly need not be intentionally and unnecessarily unpleasant in his approaches to other people. At the same time, he cannot permit politeness and caution to color or obscure the results of his research. He must look with skepticism at all existing research methods, facts, conceptions, and theories related to his work. He must be careful to explore theories or hunches that he thinks off hand are probably absurd. Basically his efforts consist of the criticism and modification, as well as the amplification, of existing knowledge.[3]

[3] For a notion of the pressures brought to bear upon a great innovating social scientist because of his critical stance, see K. H. Wolff, "Introduction," in *The Sociology of Georg Simmel*, trans. and ed. by Wolff (Glencoe, Ill.: Free Press, 1950), esp. the letter to Max Weber quoted on p. xix. See also John Wren-Lewis, "Science and Social Responsibility," *New Society*, No. 426 (November 26, 1970), pp. 957–58; Garrett Hardin, ed., *Science, Conflict and Society* (San Francisco: W. H. Freeman, 1969), esp. Parts 1, 4, 5; A. W. Gouldner, *The Coming Crisis of Western Sociology* (New York: Basic Books, 1970), esp. pp. 481 ff.; J. D. Colfax and J. L. Roach, eds., *Radical Sociology* (New York: Basic Books, 1971).

TO BE UPSETTING, WAY-BREAKING

2. *Innovation* is another tricky conception when popularly considered and then contrasted with its role in scientific investigation. If they use the word *creative* at all, most parents identify it with success in the sense of material gain, secure position, and perhaps prestige. They want their children to excel in following a beaten path. But in the social sciences, as in the physical and biological sciences and in the fine arts and the humanities, *success* means to be innovative; *creative* means to be upsetting, way-breaking; to be highly creative means to be iconoclastic. Creativity in science consists of having respect only for ideas that can be verified and of trying to replace other ideas with more tenable and accurate ones. In social science this may mean the development and testing of outrageous hypotheses about child-raising, marriage, crime, or about intergroup and interpersonal relations in a corporation, a school, or a church. Those are rarely the sorts of opportunity or exploits that parents have in mind for their children. The scientifically creative can follow beaten paths only to move out to the edges of existing knowledge. From there on, they set forth on their own. They are not mere scholars, elaborately schooled in what is already known. They are avid to go where human minds have not previously succeeded in penetrating.[4]

TO LOOK BEYOND NORMALITY
AND ABNORMALITY

3. *Mental abnormality* presents a different sort of challenge to understanding and research, a different kind of dilemma. Here the investigator has to face contrasts between popular oversimplification and dogmatism on the one hand and the infinite and subtle variability of human life on the other.

In terms of popular stereotypes, mental abnormality is an absolute matter: One is either "sane" or "nuts"; one is either "normal" or "insane." That appears to be a comforting notion for the many who are socially

---

[4] H. G. Barnett, *Innovation* (New York: McGraw-Hill, 1953) esp. Chaps. 1, 10, 13; W. F. Ogburn and S. C. Gilfillan, "The Influence of Invention and Discovery," in Ogburn, ed., *Recent Social Trends in the United States* (New York: McGraw-Hill, 1933), I, 122–66; P. A. Sorokin, *Society, Culture, and Personality* (New York: Harper & Bros., 1947), Chaps. 35–41; S. C. Gilfillan, *Sociology of Invention* (Cambridge: M.I.T. Press, 1971); D. A. Schon, *Invention and Evolution of Ideas* (New York: Barnes & Noble, 1967); A. McC. Lee, *Multivalent Man* (New York: George Braziller, 1966), esp. pp. 250–54.

labeled as being sane or normal and who cling to it, but it is inaccurate. With mental abnormality, as elsewhere, the social scientist has to look beyond stereotypes. He has to try to face social realities more intimately, with less preconception, and more precisely. He cannot accept popular stereotypes of "normality." To call strange behavior "abnormal" or an "illness" may be a serious prejudgment, a distortion of perception.[5] From cross-cultural comparisons we are learning how variable "normal" human behavior may be.[6] Significantly, psychotherapists now try to interrelate and intercommunicate with unhappy and unsuccessful people who come to them; they do not assume that such people are "sick" and try to "treat" them. Psychologists have learned that great strides may be made in understanding through attempting to perceive and interpret accurately how the deviant person sees himself and others.[7]

Detailed psychological study is not the task of the social scientist as such, but the social scientist needs to have perspective on deviant and typical mental behavior that psychologists can make available to him so that he can probe more adequately into the social contexts and significances of deviance.[8] Above all, he needs to approach the deviant curiously and perceptively, not blinded by popular stereotypes.

TO PROBE THE CRIMINAL
STEREOTYPE

4. *Criminality* presents a dilemma similar to that of mental abnormality. Once again the challenge arises from the contrast between popular oversimplification and dogmatism on the one hand and the infinite and subtle variability of human life on the other.

In terms of popular stereotypes, crime is an absolute matter: One is either a thief or honest, a dependable person or part of a "bad lot."

---

[5] See also M. B. Clinard, *Sociology and Deviant Behavior*, 3rd ed. (New York: Holt, Rinehart & Winston, 1968), p. 446; T. S. Szasz, *Myth of Mental Illness* (New York: Dell, 1967), and *Ideology and Insanity* (Garden City, N.Y.: Doubleday, 1970); T. J. Scheff, *Mental Illness and Social Processes* (New York: Harper & Row, 1967); J. K. Myers and L. L. Bean, *Decade Later* (New York: John Wiley, 1968).

[6] For cross-cultural data on mental deviations, see J. M. Murphy and A. H. Leighton, eds., *Approaches to Cross-Cultural Psychiatry* (Ithaca, N.Y.: Cornell University Press, 1965); M. K. Opler, *Culture and Social Psychiatry* (New York: Atherton Press, 1967); E. D. Driver, *Sociology and Anthropology of Mental Illness* (Amherst: University of Massachusetts Press, 1970).

[7] T. S. Szasz, *The Ethics of Psychoanalysis* (New York: Basic Books, 1965), p. 30; R. D. Laing, *The Divided Self* (Baltimore: Penguin Books, 1965), and *Self and Others*, rev. ed. (New York: Pantheon Books, 1970).

[8] B. H. Stoodley, ed., *Society and Self* (New York: Free Press, 1962), Chaps. 4 and 5; Gerald Handel, ed., *The Psychosocial Interior of the Family* (Chicago: Aldine, 1967), esp. Chaps 2, 10–12, 14–16, 20–22.

Juvenile delinquency in a "fine family" is brushed aside as "wild oats," not to be taken at all seriously. Comparable delinquency—legally defined —among members of a "bad lot" requires police action, judicial process, and perhaps a "reform school." The tendency to extend the "bad-lot" stereotype indefinitely to members of underprivileged ethnic and racial minorities is part of the persecution to which such minorities are subjected. It helps to build up a disproportionate number of police arrests and judicial records of "juvenile delinquency" and "criminality" among the oppressed.

Crime is an action or a negligence defined by law as injurious to public welfare or morality or the interests of the state. In other words, it is an offense against the criminal law as currently interpreted and implemented. This definition may be good enough for some legal purposes, but it presents great problems to the social scientist who is trying to learn more about the nature of human behavior, whether or not that behavior is called "criminal."

Of those who commit "criminal" acts, who gets caught? Relatively few. Of those who are apprehended and actually charged with crime, who are convicted? Of those who are convicted of any given offense, who are not subsequently pardoned? For that matter, what kind of sense do either the processes of our cluttered courts or our noncorrective prisons make? It is not to be wondered at that those who actually serve time in a penitentiary and who are fairly well informed about the behavior of a circle of friends are often bitter that they should be among the relatively few (guilty or not) "losers" among the many whose similar behavior might have become, with "bad luck," the basis of conviction.

The social scientist certainly does not apologize for antisocial behavior or try to justify it, but he also realizes that he cannot approach the study of even the least consequential, the most disastrous, or the most obnoxious aspects of human behavior equipped with simplistic popular stereotypes. Any adequate approach to what is called criminal or delinquent behavior once again has to be with as much unprejudiced curiosity and clear perception as possible. It has to take into consideration such a range of behavior as "wild oats," fee-splitting among professional men, both the paying and the accepting of a wide variety of bribes under many names, tax evasion, price-fixing conspiracies by merchants and manufacturers, deliberate or negligent mislabeling of commodities that cover up inferior, undetermined, or adulterated ingredients, "gentlemen's agreements" as a means through which certain ethnic and racial groups are denied access to jobs and housing, and use of governmental agencies and/or private henchmen to dominate or topple foreign governments for private gain. These acts are more costly to society than all the depredations of second-story men and other types of small-time thieves combined.[9] In addition to the dilemma posed for him by the popular stereotype and by the legal definition of crime as implemented by the courts, a social scientist studying behavior, part of which may be called criminal, is also confronted with the enticements of the sensational theories making up newspaper criminology. Plausible journalists have it that organized crime is largely in the hands of an international Italian conspiracy based in New York City, New Jersey, or Sicily, and called the Mafia.[10] Constant mythologizing about a Mafia conspiracy has been quite damaging to Italian-Americans who have no connections whatsoever with organized crime, and it has not resulted in the kind of governmental action the myths appear to demand.[11] A social scientist has to look behind and beyond such a journalistic red herring to study the realities of organized crime more directly and factually, with its *interpenetration* of political organizations and governmental agencies (local, state, federal, international) and legitimate businesses (local, state, national, international).[12]

[9] A. S. Blumberg, *Criminal Justice*, new ed. (Chicago: Quadrangle Books, 1970), esp. intro. and Chap. 8; M. B. Clinard and Richard Quinney, *Criminal Behavior Systems: A Typology* (New York: Holt, Rinehart & Winston, 1967), pp. 169–76; Quinney, "The Study of White Collar Crime," *Journal of Criminal Law, Criminology, and Police Science*, LV (1964), 208–14; Clinard, "White Collar Crime," *International Encyclopaedia of the Social Sciences* (New York: Macmillan and Free Press, 1968), III, 483–90; E. H. Sutherland, *White Collar Crime* (New York: Holt, Rinehart & Winston, 1949); Norman Jaspan and Hillel Black, *The Thief in White Collar* (Philadelphia: J. B. Lippincott, 1960); Gilbert Geis, ed., *White-Collar Criminal* (New York: Atherton Press, 1968); J. L. Albini, *The American Mafia: Genesis of a Legend* (New York: Appleton-Century-Crofts, 1971).

[10] D. R. Cressey, *Theft of the Nation: The Structure and Operations of Organized Crime in America* (New York: Harper & Row, 1969); note sharp and effective criticisms of Cressey in Albini, *The American Mafia: Genesis of a Legend;* Ralph Salerno and J. S. Tompkins, *Crime Confederation* (Garden City, N.Y.: Doubleday, 1969); Michele Pantaleone, *Mafia and Politics: The Definitive History of the Mafia* (New York: Coward-McCann, 1966); Danilo Dolci, *Man Who Plays Alone* (New York: Pantheon Books, 1969); Ed Reid, *Grim Reapers: The Anatomy of Organized Crime in America* (Chicago: Henry Regnery, 1969); Virgil Peterson, *Barbarians in Our Midst* (Boston: Little, Brown, 1952); Frederic Sondern, Jr., *Brotherhood of Evil: The Mafia* (New York: Farrar, Straus & Cudahy, 1959); Fred J. Cook, *Secret Rulers* (New York: Hawthorne Books, 1966).

[11] President's Commission on Law Enforcement and Administration of Justice, *The Challenge of Crime in a Free Society* (Washington: Government Printing Office, 1967); Gus Tyler, ed., *Organized Crime in America* (Ann Arbor: University of Michigan Press, 1962); Salerno and Tompkins, *Crime Confederation;* John Hutchinson, *Imperfect Union: A History of Corruption in American Trade Unions* (New York: E. P. Dutton, 1970); John Landesco, *Organized Crime in Chicago*, 2nd ed. (Chicago: University of Chicago Press, 1968); Ewan Mitchell, *Coping With Crime* (New York: International Publications Service, 1969).

[12] Daniel Bell, *The End of Ideology*, rev. ed. (New York: Collier, 1961), esp. pp. 138–46, discusses the "myth of the Mafia." See also Norval Morris and Gordon Hawkins, *The Honest Politician's Guide to Crime Control* (Chicago: University of

Aided and abetted by publicity-seeking crime officials locally and nationally, journalists can also find crime waves, or waves of a particular kind of crime, almost any time they need a headline story. In point of fact, really dependable and comparable statistics on crime are not to be obtained in the United States. One standard text calls the "general statistics of crime and criminals . . . the most unreliable and most difficult of all statistics." [13] Another text asserts that "available official criminal statistics, unfortunately, are of such dubious significance as to make [them] . . . extremely hazardous to the unwary." [14]

TO PENETRATE POPULAR EXCUSES
FOR PUGNACITY

5. *Violence and war*—both in times said to be of peace and of war —present the social scientist with melodramatic confusion. They are so fraught with emotional attachments and rationalizations that they have destroyed the objectivity of a great many.

Violence and war are so unthinkable to most middle-class intellectuals in peacetime that they do not permit themselves to perceive the extent to which both grow out of the nature of our present socialization processes and out of the general nature of our society. To work toward more adequate understandings of violence and war, the social scientist again must somehow free himself of popular prowar and antiwar stereotypes, our popular excuses for accepting or rejecting violence. This assertion should not be interpreted as saying that either violence or war is necessary in human society or that everyone is violent or warlike.[15] The tremendous student, veteran, and popular opposition to the Indochina War is more than a token of American resistance to war as an instrument

---

Chicago Press, 1970); John Mack, "American Criminologists and the Mafia" mimeographed, August 12, 1970; Eric Hobsbawm, "The American Mafia," *Listener*, November 20, 1969; Gordon Hawkins, "God and the Mafia," *The Public Interest*, Spring, 1969.

[13] E. H. Sutherland and D. R. Cressey, *Principles of Criminology*, 7th ed. (Philadelphia: J. B. Lippincott, 1966), p. 25.

[14] D. R. Taft and R. W. England, Jr., *Criminology*, 4th ed. (New York: Macmillan, 1964), p. 46.

[15] Leonard Berkowitz, *Aggression* (New York: McGraw-Hill, 1962), concludes that there is "no instinctive drive toward war within man [p. 25]"; Morton Fried, Marvin Harris, and Robert Murphy, eds., *War: The Anthropology of Armed Conflict and Aggression* (Garden City, N.Y.: Natural History Press, 1968); Thomas Rose, ed., *Violence in America* (New York: Random House, 1969); E. B. McNeil, ed., *The Nature of Human Conflict* (Englewood Cliffs, N.J.: Prentice-Hall, 1965).

of international policy and practice.[16] The many examples of successful nonviolent resistance in recent decades, even in the face of violence, indicate how strongly we are coming to reject violence in social action.

A social scientist cannot go along with the popular thinking that regards unauthorized violence by other people as uniformly evil while our authorized violence against other people or our own defensive violence is considered justifiable. A social scientist tries to see violence— as he tries to perceive all social behavior—in its context. For example, he tries to learn how a riot in an urban slum comes about. What relationships exist among the slum dwellers and the police, social workers, merchants, employers, and landlords? What are the slum conditions of housing, education, sanitation, personal safety, employment, and racketeering? If police power is used to suppress a riot, are the controlling powers then likely to mitigate the miseries that stimulated the riot, or will they count on the fear of force to prevent a recurrence as they forget the woes of the slum dwellers? When the police crack down on a slum racket, do government officials or businessmen help provide legitimate opportunities for employment to replace the racket, or do they merely permit the racket to be turned over to interests more friendly to the police? [17]

A social scientist as scientist also cannot go along with hysterical popular thinking about participation in war. He has many questions to ask about any war and especially about our constant preoccupation with war, about the extent to which our sciences, technologies, and education are oriented even in "peacetime" toward war.[18]

[16] Amitai Etzioni and Martin Wenglinski, *War and Its Prevention* (New York: Harper & Row, 1970); Michael Brown, *Politics and Anti-Politics of the Young* (New York: Glencoe Press, 1969); J. A. Califano, Jr., *Student Revolution: A Global Confrontation* (New York: W. W. Norton, 1969); L. S. Feuer, *Conflict of Generations* (New York: Basic Books, 1969); Daniel Walker, *Rights in Conflict* (New York: Bantam, 1968); Stephen Spender, *Year of the Young Rebels* (New York: Random House, 1969).

[17] Peter Binzen, *Whitetown, U.S.A.* (New York: Random House, 1970); Todd Gitlin and Nanci Hollander, *Uptown: Poor Whites in Chicago* (New York: Harper & Row, 1970); Gerald Suttles, *Social Order of the Slum*, rev. ed. (Chicago: University of Chicago Press, 1968); Thomas Gladwin, *Poverty: U.S.A.* (Boston: Little, Brown, 1967); Gerald Leinwand, ed., *Slums* (New York: Washington Square Press, 1970); Lee Rainwater, *Behind Ghetto Walls* (Chicago: Aldine, 1970).

[18] Noam Chomsky, *American Power and the New Mandarins* (New York: Vintage, 1969); H. L. Nieburg, *In the Name of Science*, rev. ed. (Chicago: Quadrangle Books, 1970); F. J. Cook, *The Warfare State* (New York: Collier, 1964); I. L. Horowitz, *The War Game: Studies in the New Civilian Militarists* (New York: Ballantine, 1963); J. A. Schumpeter, *The Sociology of Imperialisms* (New York: Meridian, 1955); D. K. Fieldhouse, ed., *The Theory of Capitalist Imperialism* (New York: Barnes & Noble, 1967).

TO AVOID A FAUSTIAN "COP-OUT"

6. *Social power, control, and manipulation* are the elements of the biggest games played with the greatest seriousness and absorption for the highest stakes in society. Naturally, information about how such games are played is not readily available, and those who are pawns, or even knights, in such games usually have little knowledge of the larger contexts to which they contribute and which define their careers. An outline of how the typical social manipulator does his work is set forth in the preceding chapter and related there to how people can defend themselves against such operations. Social power, control, and manipulation are presented here as a dilemma the social scientist has to face. To remain a social scientist, he cannot take the Faustian cop-outs discussed in the chapter on sociological ideologies.

Since the nature of social power, control, and manipulation is largely obscured behind the façades of institutions and other organizations, the social scientist's dilemma is whether to accept the façades or to probe behind them. To understand society's dynamics, and especially how efforts at social action succeed or fail, a social scientist has to penetrate those façades as best he can. As we saw in the preceding chapter, he proceeds by observing and analyzing basic raw materials and strategies used by manipulators—public opinions, organizational structures, personnel, mass-communications media, propaganda content, and overall and more specific strategies and societal contexts. From these the social scientist can learn how the manipulator gains and maintains social controls through social action. Where many people commonly look upon such matters as part of the "going order" of society which are not to be questioned, a social scientist may have to look at relevant aspects of society as does a power operator, in order to understand as fully as possible how such a person may achieve his goals. This may mean to treat all aspects of society—for the sake of perception only—as instruments more or less available to manipulators and utilized by them.

In other words, the dilemma here is whether to accept society merely as it appears to be, as do most human beings, or to come to a conclusion close to or beyond that of the great journalist Lincoln Steffens. As a young man visiting the California state legislature, Steffens was amazed at the contrast between what the legislature was supposed to be and what it actually was—a no-holds-barred arena in which men played for very high stakes. His immediate reaction was, "Nothing was what it was supposed to be." [19] With greater maturity, he realized that such social

[19] Lincoln Steffens, *The Autobiography of Lincoln Steffens* (New York: Harcourt, Brace, 1931), p. 47.

organizations could be seen more accurately as fitting into many different contexts and interpretations, not just into two.[20] It depended upon whether one looked at the legislature's societal façade, described in public-school textbooks, at the political power game he saw at Sacramento, at a larger financial, industrial, political, or even criminal struggle in which participants were able to utilize legislators or the legislative process for their purposes, or at the tiny bureaucratic struggles and conspiracies in the state government that depend upon legislative involvement for their outcome.

TO UNDERSTAND WHAT IT COSTS
TO "BELONG"

7. *Social legitimacy* is a term closely related to social power and control, but it requires separate treatment because it presents the sociologist with a separate dilemma. It refers to the pattern of domination and control that a society apparently sanctions at any given time. The sociologist Max Weber suggests that there are three types of social legitimacy: traditional, legalistic, and charismatic. In any given case, these types are likely to be mixed.[21]

Traditional legitimacy derives from "the authority of the 'eternal yesterday.'" In other words, it consists of customary rights, privileges, and controls long associated with certain social statuses. It gives power to tribal patriarch or chieftain or to a king who presumes to rule by divine right. Shadows of such legitimacy persist in many democratic organizations.

Legalistic legitimacy depends upon belief in the validity and reasonableness of existing legal specifications relating to controls associated with specific statuses. Such legitimacy gives power to "servants of the state" who now commonly rule modern states, even though each such ruler may also have some touch of the traditional and/or the charismatic about him.

Charismatic legitimacy is the authoritative status given to some by their personal possession of an extraordinary "gift of grace" or charisma. This gift inspires personal devotion and confidence. It may depend upon revelation, heroism, or other qualities making for individual leadership. Such legitimacy gave power to a Gandhi and an Eisenhower on the one hand, and an Adolf Hitler and a Cromwell on the other.

20 *Ibid.*, pp. 862–64.
21 Max Weber, *From Max Weber: Essays in Sociology*, trans. and ed. by H. H. Gerth and C. W. Mills (New York: Oxford University Press, 1946), pp. 78–79.

Social legitimacy is much more than popular acceptance of a pattern of justified domination through which the head of a state rules. It is the whole fabric of respected power and control relationships with which accepted members of society customarily identify themselves, and from which they get a sense of belonging and security. It is the social fabric that outsiders often call the establishment and its hangers-on. Those who cannot make it in "the establishment" may try to achieve a degree of prestige and control in terms of a subsidiary legitimate minority establishment available to them, or even in terms of an illegal or insurgent assault on the socially legitimate from without.

What is this dilemma of the social scientist as he tries to study social problems more keenly and precisely? Doesn't he want his work to be recognized as a legitimate part of societal endeavors? Shouldn't a social scientist strive for the personal and professional influence that comes from acceptance by legitimate leaders and organizations in society? These are difficult questions.

The perplexing problem here is that the social scientist has to be as accurate and as probing in his efforts to discover the nature of the socially legitimate as he is when probing the socially illegitimate and the unrecognized. He cannot let the possibility of rewards from the establishment and its hangers-on distort his judgment or his perception. In the short run, this may make more difficult his striving to have his findings respected. In a little longer run it means that he will be building the reputation for autonomous integrity basic to all durable scientific contributions.[22]

TO AVOID A LIMITING CONTEXT

8. *Relevance or social setting* may appear not to pose much of an obstacle in the study of real-life social problems, but it can. Society is such a complex of interrelated networks that the adequate study of any social problem usually reveals the involvement in it of quite unanticipated vested interests. For example, specialists in street-traffic safety have long known many ways in which to decrease our annual slaughter on the country's highways, but the implementation of their recommendations would have near-revolutionary consequences. To achieve the de-

[22] N. K. Denzin, ed., *The Values of Social Science* (Chicago: Aldine, 1970); R. L. Beals, *Politics of Social Research* (Chicago: Aldine, 1969); John Kosa, ed., *The Home of the Learned Man* (New Haven: College & University Press, 1968), esp. Kosa, "The Company of Seneca," pp. 25–50, and Franz Adler, "The Marginal Man on the Faculty," pp. 59–65; Kenneth Boulding, ed., *Peace and the War Industry* (Chicago: Aldine, 1970); I. L. Horowitz, *Professing Sociology* (Chicago: Aldine, 1968), esp. pp. 280–86, 340–54.

sirable type of traffic control would require the reorganization of the nation's traffic police training and supervisory and operational procedures, as well as revamping the structure and procedures of the related courts. Automobile operators would have to be tested more thoroughly at regular intervals. On-the-spot drunk-driver tests would have to be instituted to keep inebriates from trying to drive. No really adequate way of coping with the excessive accident rates of young drivers has been found, but this is surely not an unsolvable aspect of the problem.[23] As Ralph Nader and other reformers have pointed out, the physical structure of automobiles leaves much to be desired from the safety standpoint.[24] Old-fashioned roads and new ones designed more for efficiency or speed than safety both contribute to the total deaths, and this only starts to list some of the more obvious ramifications of one social problem and of ways to cope with it.[25] Our death toll from automobile accidents *each year* is considerably greater than our loss of soldiers in the *whole* Indochinese War or in the *whole* of World War I, respectively our fourth and third most costly wars in American lives.

The dilemma here is whether to study a social problem in a fairly restricted, and thus "safe," manner, or to try to understand it more adequately in its full context. Just to stick with our illustration, a restricted approach is what traffic-safety people have taken for a great many years, and the street-traffic death tolls have continued to mount. Until such a problem is attacked fully and in context, little else can be expected.

TO EMPATHIZE WITH THE
CULTURALLY DIFFERENT

9. *Culture shock* is our final dilemma in the sense that most people do what they can to avoid it and a social scientist in search of new knowledge about an important social problem has to be prepared to experience it.

What is culture shock? In an extreme form, and one not to be unanticipated, culture shock is the emotional reaction of a person who has gone to live in a society very different from his own. It is like being

---

23 Gerald Driessen, "Fallacy of the Untrained Driver," *Education Digest*, XXXV (1969), 43–45; R. M. Weiers, *Licensed to Kill: The Incompetent American Motorist and How He Got That Way* (Philadelphia: Chilton, 1968).

24 B. F. Goeller, *Modeling the Traffic-Safety System*, and Martin Wohl, *Putting the Analysis and Evaluation of Traffic Safety Measures Into Perspective*, prepared for the U.S. National Highway Safety Bureau (Santa Monica, Calif.: Rand Corporation, 1968).

25 M. Mueller, "Nader: From Auto Safety to a Permanent Crusade," *Science*, CLXVI (1969), 979–83; Paul Dickson, "What Makes Ralph [Nader] Run," *Progressive*, XXXIV (1970), 28–32.

dependent upon a pair of glasses—the comprehensive culture of one's native society—and then losing or breaking them and trying to get along with someone else's pair. Suddenly everything is out of focus, and it requires great effort to bring everyday affairs into focus again. As the anthropologist Philip K. Bock says, "Genuine culture shock is largely an emotional matter; but it also implies the attempt to *understand* an alien way of life, by choice or out of necessity. Since human society began, immigrants, refugees, and all kinds of travelers have been subject to varying degrees of culture shock." In answer to the question of why anyone, even a social scientist, should seek the experience of culture shock, Bock replies that "direct confrontation with another society is the best way to learn about alien modes of life or to gain perspective on one's own culture." [26]

One or more extreme experiences with culture shock in an alien land are valuable conditioning for any social scientist, but experiences with culture shock are also to be had in conducting social-scientific field research in one's own country. When we travel about our country, we tend to conclude that Americans are very much homogenized. Whether in Beverly Hills, California, or in Garden City, Long Island, they are much the same, varied only a little by those who have recent immigrant backgrounds. This is largely because we all tend to associate with our own sort of people as we move about the country. We do not really get different perspectives on human society. Even when we travel, we tend to gain the same perspective time and again from different geographical vantage points.

When students from middle-class homes go into either less or more privileged homes to interview people at some length, they experience a degree of culture shock. Out of that confusing and even painful experience, whether or not the students intended to become professional social scientists, comes a new understanding both of other people and of themselves. When white students go into nonwhite communities, the extent to which they suffer from culture shock becomes a fair measure of their intellectual and emotional gain. Nonwhite students have already had such experience to an excessive degree before coming to the university. To have vivid glimpses into the lives of the ethnically and racially different, of the occupationally contrasting, and also of the mentally retarded, damaged, and disturbed, should be part of everyone's education. It is an essential part of the social scientist's education.

There are social scientists whose research is so abstract, and even superficial, that they have never experienced the confusing wealth of strange data out of which culture shock arises. A long and distinguished

[26] Bock, *Culture Shock: A Reader,* pp. x–xi.

list of the most significant contributors to our knowledge of social problems in particular, and human society more generally, includes *only* those who have had experiences of culture shock. To the inquiring social scientist, culture shock thus represents no dilemma. He seeks it.[27]

What of those for whom a liberal education has succeeded in dramatizing adequately the variability and richness of the human heritage and human life? For them, culture shock also can represent no dilemma. For any well-educated person, culture shock is a difficult, valuable, and highly involving path he can follow with great gain to himself and to those he may serve. For those to whom it is a dilemma to be resolved through easy avoidance, experience in human affairs remains largely restricted to what can be learned from one narrow cultural viewpoint, the viewpoint available in one stratum of one ethnic group.

The consideration of these nine perplexities and ways in which social scientists can and do resolve them has hopefully demonstrated two conceptions.

Suggested on the one hand is the extent to which the social scientist must be his own most important instrument in his study of social problems in their social settings. He must know that instrument as well as he possibly can, and he must try to use it as precisely and as wisely as he can if he wishes to dedicate himself to scientific goals.

On the other hand are the broader significances of these perplexities. Need these sorts of intellectual and emotional experiences be described as being of service only to the professional social scientist? The answer to that question recurs frequently in the writings of leading education theorists. Liberal education should help all of us to achieve such kinds of objectivity and sensitivity, such sorts of empathy with those quite different from ourselves, and such ways of penetrating social façades as those that are suggested here. By knowing other people more intimately and accurately, we can come to understand ourselves better. By learning more about ourselves, we can discover how to use our senses more accurately in our efforts to understand others.

[27] R. L. Gordon, *Interviewing* (Homewood, Ill.: Dorsey Press, 1969), Chap. 3; Frances Henry and Satish Saberwal, eds., *Stress and Response in Fieldwork* (New York: Holt, Rinehart & Winston, 1969), esp. Chaps. 3 and 5; G. D. Spindler, ed., *Being an Anthropologist* (New York: Holt, Rinehart & Winston, 1970).

CHAPTER 10

How Sociologists Can Serve Man

"We do get absorbed in a lot of 'games' here! They're strange to you, I suppose, but we enjoy them." He was having some pints of ale in the English manner with an American in the Saracen's Head, a medieval, timbered inn. The inquisitive visitor had asked what the present lay members of the chapter of Southwell Minster (Church of England) do at their regular meetings in the ancient chapter house, once the meeting place of the Minster's chapter of monks.

The Nottinghamshire farmer explained that the chapter had certain parish duties, but that it was, to most of its members, as much a prestigious and friendly social club as anything. Each member occupies a labeled stall, or seat, representing an estate traditionally associated with the Minster. He was the hereditary occupant for his ancient farm in a neighboring village. He then continued in his cultivated manner: "It would take anyone a long time to learn our so-called ancient games here, and it would probably be impossible for a foreigner ever to learn to play them above reproach. They give us our 'pecking order,' our friendly social routines, our sense of belonging, and our ways of trying to keep out the unwanted."

That was the end of his discussion on the subject. He realized that his foreign visitor wanted to probe more deeply into the town's power structure, but he was not about to become an ethnological informant in greater detail. He appeared to believe that he had already carried candor as far as he wished with a stranger, even though that stranger would be gone, probably forever, tomorrow.

CANDOR ABOUT "THE GAMES
WE PLAY"

Candor about the subtleties of our social procedures—how "the games we play" are actually played—is not easy to find. Perceptive social scientists also discover quickly enough that the bigger the "game," the more its procedures are obscured or disguised. Only those chosen to carry on a given game in business, politics, the church, academia, or high society are freely instructed as insiders by sponsoring insiders in how to behave in competitions or struggles involving the control of social power.

From this it may appear that social scientists have chosen a frustrating profession. Their studies do focus principally upon the games children, women, and men play, the interaction patterns taken on or developed as people mature and try to function in society. Significant aspects of those interaction patterns are so embedded in habit, tradition, and vested interest that their accurate perception requires an act of both self-liberation and social daring. This is discussed in other chapters in various contexts, especially in connection with sociologists' ideologies and professional perplexities.

How Candid Can Social Science Become? Given this background, can social science become—often enough—a brash, young, vital, productive, unsettling, even revolutionary, existential-humanist discipline of the sort advocated here? Or must it become more and more socialized, hemmed in by orthodox views and procedures in institutionalized settings? Because of the magnitude of modern investigative and experimental operations, isn't the independent and individualistic social scientist, the mainstay of humanist sociology, obsolete? Because only highly trained specialists can know enough about a field to utilize adequately its data and theories, for whom are such expensive technicians to work? Must the work of sociological scientists inevitably produce primarily a technology that only managers of large enterprises can use? What are the optimum conditions under which a scientist can do sociological research?

The Contributions of Sociologists. This chapter deals sketchily with these questions in terms of the principal kinds of contributions sociologists are now making in our very tense and integrating American and world society. These contributions may be listed under five headings: (1) trivia, as always, and in quantity, (2) technology for management and manipulation, (3) criticisms and proposed modifications of public policy, (4) sociology for liberal education, and (5) sociology for everyman. Some may question why this list does not include such a heading as "pure sociology." Purity in this sense usually means abstraction, but to be sociological, theory has to have close reciprocal interrelations with firsthand investigations of social phenomena. Our list is meant to include sound sociological theory.

Outstanding contributions to the last three of these five—to public policy, for liberal education, and for everyman—constitute practically all the worthwhile sociological literature we have, but the first two—trivia and technology—have today the greatest bulk by long odds.

Let us look briefly at ventures in these five areas, including the high intellectual and social adventures sociologists have had and can continue to have in the last three of them:

1. TRIVIA

This topic is included for the purpose of completeness and for brushing aside, but it cannot be ignored. Its volume is oppressive. "Not philosophers but fret-sawyers and stamp collectors compose the backbone of society," [1] asserts Aldous Huxley, and so it is also with those who call themselves the scientists of human interrelationships. Blessed today are those of slight curiosity, no courage, and a penchant for ritual, for our profession provides many ways for them to achieve a respectable status without prying into controversial matters, the only matters likely to concern a scientifically motivated sociologist.

Trivia-makers have ready justifications for their scientific inconsequence and for the human irrelevance of their products. They look upon themselves as the hod carriers of science. Social science will be a vast structure. It is just now starting to take shape. Each hod of bricks somehow, somewhere, sometime, will surely be found helpful.

This is not to call all hard-working sociological hod carriers trivia-makers. The latter are the ritualistic hod carriers, those who go through elaborate and even elegant motions, but carry no bricks. Our profession being what it is, we ordinarily think it to be impolite to remark that an ornate hod, carried well, is empty. Thus too often we uncritically reinforce Huxley's dictum about fret-sawyers and collectors.

Writers of trivia are most often "approachers," or contributors to methodology. They remind one of the elegant dress and equipment of Abercrombie & Fitch hunters. They resemble ardent fishermen who spend their spare time throughout the year creating artistic gems of craftsmanship in the form of trout flies of only casual interest to trout. They

---

[1] Aldous Huxley, *Brave New World* (New York: Bantam, 1953), p. 2.

also bring to mind certain college and university presidents who look upon an athletic building, a beautiful library façade, or a highly visible computer or cyclotron as their chief showpiece, a showpiece much more controllable and less controversial than a famous professor. The sociological approachers expend endless research grants and fill many volumes with refinements of semantics, methodology, and theory which—like the fisherman-craftsman's dry flies—are for the purpose of conspicuous distinction rather than production. They always conclude their reports on the high note that they have made a ringing case for further research on the subject—that is, for more research grants. As A. H. Maslow has pointed out, definition and refinement of proper methods for science often lead "to voluntarily imposed self-limitations, to abdication from huge areas of human interests"—in short, to that contradiction of terms, a "scientific orthodoxy." [2]

Methodological purists contend that scientists should not call any conclusions "scientific" short of near certainty. Especially on publicly controversial matters, they insist upon silence until they are overwhelmed with evidence, evidence they themselves will not collect. Thus they make available to themselves a most protective negativism. This negativism easily aligns itself with establishment prejudices against science as a competing source of social authority. The negativism thus gives approachers a cheap and heady illusion of dispassionate courage. It glosses over the unconnectedness, insignificance, and irrelevance of so many of their items.[3]

2. TECHNOLOGY FOR MANAGEMENT AND MANIPULATION

The major managers and manipulators of our society have problems on which, in their opinion, sociologists can be put to some use. Statistical technicians and social engineers become media through whom the prestige of sociology as a science can be brought to bear upon problems of industry, government, churches, and civic organizations. Persons functioning as technicians—not as scientists—in mass communications, public-opinion surveying, group dynamics, social organization, social welfare, industrial sociology, and the like, are put to work converting sociological

    [2] A. H. Maslow, "Problem-Centering vs. Means-Centering in Science," *Philosophy of Science*, XIII (1946), 329.
    [3] W. J. Filstead, ed., *Qualitative Methodology: Firsthand Involvement With the Social World* (Chicago: Markham, 1970), esp. Chaps. 3–5 by Irwin Deutscher, Herbert Blumer, and M. B. Clinard; Blumer, *Symbolic Interactionism* (Englewood Cliffs, N.J.: Prentice-Hall, 1969), esp. Chaps. 1, 9, 10; Glenn Jacobs, ed., *The Participant Observer* (New York: George Braziller, 1970), esp. pp. vii–x.

theories into presumably workable stereotypes and techniques which they can merchandise. Thus do strange terms and disturbing ideas degenerate into clichés and form bases for saleable gimmicks.

As in other fields, sociologists may popularly be called scientists whether or not they are interested in pursuing scientific investigations. This one label blankets industrial engineers, technicians, specialists in teaching, administrators, do-gooders, and do-badders, as well as qualified and scientifically motivated sociological scientists.

Trivia-makers and neopositivist social engineers frequently fret in print about being grouped with do-gooders, but the confusion has its unintended merits, for it permits a degree of useful mobility within the profession. Scientific researchers and professors lend an academic authority to engineers and technicians. Engineers and technicians and administrators in turn have acquired the respectability of usefulness to the powerful in our antideviationist society. They therefore provide willy-nilly a kind of practical respectability among power seekers for sociologists as a whole, and hence a protective covering for socially irreverent scientists. In addition, under the leadership of our more responsible periodicals [4] and through liberal-arts education,[5] more of our men of affairs are coming to understand what may be gained from putting up with undependable and disturbing physical, biological, and social scientists. Whatever harm may come to the development of scientific sociology from the overweening claims of commercial market researchers, opinion analysts, personnel manipulators, and their fellows, is in part counterbalanced by their magnifying interest in whatever the term *sociology* may mean.

PRESSURES FOR "PRACTICAL RESULTS." Previous chapters discuss aspects of managerial and manipulative social technology in connection with distortions of social thought by the news conceptions of the mass media and by the claims of therapists and reformers. They also describe the managerial-bureaucratic paradigm for sociology developed for social engineers and the roles of sociological technology in social manipulation. As these considerations suggest, significant problems arise in the relations between sociological scientists and social engineers chiefly within our colleges and universities. These problems concern the involvement of faculties and students of liberal-arts colleges and graduate schools in

[4] For example, *New York Times, Washington Post, Christian Science Monitor* (Boston), *Wall Street Journal* (New York), *Time, Newsweek,* and *Fortune.*

[5] Carnegie Commission on Higher Education, *Quality and Equality: New Levels of Federal Responsibility for Higher Education* (New York: McGraw-Hill, 1969); Alvin Eurich, ed., *Campus Nineteen Eighty: The Shape and Future of American Higher Education* (New York: Dell, 1969); R. F. Goheen, *Human Nature of a University* (Princeton: Princeton University Press, 1969).

special-interest social-engineering projects. As William H. Whyte, Jr., said in *Fortune*, "The more quickly our bureaucracies grasp at the new 'tools' of persuasion, the more will the legitimate social scientist be pressured for 'practical results.' Those who would indulge in pure inquiry instead would find themselves 'deviants' from the integrated society they helped to fashion; only as lackeys would they have a function. In sheer self-defense, if nothing else, the social scientist must keep an eye on ethics." [6] On the other hand, it has been the commercialized social engineers rather than the sociological scientists who have clamored for ethical *codes*, statements so frequently found useful to the exploitative and useless to the idealistic.[7]

Rationalizations for converting sociological graduate departments into social-engineering institutes become rather precious, and at times downright cynical. The principal contentions are as follows: Outside subsidies from special interests, whether cloaked as foundation grants or not, make it possible to finance the expensive research now "necessary" for the "development of sociology." Financing includes stipends for graduate students, technical assistants, and secretaries, as well as funds for complicated computer operations and possibly also to pay report publication costs. Even though the immediate problems of such projects are technical rather than scientific, the data gathered are said to bear as well upon more "basic scientific problems." Donors (as they are often called) pay for social engineering, and they get what they pay for or do not subscribe again, but the faculties also presumably get data related to their "scientific interests," as well as facilities and funds with which to recruit and train graduate students in big-time procedures "essential" to current sociological research. But instances have already piled up that do not bear out this line of reasoning. Soap manufacturers and television entrepreneurs make professors work hard for their subsidies. "Scientific interests" are put aside indefinitely.

"COW SOCIOLOGY." How much do commercial pressures succeed in modifying the value position of academic solicitors for research funds in sociology? In a proposed misadventure, academic social engineers associated with a prestigious university institute outlined a series of investigations to determine how to carry on research more efficiently in an organizational or team setting. The proposal for the program quotes a "prominent research executive" as follows: "We must know what we want and what we expect of the research worker. We must understand his motivations and characteristics. Based on our understanding of these

6 W. H. Whyte, Jr., "The Social Engineers," *Fortune*, XLV (1952), 89. See also Whyte, *Is Anybody Listening?* (New York: Simon & Schuster, 1952), esp. Chap. 10.
7 R. W. Friedrichs, *A Sociology of Sociology* (New York: Free Press, 1970), esp. pp. 118–23; N. K. Denzin, ed., *The Values of Social Science* (Chicago: Aldine, 1970).

things, we must provide environments conducive to good results. We must use creative imagination in the administration of research. We must follow this by sound engineering and good business planning. This is effective research. This is the kind of research which means position and control of destiny tomorrow." [8] To these ideas, which sound so much more like those of industrial managers or advertising hucksters than anything worth being associated with scientific sociology, the academic social research institute says amen in these words: "It is toward such goals that the following proposal is directed." [9]

This example is extreme only in its frankness. In this project, as in many other social-engineering "researches" examined, certain rigid ideological conditions are set at the beginning that define the kinds of facts to be gathered. These conditions, in effect, command certain conclusions. A much more fundamental problem than the one stated is whether *or not* scientists can best do sociological work under a research administrator and as part of an organization consisting of one or more teams. Even more fundamental is the question, How does creative scientific work take place? For that matter, how does creative work of any kind take place? By what sorts of people? Under what kinds of conditions? [10]

Is it any wonder that academic social engineers take on the cultlike characteristics so common among business technicians, with security found in a hierarchy, a full-blown "company" ideology, a patter, a few well-worn techniques and gadgets, and a narrow routine of life? Daniel Bell notes the pride these people exhibit in what they call "strictly empirical research" with its "formidable statistical apparatus," and he adds, "Yet while researchers in this field often display a parvenu arrogance toward theory, a great deal of pretentious, senseless, and extravagant writing fills their own work, much of it inspired by the theoretical system they have taken over from Pareto." These technicians' ideology typically accepts a depersonalized view of less fortunate humanity. Bell observes: "The belief in man as an end in himself has been ground under by the machine, and the social science of the factory researchers is not a science of man, but a cow-sociology." He quotes Burleigh Gardner as follows: "The more satisfied [the worker] is, the greater will be his self-esteem, the more content will he be, and therefore, the more efficient in what he is doing." [11] How reminiscent of Aldous Huxley's *Brave New World!*

    [8] E. W. Engstrom and E. H. Alexander, "A Profile of the Man in Industrial Research," *Proceedings of the I. R. E.,* December, 1952, pp. 1637–44.

    [9] Institute for Social Research, University of Michigan, *Proposal for a Research Program on the Administration of Research Organizations,* mimeographed, April 5, 1954, p. 2.

    [10] Harold Anderson, ed., *Creativity and Its Cultivation* (New York: Harper, 1959); Bernard Barber, *Science and the Social Order,* rev. ed. (New York: Collier, 1962).

    [11] Daniel Bell, "Adjusting Men to Machines," *Commentary,* III (1947), 87–8, and *The End of Ideology,* rev. ed. (New York: Collier, 1961), p. 250.

As Whyte concludes in his study cited above, social engineering "is pro-
foundly authoritarian in its implications, for it subordinates the individual to the group" and provides "a highly appealing rationale for
conformity." [12]

Intentionally or not sociological researchers and theorists have thus
begun to develop, as one of their major products, a technology that engineers and technicians are placing at the service of special interests with
little or no regard for broader interests. Sociologists are also needed as
scientists. Those who become lackeys do not remain scientists. Thus in
our academic sociology we have the same confusion between discovering
the new and putting across the old that is having such devastating effects
in the other physical, biological, and social sciences.

Let us now turn to the areas of high adventure in sociology—public
policy, liberal education, and everyman's social ideas.

3. CRITICISMS AND PROPOSED
MODIFICATIONS OF PUBLIC POLICY

The fathers of American sociology, such as Lester F. Ward [13] and William G. Sumner,[14] were social critics who attempted to clarify issues and to
propose modifications in aspects of ongoing human society. The products
of contemporary sociologists relevant to public policy self-consciously avoid
the polemic tone of Ward's and Sumner's earlier works. They also seldom
reveal equally informed insight into human affairs. Sociologists today do
write useful papers and books on problems of broad concern—racism and

[12] Whyte, *Fortune*, p. 89.

[13] L. F. Ward, *Dynamic Sociology* (New York: D. Appleton, 1910), I–II,
Pure Sociology (New York: Macmillan, 1903), and *Applied Sociology* (Boston: Ginn,
1906). See also Israel Gerver, *Lester Frank Ward* (New York: T. Y. Crowell, 1963).

[14] M. R. Davie, *William Graham Sumner* (New York: T. Y. Crowell, 1963), esp.
Chap. 1. Sumner started out as an Episcopalian clergyman, trained well in the most
rigorous German theology of his day and deeply interested in public affairs. He
evolved into a politico-economic polemicist of a radical laissez-faire stamp. And then,
following a period of drastic self-reeducation, especially in comparative ethnology, he
finally placed himself on a road toward becoming one of our most outstanding sociologists. He himself provides the best available glimpses of his intellectual life history
in his posthumously collected essays, edited by his Yale protégé and successor, A. G.
Keller: *War and Other Essays, Earth-Hunger and Other Essays, The Challenge of the
Facts and Other Essays,* and *The Forgotten Man and Other Essays* (New Haven: Yale
University Press, 1911, 1913, 1914, 1919). Keller, as Sumner's literary executor, did
what he could to try to preserve Sumner's earlier reputation as a conservative academic
hero and to de-emphasize Sumner's increasingly evenhanded objectivity, and especially
his antimilitarism and antiplutocracy. Left-wing writers have aided Keller's effort. See
for example, B. J. Stern, "William Graham Sumner," *Encyclopaedia of the Social
Sciences,* (New York: Macmillan, 1934), XIV, 463–64. Confused liberals and
poor scholars among sociologists have similarly contributed to obscuring the older
Sumner's great insights into the nature of human society.

colonialism, intergroup relations, mass communications, community organization, the socialization of the individual, conformity and nonconformity, marital adjustments, extramarital sex, influences of housing and community layout on the routines of life, social stratification, social manipulation and exploitation, social deviation, social deprivation, individual and social maladjustment, delinquency, and crime. These works are variously quoted and interpreted by sociologists and others in roles as consultants, expert witnesses, speakers, committee members, judges, administrators, and legislators. Even more powerfully, these works are used in formal and informal education and thus influence policy-making by modifying popular culture.

As the previous discussion of technology for management and manipulation suggests, the relationship between the sociologists and the public policy-makers is a complex and sometimes problematic one. In addition to social scientists subjecting policy doctrines to criticism and suggesting modifications in them, policy-makers are trying to use "sociologists" as social engineers, to have them contribute findings and professional weight to political action efforts. Policy-makers are often annoyed at findings of autonomous sociological critics, but they have discovered how to use so-called sociologists as operations analysts, simulation experts, and specialists in tactical data systems, war-gaming, and other types of gamesmanship. As one would anticipate from such recruitment, which is largely self-recruitment, the problem of working with entrepreneurs and bureaucratic managers presents social engineers with irreconcilable problems in publicly portrayed values. How is one to function as a faithful servant of an organization or an organizational clique and still maintain himself as a credible "sociologist," believably dedicated to verified and verifiable social data and theory? "What is at stake as a result of this newly acquired influence is not the feasibility of social science, but the credibility of social scientists." [15]

The reception of research findings on mass communications, on intergroup relations, especially racism, and on housing and urban redevelopment illustrates failures and successes of sociologists in contributing to public policy formation in recent decades. The following discussion of work in these areas is concerned chiefly with contributions of autonomous sociological scientists, but it also contains some references to the consequences of certain instrumental efforts by social engineers.

In mass communications, a few social scientists and other students of public affairs have perceived, analyzed, and been concerned about the powerful drive over the years toward the integration of control and opera-

[15] I. L. Horowitz, *Professing Sociology: Studies in the Life Cycle of Social Science* (Chicago: Aldine, 1968), pp. 262–63.

tion of press, radio, and television media.[16] Sociologists have also probed other aspects of the mass media, such as the nature and significance of their staffs' working conditions and of media content,[17] but the present discussion is confined to the matter of control.

THE ASSOCIATED PRESS CASE. Hearings before the Federal Communications Commission on press-radio relations in 1941, the case of the *United States* v. *The Associated Press* and others in 1942–1945 (concerning the AP's monopolistic role), and the reports of the Luce Commission on Freedom of the Press published in 1947 [18] were important phases of public discussion and decision making regarding this trend—when it was actively being discussed.

Both the Federal Communications Commission [19] and the federal courts [20] admitted sociological evidence pro and con given by sociologists. This evidence set forth analyses of press and radio control statistics and other relevant facts and interpreted the probable consequences of the monopolistic trend. In each case the government had available studies by autonomous sociologists pointing to the restricting trend in mass communications. In each case social engineers in the employ of industrial organizations tried to portray the admitted trend as harmless and commercially imperative.

Those concerned with the constriction of competition in communications lost in both cases. The FCC slurred over the issue of press-radio integration and muddled along without a clear policy. As a result, joint press-radio control of the dominant radio and television outlets increased.[21] Even though the FCC came to limit one ownership to no more than seven AM, seven FM, and seven TV stations (five VHF, two UHF), almost all of the powerful clear-channel radio stations are owned by

[16] A. McC. Lee, "Freedom of the Press," in E. B. and A. McC. Lee, *Social Problems in America*, rev. ed. (New York: Henry Holt, 1955); Carnegie Commission on Educational Television, *Public Television: A Program for Action* (New York: Harper & Row, 1967).

[17] For a good summary, see O. R. Holsti, J. K. Loomba, and R. C. North, "Content Analysis," Chap. 16 in Gardner Lindzey and Elliot Aronson, eds., *The Handbook of Social Psychology*, 2nd ed. (Reading, Mass.: Addison-Wesley, 1968), II. Of related interest is Walter Weiss, "Effects of Mass Media of Communication," Chap. 38 in *The Handbook of Social Psychology*, V (1969).

[18] Commission on Freedom of the Press, *A Free and Responsible Press* (Chicago: University of Chicago Press, 1947), and a series of monographs.

[19] A. McC. Lee and others, expert testimony before Federal Communications Commission, July 23 and 24, 1941; A. McC. and E. B. Lee, statistical exhibits No. 52296, Federal Communications Commission, July 23, 1941, 7 sheets.

[20] A. McC. Lee, expert testimony, in *Affidavits Filed in Support of Plaintiff's Motion for Summary Judgment*, District Court U.S. Southern District, N.Y., Civil Action No. 19–163, *U.S.A.* v. *A.P. et al.*, May 25, 1943, pp. 75–170.

[21] R. B. Nixon and Jean Ward, "Trends in Newspaper Ownership," *Journalism Quarterly*, XXXVIII (1961), 3–12; Wilbur Schramm, *Mass Media and National Development* (Stanford: Stanford University Press, 1964).

networks or affiliated contractually with them. Very few TV stations are not affiliated with one of the three national television networks. In addition, so far as newsgathering is concerned, the AP and the United Press International are the only comprehensive services between which to choose. Both are newspaper-controlled.

THE MARSHALL FIELD CASE. Oddly enough, even though the federal government won the AP case in the U.S. Supreme Court, the result was much the same after a short time as if the AP had won. This was the famous Marshall Field case in behalf of Field's *Chicago Sun* and other papers that had been denied AP service (membership in the AP as a producers' cooperative). By easing the rigidity of the AP's contractually established monopoly, by opening its membership to all financially qualified media, the U.S. Supreme Court enabled the AP to become a more inclusive representative in newsgathering of the existing daily-newspaper owners. As far as gains in variety of viewpoint in newsgathering or among daily newspapers were concerned, the continued decline in competition and the tight integration of daily newspapers into the American business community counteracted the victory. The AP decision made possible only a few quite temporary gains in the competition of ideas and versions of the news.[22]

THE LUCE COMMISSION REPORT. In 1943–1947 the Luce Commission on Freedom of the Press operated under a subsidy from Time, Inc., and the Encyclopaedia Britannica, Inc., with the funds paid through the University of Chicago. Robert M. Hutchins, as chairman of the commission, contends that none of those organizations "had any control over or assumed any responsibility for the progress or the conclusions of the inquiry." [23] Hutchins visualized the mass-communications problem of the time especially in these terms: "Anybody with nothing to say can say it by mass communication if he has a knowing press agent, or a considerable reputation, or an active pressure group behind him, whereas, even with such advantages, anybody with something to say has a hard time getting it said by mass communication if it runs counter to the ideas of owners, editors, opposing pressure groups, or popular prejudice." He expressed the hope that the Commission's report would help "in obtaining a hearing for ideas, not in adding to the confusion of tongues." [24]

Hutchins, as one bemused by plausible ideas and with little respect for fact-grubbing, did not use any of the social-scientific critiques of the

---

[22] Edwin Emery *et al., Introduction to Mass Communications,* 2nd ed. (New York: Dodd, Mead, 1965), Chap. 14.

[23] R. M. Hutchins, "Foreword," in Commission on Freedom of the Press, *A Free and Responsible Press* (Chicago: University of Chicago Press, 1947), p. v.

[24] *Ibid.,* p. viii.

media then available.[25] On the contrary, he had the staff interview "members of the industries, government, and private agencies concerned with the press," and the commission itself "held 17 two-day or three-day meetings and studied 176 documents prepared by its members or the staff." [26] Thus, lofty statesmanship and moral philosophy, a lack of relevant facts on threats to press-radio-television freedom, and an unwillingness to appear aggressive or radical blunted the impact of the Luce Commission reports. The prestige of the Commission's membership helped to stir discussion, but its proposals offered little with which to work for improvement. The proposals were largely efforts to reason with those who had control. As Hutchins himself admitted, "The Commission's recommendations are not startling. The most surprising thing about them is that nothing more surprising could be proposed." [27] For example, since the mass media are becoming so like-minded, the Commission called for them to "accept the responsibilities of common carriers of information and discussion." [28] Its chief recommendation to owners and the public had to do with staff education. This recommendation helped to strengthen further the development of mass-media representation within the academies in the form of schools and institutes of journalism and mass communications. The faithful academics who staff these units provide a wealth of social-engineering data and sophisticated and "objective" special pleading for the industry.[29]

In a sense, the Luce Commission reports helped to remove mass-communications studies of a controversial sort from the agendas of sociologists. Those studies are increasingly the province of the social engineers who staff the mass-communications schools and institutes.

INSTRUMENTS OF ORTHODOXY AND OF CHANGE. In contrast with this tale of failure, the intergroup relations situation is strikingly different for

[25] For example, Helen MacGill Hughes, *News and the Human Interest Story* (Chicago: University of Chicago Press, 1939); H. L. Ickes, ed., *Freedom of the Press Today: A Clinical Examination by Twenty-Eight Specialists* (New York: Vanguard, 1941); C. D. MacDougall, *Hoaxes* (New York: Macmillan, 1940); L. C. Rosten, *The Washington Correspondents* (New York: Harcourt, Brace, 1937). Important penetrating surveys and critiques of the press had also been written by informed journalists of note, such as George Seldes, *Freedom of the Press* (Indianapolis: Bobbs-Merrill, 1935). Seldes, treated with respect by newspapermen, was also apparently ignored by the Luce Commission. (See the editorial on Seldes' book, "Welcome Criticism," *Editor & Publisher*, LXVIII, No. 19 (Sept. 21, 1935), 26, and F. L. Martin, dean of the University of Missouri School of Journalism, "Shop Talk at Thirty," *Editor & Publisher*, LXVIII, No. 30 (Dec. 7, 1935), 44. [*Editor & Publisher* is the leading newspaper trade journal.]).

[26] Hutchins, "Forward," in *A Free and Responsible Press*, p. vi.

[27] *Ibid.*, p. 8.

[28] Commission on Freedom of the Press, *ibid.*, p. 92.

[29] Note proindustrial slant of the official journal of the journalism professors, *Journalism Quarterly.*

a basic reason. Sociologists, psychologists, and anthropologists have educated many thousands of college students with regard to race, racism, interethnic relations, and other aspects of intergroup relations. This educational work is one of our greatest accomplishments, but we have not done nearly as much work on the growing pall of orthodoxy in mass communications, and we generally give much less attention to the latter in our college texts. Our "researchers" have done more to solve technical problems in psychological warfare and for advertising and public-relations purposes than to help students understand propaganda and other aspects of social manipulation which directly bear upon them. In other words, we have done more to promote than to dispel the growing pall of orthodoxy.

SOCIOLOGY IN THE SUPREME COURT. Kenneth B. Clark and his associates for the first time had social-psychological findings of sociologists and psychologists admitted as evidence and used as the major basis for a decision by the U.S. Supreme Court.[30] The resulting unanimous decisions, read by Chief Justice Earl Warren on May 17, 1954, have had sweeping consequences in school desegregation throughout the United States. The educational work done by social scientists over the years since 1896, plus the changed international status of the United States, combined to provide the foundation for the elimination of the Plessy "separate but equal" doctrine.[31] This reference to historical preparation is not meant to belittle the hard-won accomplishment of Clark and his associates and of the National Association for the Advancement of Colored People; rather, it is meant to help place it in a broader perspective. As James Reston commented in the *New York Times* with regard to the decision, the "court's opinion read more like an expert paper on sociology than a Supreme Court opinion." [32] These high-court decisions constitute a formal recognition of participation in policy-making beyond anything previously achieved by sociologists in public affairs in this country.

WRESTLING WITH MAJOR ISSUES. From these two instances it should be clear that sociological findings make their greatest impact upon public policy when they are simultaneously moving through educational, popular, and policy-influencing channels. Such a success as that in the desegregation decisions does not arise from little social engineering manipulations.

[30] K. B. Clark *et al.*, "The Effects of Segregation and the Consequences of Desegregation: A Social Science Statement," *Appendix to Appellants' Briefs*, U.S. Supreme Court (October 1952), *O. Brown et al.* v. *Board of Education of Topeka, Kansas*, and other cases. For a summary and interpretation of testimony by expert witnesses in these cases, see Clark, "The Social Scientist as an Expert Witness in Civil Rights Litigation," *Social Problems*, I (1953), 5–10.

[31] *Plessy* v. *Ferguson*, U.S. Supreme Court, 1896.

[32] James Reston, "A Sociological Decision," *New York Times*, May 18, 1954, p. 14.

On the contrary, it comes from wrestling with a major issue of human existence.

This is not to imply that success with the desegregation decisions was more than a battle won in a long and continuing struggle, the struggle for no less than equal opportunities for all without reference to race or color. While the struggle continues in the schools, it currently has other crucial focal points in employment and in housing through urban and rural redevelopment. For sociologists, schooling, employment, and housing can scarcely be separated; they are all integral parts of individual and family life.

Sociological research and teaching are contributing to this broader struggle both substantively and evaluatively. Substantively, sociologists continue to find and interpret evidence that verifies and emphasizes the contributions to social health of desegregation in all aspects of social life.[33] On the evaluative side, sociologists produce articles and books that point time and again to contrasts between the alleged purposes of programs to improve employment or housing for the underprivileged and the actual consequences that follow. As the sociologist Mel Ravitz sums up such findings, "Despite the millions of dollars of federal grants, state aid, and local funds we have spent over the past twenty years for urban renewal, public housing, delinquency control, anti-poverty efforts, we have little tested evidence that all this money has made a significant impact in improving the lives of the mass of urban citizens."[34] When two other sociologists first revealed that housing segregation in Detroit "had increased steadily since 1930," and then that "Detroit was fast becoming a city of dependents—dependents who must be supported on a constantly shrinking tax base,"[35] they were fired from their positions with a state university institute. Their generalization applied just as well to a great many other American cities.[36]

[33] K. B. Clark, *Dark Ghetto* (New York: Harper & Row, 1965), esp. Chap. 9; E. F. Frazier, *Race and Culture Contacts in the Modern World* (New York: Alfred A. Knopf, 1957); Nathan Glazer and D. P. Moynihan, *Beyond the Melting Pot* (Cambridge: M.I.T. Press, 1963); Gardner Lindzey and Donn Byrne, "Measurement of Social Choice and Interpersonal Attractiveness," Chap. 14 in Lindzey and Aronson, *The Handbook of Social Psychology*, II, and W. J. McGuire, "The Nature of Attitudes and Attitude Change," Chap. 21 in *ibid.*, III (1969).

[34] Mel Ravitz, "The Crisis in Our Cities: An Action Perspective," in Leonard Gordon, ed., *A City in Racial Crisis* (Dubuque, Iowa: W. C. Brown, 1971), p. 159.

[35] T. F. Hoult, " 'Race and Residence' Reviewed After the Riot," in Gordon, *ibid.*, pp. 14–15. Hoult refers also to A. J. Mayer's work. See also Mayer and Hoult, *Race and Residence in Detroit* (Detroit: Wayne University Institute of Urban Studies, 1962).

[36] D. O. Cowgill, "Trends in Residential Segregation in American Cities, 1940–1950," *American Sociological Review*, XXI (1956), 43–47; K. E. Taeuber, "Negro Residential Segregation: Trends and Measurements," *Social Problems*, XII (1964), 42–51; W. G. Marston, "Social Class as a Factor in Ethnic and Racial Segregation," *International Journal of Comparative Sociology*, IX (1968), 145–53; Reynolds Farley

Just what might appear as evidence of sociological contribution in this situation of spreading inner-city blight, spreading rural decay, and suburban affluence, it is difficult to predict. At any rate, sociologists, journalists, and concerned politicians are at least succeeding in making more vividly apparent the appalling tendencies and their probable consequences not only in delinquency, drug addiction, crime, and violence, but also in the brutalization of our society as a whole. They share with Kenneth B. Clark the view that "Every time a Negro sees a group of secretaries—white and Negro—chatting over lunch; or children—white and Negro—walking together to school, he feels that hope is possible. Every time his white friend shows he is not afraid to argue with him as with anyone else, he sees that freedom is possible, that there are some for whom race is irrelevant, who accept or reject a person not as a Negro or a white, but in terms of himself. Only so can the real confinements of the ghetto be broken. The Negro alone cannot win this fight that transcends the 'civil rights struggle.' White and Negro must fight together for the rights of human beings to make mistakes and to aspire to human goals. Negroes will not break out of the barriers of the ghetto unless whites transcend the barriers of their own minds, for the ghetto is to the Negro a reflection of the ghetto in which the white lives imprisoned. The poetic irony of American race relations is that the rejected Negro must somehow also find the strength to free the privileged white." [37]

Here are some other questions of public policy with which sociologists are now dealing: How can society best adjust itself to psychological deviants—criminal, sexual, deficient, and other? [38] Is police brutality inevitable, even defensible, something the busy and anxious world cannot help but permit the defenseless to suffer, or can the police gain a new and more mature understanding of their social responsibilities? [39] What

---

and Taeuber, "Population Trends and Residential Segregation Since 1960," *Science,* CLIX (1968), 953–56; Taeuber, "The Effect of Income Redistribution on Racial Residential Segregation," *Urban Affairs Quarterly,* IV (1968), 5–14.

[37] Clark, *Dark Ghetto,* p. 240. See also, Clark and Jeannette Hopkins, *A Relevant War Against Poverty* (New York: Harper & Row, 1970), esp. Chap. 6; M. M. Gordon, *Assimilation in American Life* (New York: Oxford University Press, 1964), esp. Chap. 8.

[38] A. S. Blumberg, *Criminal Justice* (Chicago: Quadrangle, 1967); Simon Dinitz and W. C. Reckless, eds., *Critical Issues in the Study of Crime* (Boston: Little, Brown, 1968); R. D. Knudten, ed., *Criminological Controversies* (New York: Appleton-Century-Crofts, 1968); Gresham Sykes, *Crime and Society,* 2nd ed. (New York: Random House, 1967); J. H. Gagnon and William Simon, eds., *Sexual Deviance* (New York: Harper & Row, 1967); Michael Schofield, *Sociological Aspects of Homosexuality* (Boston: Little, Brown, 1965); R. M. Elman, *The Poorhouse State* (New York: Dell, 1968).

[39] Arthur Niederhoffer and A. S. Blumberg, eds., *The Ambivalent Force* (Waltham, Mass.: Ginn, 1970); Niederhoffer, *Behind the Shield* (New York: Doubleday, 1967); Blumberg, *Criminal Justice;* Paul Chevigny, *Police Power: Police Abuses in New York City* (New York: Pantheon, 1969); L. H. Whittemore, *Cop: A Closeup of Violence and Tragedy* (New York: Holt, Rinehart & Winston, 1969).

about the atomism and anonymity of urban life?[40] Just what does rural decay mean to human beings and their families?[41] Can we have community planning for living and not just for architectural effects?[42] How can we achieve more satisfactory marriage and divorce patterns?[43] Can lonely men and women of the latter twentieth-century decades learn enough about propaganda and social manipulation so that they can take active and useful roles in their community's political and social life?[44] How can sociologists contribute more to international understanding?[45]

These questions suggest some of the major policy areas to which sociologists are now making research contributions. If more would devote less of their efforts to fancy methodological footwork and to dehumanized engineering and more to great human concerns, sociology would be less likely to fall in this country into the formalism and abstract speculation to which so many European and American colleagues have frequently been so prone.

Let us now look at sociological products which function even more directly to facilitate culture modifications.

4. SOCIOLOGY FOR LIBERAL EDUCATION

In speaking of the competitive situation of sociology among campus disciplines, a sociologist points to how sociological debates often confuse "nonsociological academic folk, whose bewilderment is brought about by

[40] Eric and Mary Josephson, eds., *Man Alone* (New York: Dell, 1962), esp. Chap. 6.

[41] H. M. Caudill, *Night Comes to the Cumberlands* (Boston: Little, Brown, 1963); Thomas Gladwin, *Poverty U.S.A.* (Boston: Little, Brown, 1967); John Fetterman, *Stinking Creek* (New York: E. P. Dutton, 1970); Paul Good, *The American Serfs* (New York: G. P. Putnam's Sons, 1968).

[42] Jewel Bellush and M. Hausknecht, eds., *Urban Renewal* (New York: Doubleday, 1967); Sylvia F. Fava, ed., *Urbanism in World Perspective* (New York: T. Y. Crowell, 1968), esp. Part 5; Donald Foley, *Controlling London's Growth* (Berkeley: University of California Press, 1967); H. J. Gans, "Urban Poverty and Social Planning," in P. F. Lazarsfeld, W. H. Sewell, and H. Wilensky, eds., *The Uses of Sociology* (New York: Basic Books, 1967); Scott Greer, *Urban Renewal and American Cities* (Indianapolis: Bobbs-Merrill, 1965); Roy Lubove, *The Urban Community* (Englewood Cliffs, N.J.: Prentice-Hall, 1967); S. B. Warner, Jr., ed., *Planning for a Nation of Cities* (Cambridge, Mass.: M.I.T. Press, 1966); S. D. Berger, *The Social Consequences of Residential Segregation of the Urban American Negro* (New York: Metropolitan Applied Research Center, 1970).

[43] Jerold Heiss, ed., *Family Roles and Interaction* (Chicago: Rand McNally, 1968); M. E. Spiro, *Children of the Kibbutz* (New York: Schocken Books, 1965); Lewis Yablonsky, *The Hippie Trip* (New York: Pegasus, 1968).

[44] See the discussion and bibliographical notes in Chapter five.

[45] Amitai Etzioni and Martin Wenglinsky, eds., *War and Its Prevention* (New York: Harper & Row, 1970); John Kosa, ed., *The Home of the Learned Man* (New Haven: College & University Press, 1968); Gene Sharp, *Exploring Nonviolent Alternatives* (Boston: Porter Sargent, 1970); K. T. Fann and D. C. Hodges, eds., *Readings in U.S. Imperialism* (Boston: Porter Sargent, 1971).

a field that sometimes appears to strive to be at once scientific fish, humanistic flesh, and reformistic fowl." [46] As it has been shown, this apparent confusion arises out of efforts by some sociologists to ride piggyback on either the scientistic or the humanities bandwagon to academic "respectability" or on a reformistic bandwagon to popular acclaim.

A great many sociologists do something much more appropriate in their teaching than merely taking one of those three sectarian positions. As they perceive it, their assignment is not at all so clear-cut or so unpretentious as that which most other professors believe they should undertake. Sociologists face students who think they already know a great deal about society and human interrelationships. Young men and women now have derived this from their parents, home community, religious precepts, friends, "sociological" novels, and "sociological" exposés on television, in newspapers and magazines, and in books. When sociologists face such students, they deal with subjects often discussed in literature classes, in sermons, at home with parents, and in peer-group "bull" or "rap" sessions.

Sociologists profess to have a better way to learn about human affairs than through traditional wisdom, religious inspiration, logical deduction, or speculation. In doing so, they undertake three major duties with their general undergraduate students. They (1) introduce them to how sociologists contribute to knowledge, (2) acquaint them with some major findings and typical studies, and (3) inform them about how sociologists, as social scientists and as participants in Western culture and learning, synthesize what they have discovered with what others have to offer about man's behavior in society. In doing these three things, they assume the obligation to serve as higher critics of inherited social and moral philosophy and to help students to build socially relevant findings of scientists into their altering perspectives on man in society and themselves in particular. This obligation is carried out in part by well-chosen text materials, but the impact of scientific thinking about society is so reorganizing intellectually to those who absorb it that classroom discussion and skilled teaching are essential to make the experience as rich as it can be.

Some sociologists, especially trivia-writers and ultraempiricists, ape mathematicians and physicists in still another respect and treat textbooks as beneath their lofty notice. Many a textbook should be sneered at as an unhappy, half-baked jumble of folk wisdom, a middle-class version of morality, scientistic pretentiousness, social fads of the time, and variable amounts of unassimilated sociological findings. It must also be

---

[46] C. H. Page, "Sociology as a Teaching Enterprise," in R. K. Merton, Leonard Broom, and L. S. Cottrell, Jr., eds., *Sociology Today* (New York: Basic Books, 1959), p. 587.

added, in contrast, that a very large share of the key works in sociology were written originally for liberal-arts students to hear or read.

Many contemporary textbooks lack the integration that comes from long working and reworking of materials. This lack derives in part from having too few sociologists now devoting themselves primarily to the formulation of sociological data, theories, and perspectives for college lecture and text purposes and for everyman. Too many lectures and texts are now just compilations. We are getting too many nonbooks or undigested aggregates.

This position with regard to what the sociology professor contributes to a liberal-arts education should not lead anyone to conclude that the suggestions on synthesis all sociology professors might offer should or would be the same. As the present book indicates quite fully, sociology is a way of searching for knowledge; it is not a body of doctrine or of dogma. It is a way of finding information and tentative theories with which to bring traditional social wisdom into a more accurate relationship with society and human relations as they are existing and evolving today. The vast complexities of social man, human groups, and society, as well as those of adjacent disciplines, make this a highly tentative process. Thus the views any professor and his students express in a class in sociology are part of the discussional process in Western society in which sociological findings are being weighed, interpreted, and related to those of cultural anthropology, history, social philosophy, psychology, and literature.

5. SOCIOLOGY FOR EVERYMAN

The elitist sees no virtue in the crude *demos,* the common mass of mankind. "No art form, no body of knowledge, no system of ethics is strong enough to withstand vulgarization. . . . At its worst, mass culture threatens not merely to cretinize our taste, but to brutalize our senses while paving the way to totalitarianism." [47] Curiously enough, these are the statements of a professional sociologist. He neglects the intimate and reciprocal relationships between the intellectuals in any field and their time, place, and culture. Intellectuals are embedded willy-nilly in mass society by derivation, kinship, and routines of life, regardless of the extent to which they may have been able to separate or even alienate themselves from it. They serve society by focusing attention on artistic and scientific accomplishments, by staffing educational and research in-

---

[47] Bernard Rosenberg, "Mass Culture in America," in Rosenberg and D. M. White, eds., *Mass Culture: The Popular Arts in America* (Glencoe, Ill.: Free Press, 1959), pp. 5, 9.

stitutions and activities, and by criticizing and preserving the cultural heritage. Their tastes and senses, however, always owe a debt to current mass man in his amazing variety.

A cultured elite surely has no monopoly on creativity, or even control of it, in any society. Often those with both sufficient biological endowment and adequate motivation to be creative appear in depressed and exploited pockets of the masses, not among the assimilated ranks of a cultured elite.[48] Some of the more conservative sociologists, interestingly enough, have developed rather democratic views of innovation. For example, W. F. Ogburn concludes that "the existing culture is the mother of inventions." [49] A. G. Keller regards the great man as "the product of his time and place, and his greatness consists in his insight, or lack, in producing a variation—in anticipating some massive movement [in human affairs, social structure, art, science, ideas] that is about to take place anyhow." [50]

THE VIRTUES OF VULGARIZATION. Thus vulgarization is an end-product to be sought by sociologists and is not to be avoided, and it certainly requires their understanding, and where possible, cooperation. The audiences for sociological research findings are (1) technical and professional colleagues, (2) students and other serious listeners and readers, (3) popularizers to larger audiences, and (4) popular communicators to mass audiences as they absorb or are influenced in their thoughts by more scientific or scientifically modified views of society, usually by way of the popularizers. Popular communicators are the ones who provide the prevalence for ideas that can modify culture.

There are at least four ways to look at writing about sociology for a general audience: (1) You can insist that all sociology of any consequence is for specialists. It has to be written precisely, and only inaccurate and superficial reinterpretations can be presented to the general public. (2) You can say that sociology is much too complicated for interpretation below the level of college freshmen or sophomores. (3) You can state that it should be done, that it can be done, and then sit and wonder what in the world we have to say to everyman. Publishers inform me that any number of popular books about sociology have been unsuccessfully attempted. Finally, (4) you can take the position of professional writers for general audiences that any major idea can be translated.into simple enough English for the understanding at least of readers of *Time, Newsweek, The Atlantic Monthly,* and *The Saturday Review.* When you

---

[48] L. A. Coser, *Men of Ideas* (New York: Free Press, 1965); J. C. Gowan, G. D. Demos, and E. P. Torrance, *Creativity: Its Educational Implications* (New York: John Wiley, 1967).

[49] W. F. Ogburn, *Social Change,* 2nd ed. (New York: Viking, 1950), p. 83.

[50] A. G. Keller, *Societal Evolution,* rev. ed. (New York: Macmillan, 1931), p. 92.

tell such writers that this popularization has rarely been attempted successfully in sociology, they try to raise what they consider to be embarrassing questions about whether or not sociologists really have something of importance to say, whether or not they have merely put ordinary ideas into a pseudo-technical language.

Perhaps the situation is more than a little due to what the sociologist Peter L. Berger calls the "grim humorlessness" [51] of social scientists. More likely it is true because of the touchy nature of the materials with which social scientists deal, the very fabric of society, and therewith, that which gives a sense of security to its members.

EVERYMAN'S INTERESTS IN SOCIOLOGY. Those of us who have fairly detailed knowledge of sociology and have taught sections of introductory sociology and social problems know that there are basic theoretical issues and theories in sociology that fascinate freshmen and sophomores from other departments. What interests majors in business administration, education, and journalism is likely to be of concern to at least fairly literate general audiences. Reference is to such topics as societal, cultural, and personal relativity, discontinuities in age roles, the class and caste structuring of societies, the semiautonomous nature of human groups, and the strange characteristics of social distance, attitudinal multivalence, and morals-mores contrasts.

These complicated and controversial topics suggest possible reasons why sociology for everyman has been slow in coming and why it has been achieved chiefly in the form of polemics and discussions of specific problems and issues. At any rate, the dissemination of sociological findings has proceeded substantially beyond the first two spheres mentioned above, which included colleagues, students, and serious readers.

Media for popularizing social scientific findings for larger audiences include Public Affairs Pamphlets,[52] the English weekly *New Society*,[53] and the American monthly *Society* (formerly *Trans-Action*).[54] In addition, since 1938 the American Sociological Association [55] has somewhat

[51] P. L. Berger, *Invitation to Sociology* (Garden City, N.Y.: Doubleday, 1963), p. 164.

[52] The Public Affairs Committee, 381 Park Avenue South, New York, N.Y. 10016, has published about five hundred pamphlets on a wide range of social and personal concerns since 1936, each with an average circulation of about one hundred thousand. Each pamphlet is carefully checked by leading specialists prior to publication.

[53] Called a mixture of journalism and social-scientific analysis, published by New Society Publications, 128 Long Acre, London WC2E 9QH, England.

[54] Popular articles on research results written chiefly by social scientists, published since 1963, now located at Rutgers University, New Brunswick, N.J. 08901.

[55] For reports on early years of this work, see *American Sociological Review*, IV (1939), 264–66; V (1940), 104–5, 413–14; VI (1941), 95–97, 260–61; VII (1942), 90–92, 230; VIII (1943), 80–81.

systematically made its convention papers and proofs of forthcoming journal articles available to working press representatives for reinterpretation. In another manner, the inclusive *Sociological Abstracts* [56] facilitates dissemination by providing libraries, including subscribing periodicals, with exhaustive sets of summaries of sociological contributions suitably indexed for quick reference.

With the rise of relatively inexpensive paperbound book publication, volumes especially on specific social problems have more and more commonly been written by sociologists for a popular, as well as a student, market. These contributions are becoming quite influential in policy-making with regard to urban tensions, race relations, housing, community planning, drug abuse, sexual problems, delinquency and crime, and mental deviation. Stuart Chase's *The Proper Study of Mankind*,[57] Vance Packard's *The Status Seekers*,[58] William H. Whyte's *The Organization Man*,[59] and Peter L. Berger's *Invitation to Sociology* are examples of the extent and the manner in which more general sociological theories and problems can be made attractive to popular audiences. Critics quarrel with these and other books of the sort on a variety of scores—superficiality, straining for literary effects, sensationalism—but they carry many sociological findings into general discussions and arouse interest in more systematic treatments.

It is difficult to characterize the tide of "sociological" novels, especially those by ethnic and black writers, which have done much to widen American social horizons. They have increased the challenge to sociologists to meet literary realism and vividness with ever more precise description and more basic and tenable analysis.[60]

SOCIOLOGISTS SERVING MAN. As we rush through the latter decades of the twentieth century, sociologists are serving man with more and more accurate perspectives on the individual in society, on groups and group processes, and on cultural and societal influence and change. They do this by providing information, theory, and counsel to educators, psychotherapists, social workers, social planners, and major policy-makers in government, business, and voluntary organizations. They do this by

[56] Published since 1952, 73 Eighth Avenue, Brooklyn, N.Y. 11215. It now consists of eight issues a year, plus an annual index, and covers books and articles published all over the world in many languages, arranged by specialties.

[57] Stuart Chase, *The Proper Study of Mankind*, rev. ed. (New York: Harper, 1956).

[58] Vance Packard, *The Status Seekers* (New York: David McKay, 1959). Subtitle: *An Exploration of Class Behavior in America and the Hidden Barriers That Affect You, Your Community, Your Future.*

[59] W. H. Whyte, Jr., *The Organization Man* (New York: Simon & Schuster, 1956).

[60] See Jacobs, *The Participant Observer;* Filstead, *Qualitative Methodology;* G. J. McCall and J. L. Simmons, eds., *Issues in Participant Observation* Reading, Mass.: Addison-Wesley, 1969).

bringing a broader societal perspective and a more integrated conception of human interrelationships to historians, social philosophers, political scientists, educational theorists, economists, anthropologists, and belletrists. They do this by furnishing serious popular writers of books, periodical articles, and newspaper columns with the data and theory with which to criticize and help modify traditional folk beliefs and policy theories. And they do this by their own public statements and their impact upon teachers and texts in all levels of our schools.

These opportunities for sociological service require firsthand knowledge of the arenas where both popular and special knowledge about humanity is most necessary. These arenas concern disciplines in addition to sociology. No scientific study of man is without its contribution to an understanding of human society. As cotrustees of the liberal-arts heritage of our universities and of the social philosophical heritage of the West in our society, all social scientists need to keep their eyes trained and to encourage their students to keep their eyes trained—as many of them already are—upon the great and pressing problems and challenges of man's life in contemporary society. Thus they can help create social sciences to serve the needs of man rather than to aid the manipulations of present and future elites and tyrants, such as those in Huxley's and Orwell's nightmares.[61]

[61] See Aldous Huxley, *Brave New World,* and George Orwell, *1984* (New York: Harcourt, Brace, 1949).

NOTE: Parts of this chapter were rewritten from A. McC. Lee, "Sociologists in an Integrating Society: Significance and Satisfaction in Sociological Work," *Social Problems,* II (1954–1955), 57–66, by permission of the Society for the Study of Social Problems.

CHAPTER II

Some Things People
Need to Know

Our young rebels cry out against an "establishment" that rules through "hypocrisy." Our militant blacks steel themselves to action against white racist "hypocrisy." Our more activist women prod their less concerned sisters of the majority sex to join in destroying the sexist "hypocrisy" through which men dominate society and exploit females.

The cry is an old one. Matthew quotes Jesus as saying, "Woe unto you, scribes and Pharisees, hypocrites! for ye make clean the outside of the cup and of the platter, but within they are full of extortion and excess." [1]

The term *hypocrite* derives from a Greek word meaning to mimic or to play a part. It has come to refer to a person who assumes a false appearance, who pretends "to be what he is not, or to feel or believe what he does not actually feel or believe; especially, a false pretender to virtue or piety." [2] Thus the clean "outside of the cup" hides such contrasting inwards as "extortion and excess." The alleged liberalism of the establishment in our society hides an exploitative "system" of which neocolonialism and neoimperialism are its worst excesses. White "liberalism" hides what amounts to a conspiracy of repression and exploitation against the blacks. Male plausibility hides male chauvinism.

Those are what the cries of dissent and the cries for reform are saying, but just what is hypocrisy as a societal phenomenon? How common is it? Why are people so surprised at being called hypocrites? What do those who revolt against hypocrisy say they are trying to accomplish? What are they likely to achieve?

[1] Matthew, 23: 25.
[2] *Century Dictionary* (New York: Century, 1914), III, 2954.

WE ARE ALL HYPOCRITES

Hypocrisy designates as ugly a characteristic all socialized human beings develop as they grow up and participate in a variety of social groups within any given society. Behind hypocrisy is multivalence, or many-valuedness, or even many-mindedness. More specifically, both sincerity and hypocrisy can arise from another person's multivalence: the "sincerity" you may like, and the "hypocrisy" you may fear as a threat to your emotional, intellectual, or economic security.

Pointing to this relationship of terms is not to be taken as an effort to apologize for outworn or overly rigid establishment values, racism, or sexism. It is an attempt to place the idea more squarely in the context of everyone's everyday human experiences. We are all hypocrites.

Society is multivalent. Any society, even quite a simple one, has a multiplicity of conflicting moral values. Our society has a complex establishment with its sets of values, and it also has youth groups, each of which flowers with a variation on the common societal stock of values. Segregation and exploitation have made white and black values contrast. The sexes partly mill around in one-sex social groups that reinforce their members' sex-related values.

Those contrasts in value orientation among relatively exclusive and somewhat homogeneous groups do not comprise the whole story of multivalence. Each individual, as he matures, is assimilated in turn into family, sibling, peer, and other groups, and each of these groups has its own rather distinct and contrasting value patterns embedded in a group culture. These early groups then become prototypes of later groups succeeding them in the adult world in which the expectation that we "act maturely" means that we "act like the rest of us" in the given group. The early groups are prototypes in the sense that habit patterns for action and belief typical of the group and taken on in the earlier group are assumed by maturing people to be subsequently appropriate for use in other similar groups, groups that are taken to be approximate successors to the prototype.

Boys playing freely with their friends do things they would never do before their siblings; their behavior would also appear even more strange or outrageous to their parents. A study of boys' play groups is helpful to achieve an understanding of a football team's spirit, an infantry squad's morale, a male poker-club's verbal patter, the formal and informal talk during a meeting of a corporation's salesmen, *but it does not tell much about how the same men function as husbands and fathers.* Thus people who grow up within any society and become somewhat normal participants in a range of its groups, with their contrasting value orientations, achieve unexceptional normality by becoming multivalent. Multivalent society requires its members to be multivalent. If a mono-valent society is possible, it has not at any rate been tried.[3]

VALUE CONFLICTS ARE NOW
MORE OBVIOUS

In less tense times and especially in the more tradition-encrusted societies, contrasts among group values—group cultures—are rarely per-ceived as a problem. Many times "social distance" obscures such con-trasts. Social distance refers to how people with contrasting values live and work in relatively close physical proximity and still are aware only superficially of what each other is like. It is social unawareness, ignor-ing, lack of empathy, nonparticipation. It permits white investment bank-ers to commute between Wall Street and Greenwich or Short Hills, even to be jovial with black employees or associates, and not really to be aware of the nature and significance of the worlds of Harlem or Newark through which they travel each workday.[4] When the contrasts are ap-parent, they are often rendered beyond question by ready-made rational-izations long present in societal and group cultures.

Class-ism, racism, and sexism are parts of those traditional culture-carried rationalizations. They are ancient rationalizations. They exhibit within them fossilized remains of tribalism. Such intergroup tension was once of "a primitive type based upon crude criteria, and expressed in murder and robbery of the alien" and the stealing of women. Now it extends "to many and variegated modes characteristic of civilized peo-ples, often based upon criteria equally crude, even if expressed, in gen-eral, in less violent ways."[5]

Questions we now confront are, How does it happen that these ancient rationalizations are now so subject to attack? After millennia of their employment as morale-builders and soporifics in intergroup relations and struggles, in social domination and exploitation, what is

[3] A. McC. Lee, *Multivalent Man* (New York: George Braziller, 1966), esp. Chaps. 1–7; see also P. A. Sorokin, *Society, Culture, and Personality* (New York: Harper, 1947), esp. Chap. 19.

[4] R. E. Park and E. W. Burgess, *Introduction to the Science of Sociology*, 2nd ed. (Chicago: University of Chicago Press, 1924), esp. pp. 282–87; E. T. Hiller, *Principles of Sociology* (New York: Harper, 1933), esp. pp. 252–63, and *Social Relations and Structures* (New York: Harper, 1947), pp. 640–45. See E. S. Bogardus's early effort to quantify "social distance" in *The New Social Research* (Los Angeles: Jesse Ray Miller, 1926), Chap. 10. For a recent summary of such quantification, see Michael Banton, *Race Relations* (New York: Basic Books, 1967), Chap. 13.

[5] W. G. Sumner and A. G. Keller, *The Science of Society* (New Haven: Yale University Press, 1927), I, 360–61.

making right now for the reexamination and revision of class-ism, racism, and sexism?

After all, our moral idealizations have always promised a great deal more to underdogs than many individuals and groups in preferred positions found it necessary to grant. Even until today, the following dictum of that great social observer and satirist of the mighty, Niccolò Machiavelli, is often verified so far as current behavior is concerned: ". . . for how we live is so far removed from how we ought to live, that he who abandons what is done for what ought to be done, will rather learn to bring about his own ruin than his preservation." [6] He did recognize, it needs to be added, that even without modern mass media prying into his affairs, a prince had to be able to disguise well his faithlessness, "to be a great feigner and dissembler." [7] Our societal morals are the clean "outside of the cup" that many times hides the "extortion and excess" a racism, class-ism, sexism, or whatever else might be within. We even have institutionalized and routinized large-scale moralistic feigning and dissembling in the activities of the so-called public-relations profession.

KNOWLEDGE FOR ACTION. These rather harsh descriptive statements are not meant to carry the impression that deception is "natural" and that it is thus difficult or impossible to change such behavior to something else. Gunnar Myrdal warns against such a conclusion when he criticizes many American social scientists for having what he calls a "naturalistic and, therefore, fatalistic philosophy" [8] or for permitting a functional description to "lead to a conservative teleology." [9]

In contrast with a merely descriptive approach to society, Myrdal makes a plea in social science for what can also be called "the clinical study of society." [10] This is an approach that owes much to the intimate observation of spontaneous behavior. It is the study of social groups and society at times when efforts are being made to change them. It focuses upon dynamics and discards static and functional approaches. It assigns only slight uses to such methods as opinion or so-called attitude surveys; instead, it is behavioral in the special sense that it stresses spontaneous reactions to efforts at reform or manipulation. From this approach one can learn a great deal about how society can be changed. This approach gets behind opinions and propaganda to what people are

[6] Niccolò Machiavelli, "The Prince," trans. by Luigi Ricci, rev. by E. R. P. Vincent, in *The Prince and the Discourses,* ed. by Max Lerner (New York: Modern Library, 1940), p. 56. See also F. Flora and C. Cordiè, eds., *Tutte le Opere di Niccolò Machiavelli* (Verona: Arnoldo Mondatori Editore, 1949), I, 48–49.

[7] *Ibid.,* p. 64.

[8] Gunnar Myrdal, *Value in Social Theory,* ed. by Paul Streeten (New York: Harper, 1958), p. 143.

[9] *Ibid.,* p. 151.

[10] Lee, *Multivalent Man,* Chap. 22.

actually doing and are likely to do. Regardless of what the approach might be called, it is essential to a more dynamic social science.

WHY A REVOLT NOW?

With that caveat in mind, let us turn again to the question about "why *now*" the revolution against the exploitation of differences in social values and viewpoints. The arts of feigning and dissembling as practiced by those in preferred positions in our society have not at all kept abreast with the march of literacy and popular education among the world's youth, nonwhites, and women. The masses are rising. They are invading vertically the citadels of power. Without those in preferred positions giving up a substantial part of their invidious social power and prestige, without their learning the arts of democratically representative leadership, they cannot now possibly keep abreast of that march, that invasion.

Public-relations word juggling no longer can cover credibility gaps between what a Presidential spokesman says and what is reported or eventually "seeps back" from the battlefront. It can no longer disguise efforts to cover up oil or fruit or steel or automobile power plays abroad and at home.[11] It can no longer maintain discredited union leaders in power.

As propagandas and manipulative maneuvers wear thinner and become more transparent, the stark need for more fundamental social reorganization becomes all the more pressing. Only with a redistribution of power and privilege in our society and throughout the world, only with greater egalitarianism and with more clearly representative social controls and controllers, can the current cries of dissent be stilled for any substantial period.

Television, sophisticated picture and news magazines, vivid "sociological" novels and short stories, stimulating "science" or "speculative" fiction,[12] a wealth of paperback exposés, reports, and symposia, the threat of the draft, implausibly explained undeclared wars, together with vast student enrollments, have combined to give us our most clear-eyed gen-

[11] Morton Mintz and J. S. Cohen, *America, Inc.* (New York: Dial, 1971); R. L. Heilbroner *et al.*, *In the Name of Profit* (New York: Doubleday, 1972); M. J. Green *et al.*, *The Closed Enterprise System* (New York: Grossman, 1972).

[12] Benjamin Appel, *Fantastic Mirror: Science Fiction Across the Ages* (New York: Pantheon, 1969); Bernard Rosenberg and D. M. White, eds., *Mass Culture* (Glencoe, Ill.: Free Press, 1959), pp. 187–224; Coulton Waugh, *The Comics* (New York: Macmillan, 1947); Frederic Wertham, *Seduction of the Innocent* (New York: Rinehart, 1954).

eration. What their professors do not, cannot, or will not teach them, they try to learn themselves. It is a generation on whom old rationalizations of inequality and inequity are more wasted than ever before. One need *not* look at our youth starry-eyed, as does Charles Reich in *The Greening of America,* and assert that they have reached a mystical and utopian stage, "Consciousness III," the spread of which will automatically solve all human problems.[13]

Our youth have no easy panacea, but they do carry a greater *leverage* for change than the immediately preceding generations. Admittedly, a few of them are highly publicized hippies and dropouts, drug addicts and members of what may be futile programs, but there are millions of others. The others in varying degrees are determined to help build a saner society less tied to war, less linked to colonialist exploitation, less enmeshed in inequality than was the society into which they were born. They have ideas about what such a difficult effort will cost them and society, but they also have ideas about how much they, their future families, and their society will gain from that effort. A great many of them want to make the effort regardless of the initial cost. They want our occupancy of spaceship Earth to continue and to become less painful for more of their fellow passengers.[14]

What we are seeing then is the growing impact of people no longer so enshrouded as were their predecessors in "social distance." Time was when a famine in China or a disastrous flood in Pakistan was a ho-hum news story of little moment in the United States. Today we can almost smell the stench of rotting human bodies, and we do hear the whimper of a starving child in our own living room. We see police dogs turned upon dissenting Americans. We see battles between police or National Guardsmen and students on our own college campuses. We are practically at the sickening spectacles of our national political party conventions with their classical degradations of democracy. We see *real* bullets hit *real* people—not actors—and see them *die.* We are at press conferences that are much more believably revealing of credibility gaps than are even brilliant pieces of journalistic candor.

How far can the destruction of social distance be carried? To what extent will its destruction continue to mean a growth in social empathy and understanding among the groups in our society and world? These are some of the things that we need to know. These are some of the things that inquiring social scientists should now be studying so that they can help us to guide social policy.

[13] Charles Reich, *The Greening of America* (New York: Random House, 1970).
[14] Garrett de Bell, ed., *The Environmental Handbook* (New York: Ballantine, 1970).

THE REVOLT AGAINST
MULTIVALENCE

How far can the revolt against societal multivalence go? To what extent are we likely to continue to preserve and to try to live by and with such fossils of tribalism as intergroup hostility, otherwise called group-centrism or group-egotism or ethnocentrism?[15] Apologists for group-egotism praise its contribution to the participant individual's sense of identity with one specific part of a pluralistic society.[16] But what of its costs in intergroup hostility, exploitation, and bloodshed? Think of the untold millions of African blacks, American Indians, Arabs, Armenians, Basques, Bretons, French Canadians, French Huguenots, Indian Indians, Irish dissenters, Irish Roman Catholics, Jews, Poles, Scots, Sicilians, Welsh, and so many other ethnic groups who have died or lived in deprivation because of their group identity! Social scientists, a brief list of propositions and questions that appear to be much more that we need to learn.[17]

How far can the revolt against individual multivalence go? Our youth are questioning not only intergroup differences in value, with their consequent hostilities and exploitations, but also our internalizations of those differences, with consequent hypocrisy and "mature" rationalizations of inconsistencies in belief and action. Psychiatrists, psychologists, cultural anthropologists, and sociologists, as well as biographers and novelists, poets and short-story writers, have explored aspects of this situation, but there is much more for us to learn. No simple pathway to the alleged monovalence of a bigot or a saint appears to be the answer. Individual multivalence has not been inspected as fully and as objectively

[15] G. P. Murdock, "Ethnocentrism," *Encyclopaedia of the Social Sciences,* (New York: Macmillan, 1931), V, 613–14; D. J. Levinson, "The Study of Ethnocentric Ideology," Chap. 4 in T. W. Adorno *et al., The Authoritarian Personality* (New York: Harper, 1950); John Dollard, "Hostility and Fear in Social Life," *Social Forces,* XVII (1938), 15–26; T. F. Pettigrew, "Personality and Sociocultural Factors in Intergroup Attitudes: A Cross-National Comparison," *Journal of Conflict Resolution,* II (1958), 29–42.

[16] H. M. Kallen *et al., Cultural Pluralism and the American Idea* (Philadelphia: University of Pennsylvania Press, 1956); M. M. Gordon, *Assimilation in American Life* (New York: Oxford University Press, 1964), pp. 13–18, 132–59, 239–45, 261–65.

[17] Gustavus Myers, *History of Bigotry in the United States,* ed. and rev. by H. M. Christman (New York: Capricorn, 1960); H. S. Commager, ed., *The Struggle for Racial Equality* (New York: Harper & Row, 1967); Jacques Barzun, *Race: A Study in Superstition,* rev. ed. (New York: Harper & Row, 1965); T. F. Gossett, *Race: The History of an Idea in America* (Dallas, Texas: Southern Methodist University Press, 1963); Banton, *Race Relations,* provides international comparisons; Philip Mason, *Race Relations* (London: Oxford University Press, 1970), offers a brief, scholarly summary of facts, theories, and issues; L. H. Masotti *et al., A Time to Burn? An Evaluation of the Present Crisis in Race Relations* (Chicago: Rand McNally, 1969).

—as irreverently—as it now should be. This is still another matter on which social scientists can help people.

CURRENT CHALLENGES TO SOCIAL SCIENTISTS

In addition to the revolt of youth, blacks, and women against the class-ist, racist, and sexist implications of entrenched societal multi-valence, what other pressing symptoms of coming social reorganization are upon us? What are other things that people need to know about and on which social scientists have provided some aid but can dig for much more? Here are some of these more basic current challenges to social scientists, a brief list of propositions and questions that appear to be emerging from social inquiry and societal conflict at the present time.

1. Man is finite, fallible, adaptable, and he lives in what amounts to a closed "system," spaceship Earth. Does this mean that his self-destruction is as predictable as that of yeast plants in a bottle of ferment-ing grape juice? Man, like yeast, pollutes his environment. When yeast plants have converted sufficient grape juice into wine alcohol, the yeast die. Will man's belated but still possible assimilation of science into his social patterns of thought make the difference? [18]

2. Culture is durable, multivalent, useful when adapted to life conditions, and destructive of its carriers when it is crystallized and thus unadapting. Can a culture be kept from a deadening crystallization? How can a crystallizing culture have the breath of life—change—again suffused into it? [19]

3. No group or groups can provide leadership in a society without depending upon popular acceptance of appropriate myths. Do all myths, even those associated with democracy, wear out? How? Can they be revived? How? Do all individuals and groups in positions of control forget their dependence upon the credibility of a myth? [20]

4. Man can only thrive when he has *verifiable* life myths with which to organize, dramatize, and embroider his routines. How many ways of

[18] De Bell, *The Environmental Handbook;* Robert and Leona T. Rienow, *Moment in the Sun* (New York: Dial, 1967); American Friends Service Committee, *Who Shall Live? Man's Control Over Birth and Death* (New York: Hill & Wang, 1970); Jacques Ellul, *The Technological Society,* trans. by John Wilkinson (New York: Vintage Books, 1964), presents a technique-determinist view of our past and future.

[19] A good start for an exploration of this topic is A. L. Kroeber, *Anthropology,* rev. ed. (New York: Harcourt, Brace & World, 1948), Chaps. 9 and 10; Peter Farb, *Man's Rise to Civilization* (New York: E. P. Dutton, 1968), based upon North American Indian history and ethnography.

[20] See Walter Lippmann, *Public Opinion* (New York: Macmillan, 1922); M. E. Olsen, ed., *Power in Societies* (New York: Macmillan, 1970).

verifying those myths now appear to be acceptable? Can an existential-humanist social science furnish such a process of verification and also of modification, a kind of perpetual basis for myth renewal? How scientifically defensible can such verification become? [21] As this book attempts to indicate in considerable detail, that process can be carried a long way through the development of an existential-humanist social science. It may be our one chance for survival.

5. Social change rarely finds expression in changed symbols, but it often does in the redefinition of existing symbols. How tenably can our treasured symbols now be reinterpreted so that they can continue to serve as tokens of a viable society? Is the effort worth it? Or must we just wait and face the kind of cataclysm in which old symbols get brushed aside and replaced with a "new" set? [22]

6. Social change is a tricky matter. Faith that it always takes place with sedate gradualism is misplaced. Even when things appear to remain the same, subtle or even fundamental changes may well be in the making or well on their way.[23] When changes do come, they can be quite dramatic, and even revolutionary. Can we learn more about social change in its many paces and manifestations—not so that we may foolishly try to forestall it, but rather, so that we may learn how more wisely to welcome it and to live with it?

[21] Herbert Blumer, *Symbolic Interactionism: Perspective and Method* (Englewood Cliffs, N.J.: Prentice-Hall, 1969), esp. Chaps. 1, 8–10.

[22] As the historian J. H. Plumb has put it, "Knowledge and understanding should not end in negation, but in action." (*The Death of the Past* [Boston: Houghton Mifflin, 1969], p. 106.) He adds [p. 145], "The old past is dying, its force weakening, and so it should. Indeed, the historian should speed it on its way, for it was compounded of bigotry, of national vanity, of class domination. . . . May history step into its shoes, help to sustain man's confidence in his destiny, and create for us a new past as true, as exact, as we can make it, that will help us achieve our destiny, not as Americans or Russians, Chinese or Britons, black or white, rich or poor, but as men."

[23] In speaking of the adaptation of constitutional interpretation to societal change, Justice W. O. Douglas notes that justices "like Brandeis, Cardozo, Hughes, Murphy, Stone and Rutledge . . . knew that all life is change and that law must be constantly renewed if the pressures of society are not to build up to violence and revolt." (*An Almanac of Liberty* [Garden City, N.Y.: Doubleday, 1964], p. 104). See also P. A. Sorokin, *Society, Culture, and Personality* (New York: Harper, 1947), esp. Chaps. 28–34, 39–47; H. G. Barnett, *Innovation: The Basis of Cultural Change* (New York: McGraw-Hill, 1953), esp. Chap. 14; Robert Boguslaw, *The New Utopians: A Study of System Design and Social Change* (Englewood Cliffs, N.J.: Prentice-Hall, 1965), esp. Chap. 8.

Index

A–B–C pattern, 148, 154
Abnormality, 120, 168, 169
Abortions, 73
Abraham, C. M., xiv
Absolutes, 162, 166, 168
Academic certification, 82, 88–89, 114
Academic hierarchies, 76, 134, 141, 181
Academic rationalizations, 83
Accidents, automobile, 177
Adamic, Louis, 150
Adams, J. P., 51
Adams, Walter, 12
Addicts Anonymous, 30
Adler, Franz, 176
Administration, 74, 90, 131, 151, 184, 186, 188
Adorno, T. W., 208
Advertising, 18, 68, 95, 143, 149–51, 154, 158, 186
Advocacy services, 153
Albig, William, 140
Albini, J. L., 42, 171
Alcoholics Anonymous, 30
Alexander, E. H., 186
Alienation, 48, 55, 57–65
Alienist, 57, 59
Alpervitz, Gar, 130
Alsop, Stewart, 81
Altstein, Sadie, xiv
American Arbitration Association, 47
American Association of University Professors, 152
American Civil Liberties Union (ACLU), 152
American Friends Service Committee (AFSC), 84, 93, 209
American Psychological Association, 136

American Sociological Association (ASA), 107, 136, 199
American Sociological Society (ASS), 134, 136–37
American Sociologist, 107
Amerindians, 45, 74, 93, 95, 208–9
Anarchism, 91, 116–17, 132
Anderson, C. H., xiv
Anderson, Harold, 186
Anomie, 58
Anthropology, 104, 128, 135, 178, 192, 197, 201, 208
"Anti-family society," 72–73
Anti-intellectualism, 11–14, 114
Apologists, 113–14
Appeal, 148, 154–56, 158
Appeasement, 157, 159
Appel, Benjamin, 206
Aptheker, Herbert, 46
Arabs, 208
Arendt, Hannah, 45, 80
Arensberg, C. M., 40, 165
Argow, W. W., 155
Argumentum:
  ad hominem, 148
  ad ignorantiam, 149
  ad invidiam, 149
  ad verecundiam, 148–49
Argyle, Michael, 66
Aristotle, 58, 110, 123
Armenians, 208
Aron, Raymond, 4
Aronson, Elliot, 48, 68, 69, 147, 149, 154, 189, 193
Aronson, S. H., 137
Art, 55, 69, 95, 168
Artists, 66, 72, 74, 94, 96, 101, 109

Asbury Park, N.J., 50–51
Aspirations, 101, 108, 117
Associated Press (AP), 189–90
Atlantic Monthly, 198
Auchincloss, Kenneth, 158
Audiences, 149–54, 198–99
Authoritarianism, 67, 79–80, 85, 100, 118,
    164, 183, 187
Autobiography, 35–36
Automation, 58, 84
Autonomy, 5, 12–15, 21, 55, 58, 63, 76–
    77, 79, 89, 93, 96, 102–11, 124, 126–
    27, 132–33, 136, 176, 188–89
Aveling, Edward, xi, 4
Avorn, J. L., 146

Babbitt, Irving, xiv
Baillie, J. B., 57
Bales, R. F., 33
Baltzly, A., 79
Balzac, Honoré de, 39
Band-wagon techniques, 148–49
Banton, Michael, 204, 208
Barber, Bernard, 6, 123, 186
Barnes, H. E., x, 8, 70, 80, 81, 128
Barnett, H. G., 168, 210
Barritt, D. P., xiv
Barron, M. L., xiv, 24
Barth, Karl, xiii
Bartlett, F. C., 140
Barzun, Jacques, 208
Basques, 208
Beals, R. L., 176
Bean, L. L., 169
Beard, C. A., x, 81, 131, 132
Beard, M. R., 131
Beauvoir, Simone de, xi
Becker, Ernest, 9
Becker, Howard, 8, 70, 128
Bell, Daniel, 23, 58, 113, 114, 171, 186
Bell, Garrett de, 207, 209
Belletrists, 128–29, 201, 208
Bellush, Jewell, 73, 195
Bender, Joseph, xiv
Bendix, Reinhardt, 82, 106, 107
Benedict, Ruth, 128
Benét, S. V., 102
Benigni, Umberto, 115, 140
Bennis, W. G., 50, 90
Berelson, Bernard, 68, 121, 140, 156
Berger, J., 125
Berger, P. L., 66, 70, 116, 118, 129, 199
Berger, S. D., 195
Berkeley Journal of Sociology, 110
Berkman, Alexander, 91
Berkowitz, Leonard, 83, 172
Berle, A. A., Jr., 130
Bernays, E. L., 140, 146
Biases, 130, 140
Biddle, B. J., 32
Bierstedt, Robert, 129
Big lie, 157, 159
Big tent, 157–59

Billington, R. A., 46
Binzen, Peter, 173
Biographies, 70, 208
Birth control, 73
Birth rate, 56, 73
Black, Hillel, 171
Blackburn, T. R., 13
Black Muslims, 30
Black Panthers, 30
Black revolts, 20, 46, 93, 113, 130, 138,
    151
Blacks, 46, 48, 51, 63, 71–72, 74, 83, 95,
    100, 154, 156, 159, 178, 200, 202,
    204, 208
Blumberg, A. S., xiv, 67, 171, 194
Blumenstock, Dorothy, 140
Blumer, Herbert, x, xiv, 5, 9, 126–27, 147,
    154, 156, 183, 210
Boas, Franz, 108, 128
Boccaccio, Giovanni, xii
Bock, P. K., 40, 165, 178
Bodart, G., 79
Boeth, Richard, 67
Boffey, P. M., 13
Bogardus, E. S., 204
Bogart, E. L., 80
Boguslaw, Robert, 210
Bonaparte, M., 14
Bond, 148
Booth, Arthur, 19
Boring from within, 146
Bottomore, T. B., 58
Boulding, K. E., 23, 176
Bouma, Donald, 49
Bourne, P. G., 71
Bowers, R. V., 106
Boyd, Andrew, 17
Bradford, L. P., 50
Brady, R. A., 81
Brainwashing, 23, 68–70, 121
Brandeis, L. D., 210
Bretons, 208
Bribes, 152, 170
Broom, Leonard, 196
Brown et al. v. *Board of Education of
    Topeka, Kansas,* 192
Brutalization, 57, 93, 158
Buchanan, R. H., xiv
Burch, W. R., Jr., xiv
Burckhardt, Jakob, 107
Bureaucracy, 3, 21, 104, 126, 185
Bureaucratization, 100, 113, 124–25
Bureaucrats, 66, 104, 106–9, 127, 129,
    144, 188
Burgess, E. W., x, 123, 126, 136, 137,
    204
Burke, Kenneth, 57
Burnham, David, 57
Bury, J. B., 4, 60
Business, 55–56, 181, 190, 200
    planning, 186
    technicians, 186
    (*see* Capital)
Byrne, Donn, 193

Cabell, J. B., 132
Califano, J. A., Jr., 173
Calley, William, 158
Camus, Albert, xi
Canadians, French, 208
Cannell, C. F., 33
Capital, 118, 131, 157 (*see* Business)
Cardozo, B. N., 210
Carnegie Commission on Educational Television, 189
Carnegie Commission on Higher Education, 184
Carnegie Corporation, 125
Cartwright, Dorwin, 32
Case, C. M., 128
Case-making, 149
Casey, R. D., 140
Catalyst, 110
Catchwords, 58, 64
Caudill, H. M., 195
Censorship, 157, 159
Certainty, quest for, 161–62
Chafee, Zechariah, Jr., 87
Chall, L. P., xvi, 120
Change of pace, 157–58
Chapin, F. S., 33, 128
Chapman, S. H., xiv, 17, 119, 137
Charisma, 36, 97, 175–76
Chase, M. T., 48
Chase, Stuart, 48, 200
Chevigny, Paul, 194
Chicago Commission on Race Relations, 46
Chicago Sun, 190
Child rearing, 25, 74, 168
Children, 65, 71–75
Chomsky, Noam, 91, 132, 146, 173
Christianity, 79, 116, 118
Christman, H. M., 162, 208
Chugerman, Samuel, 35
Churches, 66, 79, 140, 147, 152, 168, 181, 183
Cicourel, A. V., 33
Civil War, 46, 130
Clark, K. B., xiv, 47, 83, 192–94
Clarke, A. C., 23
Clemens, S. L., x, 39
Clews, J. C., 115
Clinard, M. B., 93, 169, 171, 183
Clinical study of society, 22, 32, 43–52, 54, 155, 205
Cohen, J. S., 130, 206
Coleman, J. S., 125
Colfax, J. D., xiv, 167
Collier, John, 45
Commager, H. S., 208
Commission on Freedom of the Press, 189–91
Commission on Human Relations, 48
Common man, 85, 88, 92, 95–96, 148
Common sense, 69, 115
Communications, 49, 54, 56, 91, 115, 127, 134, 148, 160 (*see* Mass communications)

Communications media, 65, 143, 145, 149–54
Communism, 70, 91–92, 132, 146, 154, 157–58
Communities, 42, 48, 50–51, 59, 66, 73–74, 76, 97, 122, 129, 147, 178, 196
Community Confrontation & Communication Associates (CCCA), 48–49
Compromise, 83–84, 101, 159
Computerization, 21–23, 76, 125, 185
Comte, Auguste, 4, 8
Conformism, 67–68, 99–100, 111, 116–17, 156
Confrontations, organized, 47–52, 78, 159
Connell, K. H., xiv
Connery, D. S., 17
Conspiracy, 15–17, 132, 202
Consultants, 61, 76, 92, 129, 133, 143, 188
Content analysis, 147–49, 157, 189
Controversy, 83, 106, 164, 166
Cook, F. J., 14, 171
Cookson, John, 78
Cooley, C. H., x, 35–36, 76, 108, 127–28
Co-optation, 51–52
Copernican paradigm, 123
Cordiè, C., 205
Coser, L. A., 133, 198
Cottrell, L. S., Jr., 196
Courtiers, 87–98, 133–34
Cowan, Antonia, 60
Cowan, J. C., 198
Cowgill, D. O., 193
Crane, Diana, 6
Creativity, 2, 12–14, 21, 40–41, 55, 64, 94–96, 102, 109, 129, 168, 198
Credibility gap, 129, 159, 207, 209
Cressey, D. R., 171–72
Crime, criminals, 41, 51, 64, 72, 93, 120, 135, 166, 168–72, 202
    organized, 164, 171 (*see* Mafia)
    white-collar, 135, 170
Criminal law, 93, 170
Criminology, 120
Crisis:
    ideological, 122, 130–33
    social, 130–33, 138
Criticism, 53, 75, 86, 110, 121, 133, 152, 166–67, 181, 187–96, 201
Cromwell, Oliver, 175
Cross-cultural comparisons, 59, 162, 169
Culture:
    group, 68, 82, 85, 102, 104, 112, 138, 178, 203–4 (*see* Subcultures)
    mass, 55, 64, 67, 69, 97, 197
    multivalent, 116–17
    play, 26
    popular, 53, 84, 138, 155, 198
    societal, 68, 92, 102, 104, 112, 117, 142, 154, 162, 197, 204, 209
Culture shock 40–41, 165–66, 177
Curiosity, 76–77, 170, 182
Curtis, L. P., Jr., 16
Cutler, J. E., 46

Cutlip, S. M., 145
Cybernetics, 125

Darwin, Charles, 14
Darwin, Francis, 14
Data-retrieval systems, 33, 56, 76
Daughters of the American Revolution, 30
Davie, M. R., x, 46, 81, 102, 107, 121, 128–29, 187
Davis, Jerome, 128
Dawson, C. A., 128
Deaths, 78, 113
  accidental, 78, 177
  military, 78, 80
Deetz, James, 32
Definition, trap of, 113–15
Dehumanization, 1–2, 4, 7, 79, 134–36, 186
Delinquents, 64, 72, 74, 120, 200
  juvenile, 170
Democracy, 79, 88, 97, 99–102, 118, 127–28, 130, 133, 136, 148, 154, 160, 209
  humanist, 131–32
  participatory, 7, 43–45, 89, 91, 93, 110, 162, 198, 206–7
Demonstrations, 43–44, 78
Demos, G. D., 198
Denzin, N. K., xiv, 176, 185
Deprivation, relative, 64, 74, 117, 208
"Destroyers," 50
Deutscher, Irwin, 183
"Deviant" behavior, 67, 109, 120, 169
Devlin, Bernadette, 17
Dewey, John, x, 10, 20, 76, 99–100, 128, 161–62
Dickens, Charles, 39
Dickson, Paul, 177
Dictatorship, 87, 97, 132
Dinitz, Simon, 194
Disch, Robert, 15
Disinvolvement, 57, 59
Dissent, 100, 166, 206–7
Doctoral dissertations, 126
Dodd, Martha, 81
Dodd, W. E., 81
Dodd, W. E., Jr., 81
Dolci, Danilo, xiv, 41–45, 51, 60, 171
Dollard, John, 127, 208
Domhoff, G. W., 132
Doob, L. W., 140
Dorfman, Joseph, 35
Dostoevski, F. M., 39
Douglas, W. O., 210
Dovring, Karin, 140
Downs, Anthony, 24
Dramaturgy, 70, 125
Dreiser, Theodore, 132
Driessen, Gerald, 177
Driver, E. D., 169
Dropouts, 63, 93, 207
Drugs, 51, 56, 66, 74, 164, 207
DuBois, R. D., 48

Dunham, Barrows, 10
Dunham, H. W., 127
Dupertuis, C. W., 16
Durkheim, Émile, 60, 108, 128
Dynamic relationism, 115–16

Earle, E. M., 100
Eastern Union of Radical Sociologists Newsletter, 110
Ecology, 56, 72, 159
Edman, Irving, 6, 88
Education, 1, 3, 9–14, 16, 23–27, 33–35, 42, 44, 53, 57, 63–64, 69, 71, 73, 79, 91, 94, 99–100, 105, 113, 115, 118, 121, 133–34, 140–41, 151, 159, 162–63, 168, 173, 179, 181–82, 184, 197, 200–201
Edwards, O. D., 16, 71
Egalitarianism, 84, 162, 206
Ehrlich, Anne, 63
Ehrlich, Paul, 63
Einstein, Albert, 2, 14, 123
Eisenhower, D. D., 7, 11, 175
Elites, 55, 64, 69, 83, 87, 90–92, 94, 97–98, 110, 112, 132, 198, 201
Elitism 87–91, 127, 197
Ellis, Havelock, 120
Ellul, Jacques, 69, 115, 121, 140, 209
Elman, R. M., 194
Emery, Edwin, 190
Emotion, 95, 155, 203
Empathy, 47–48, 160, 177–79, 204, 207
Employment, 25–27, 44, 65, 74, 135, 172–73
Encyclopaedia Britannica, Inc., 190
Engels, Friedrich, 91, 114
Engineering, 72, 152, 184, 187
England, R. W., Jr., 172
English, 66, 71, 83, 97, 180, 198
Engstrom, E. W., 186
Enterprise, 94, 104–6, 109
  free, 97–98, 118
Entrepreneurs, 94, 96, 106–8, 117, 126, 128, 130, 141, 143–44, 146, 188
Environment, 2, 57, 66, 78, 95–96, 110, 113, 117, 156, 186, 209
Epicurus, 110
Epstein, B. B., 16
Erasmus, Desiderius, xii
Erikson, E. H., 102–3, 128
"Establishment" circles, 47, 61, 71, 133, 158, 176, 183, 203
Ethic, Protestant, 118
Ethical norms, 162, 185, 197
Ethnic groups, 15–17, 40–41, 51, 74, 81, 90, 93, 105, 108–9, 149, 154, 156, 167, 170, 178–79, 200, 208
Ethnocentrism, 10, 15–17, 208
Ethnology, 187
Ethnomethodology, 125
Etzioni, Amitai, 173, 195
Eupsychian management, 62
Eurich, Alvin, 184

Existential humanists, 5, 127, 132, 181
Existentialism, x–xii, 31, 55, 112, 129, 210
Experience, 28–30, 41, 69, 75, 162
Exploitation, 46, 57, 63, 74, 129, 185, 188, 202–4, 207
Extermination camps, 80

Façade, societal, 175, 179
Fairchild, H. P., 62
"False consciousness," 114
Family, 56, 65, 71–75, 119, 168, 203
Fann, K. T., 195
Farb, Peter, 209
Faris, R. E. L., 127
Farley, Reynolds, 193
Fascism, 97, 132
Faunce, W. A., 58
Faustian compromises, 133, 174–75
Fava, S. F., 120, 137, 195
Fay, S. B., 80
Federal Communications Commission (FCC), 189
Federal Data Center, 66
Federal Office of War Information, 150
"Fellow travelers," 144–45
Ferracuti, Franco, 82
Ferrarotti, Franco, xiv, 106, 117
Ferry, W. H., 130
Fetterman, John, 195
Feuer, L. S., 173
Field, Marshall, 190
Fieldhouse, D. K., 173
Filler, Louis, 132
Filstead, W. J., 183, 200
Finer, Herman, 94
Flora, F., 205
Foley, Donald, 195
Folk theories, 46–47, 75, 117–19, 196, 201
Foote, N. N., xiv
Ford Foundation, 47
Forster, Arnold, 16
Fosdick, H. E., 79
Foundations, 55, 94, 134, 146, 152–53, 185
Fournier, Elizabeth, xiv
France, Anatole, 39
Franco, Francisco, 85
Freedom, 14–15, 65, 131
Freud, Anna, 14
Freud, E. L., 14
Freud, Sigmund, 14, 95, 108, 120
Freudianism, 62, 118
Fried, Morton, 80–81
Friedrich, C. J., 31, 95
Friedrichs, R. W., 105–6, 110, 185
Friends, Religious Society of, 48
Fritzsche, Hellmut, 13
Fromm, Erich, xiii, 58–59, 62
Fronts, 144, 146
Fulbright, J. W., 11–12, 20, 146
Fuller, Buckminster, 22

Functional analysis, 124–25, 128, 205
Functional-systemic paradigm, 126

Gagnon, J. H., 194
Gamesmanship, intellectual, 69, 129, 188
Gandhi, M. K., 2, 41, 79, 175
Gans, H. J., 195
Gardner, Burleigh, 186
Gardner, Ernest, 13
Garfinkel, Harold, 125
Geis, Gilbert, 171
Geismar, Maxwell, 132
Generation gap, 23–26, 129, 163
Gentlemen's agreements, 159, 170
Gerth, H. H., 60, 106, 175
Gerver, Israel, 187
Gettys, W. E., 128
Gibbon, Edward, 110
Gilfillan, S. C., 168
Ginsberg, Morris, 4, 61
Ginzberg, Eli, 23
Gitlin, Todd, 173
Gladwin, Thomas, 173, 195
Glass, J. F., 64, 166
Glazer, Nathan, 193
Glittering generalities, 64, 143
Goeller, B. F., 177
Goffman, Erving, 70, 125
Goheen, R. F., 184
Goldaber, Irving, xiv, 33, 41, 45, 48–51
Goldman, Emma, 91
Goldsby, R. A., 15
Golembiewski, R. T., 32
Good, Paul, 195
Goode, W. J., 35
Goodman, Paul, 91
Gordon, Leonard, 193
Gordon, M. M., 15, 74, 194, 208
Gordon, R. L., 179
Gorer, Geoffrey, 66
Gossett, T. F., 15, 46, 208
Gossip, 150–51
Gottman, Jean, 74
Gould, Julius, 114, 162
Gouldner, A. W., 11, 54, 62, 105–6, 125, 167
Graham, J. A., 32
Green, M. J., 146, 206
Green, Philip, 80
Greer, Scott, 73, 195
Grimshaw, A. D., 46
Gross, Llewellyn, 125
Group conversation method, 48
Group dynamics, 62, 183, 203
Groups, 32–33, 42, 47, 57, 68, 104, 120, 147, 199, 203–4, 209
    adversary, 49
    peer, 142, 196
    "problem," 61
Guérin, Daniel, 91, 132
Guilt by association, 149
Guilt by heredity, 149
Gumplowicz, Ludwig, 128

Hacker, Andrew, 130
Hadden, J. K., 74
Hallowell, A. I., 128
Hamilton, Alexander, 100
Hamilton, C. V., 12
Hamilton, W. H., 87
Hammond, P. E., 33
Hampden-Turner, Charles, 114
Handel, Gerald, 169
Hardin, Garrett, 167
Hare, A. P., 32
Harris, Marvin, 32, 80, 82
Hausknecht, M., 73, 195
Hawkins, Gordon, 171–72
Hedges, J. B., 46
Hegel, G. F. W., 57, 59, 81
Heidegger, Martin, xi
Heilbronner, R. L., 206
Heisenberg, Werner, 161
Heiss, Jerold, 195
Heizer, R. F., 32
Heller, C. S., 17
Henderson, Howard, xiv
Henderson, L. J., 6
Henderson, L. T., xiv
Henry, Frances, 179
Heresy, 114, 116
Herman, E. S., 71
Hersh, S. M., 71, 80
Herskovits, M. J., 11, 46
Heuristics, 110
Hiller, E. T., 204
Himelhoch, Jerome, 120, 137
Hinsie, L. E., 59
Hippies, 56, 67, 207
History, 3–4, 64, 78, 81, 116, 128, 131, 162, 197
Hitler, Adolf, 81, 85, 88, 157, 175
Hobsbawm, Eric, 172
Hodges, D. C., 195
Hoffman, Abbie, 69
Hoffman, Robert, 91
Hofstadter, Richard, 45, 114, 152
Holden, David, 17
Hollander, Nanci, 173
Holsti, O. R., 149, 189
Homans, George, 124
Homes, 56, 65, 71–75, 173, 178
Hooton, E. A., 16
Hopkins, Jeannette, 194
Horowitz, David, 146
Horowitz, I. L., 11, 38, 105, 107, 132, 146, 173, 176, 188
Hot potato, 157
Hoult, T. F., 193
Hovland, C. I., 126
Howe, R. L., 48
Hughes, C. E., 210
Hughes, E. C., 64
Hughes, H. MacG., 191
Huguenots, French, 208
Hull, Raymond, 24
Hulme, T. E., 60
Hulse, F. S., 32

Human Factor, The, 110
Humanism, ix–xiv, 4, 7, 30–31, 55, 76, 91, 112, 126–32, 181, 210
Humanist-existential paradigm, 124, 128–29, 133–34, 138
Human relations, 49, 59, 62, 70, 96–97, 129, 132
Human resources, 26–27, 43, 59, 97, 147, 158, 160–61
Human survival, 9, 27, 96, 110
Hummel, William, 149
Humor, 159, 199
Humphrey, N. D., 46–47
Huntress, Keith, 149
Hutchins, R. M., 190–91
Hutchinson, John, 171
Hutchinson, R. E., 32
Hutter, Mark, xiv
Huxley, Aldous, 42, 182, 186, 201
Hypocrisy, 91, 129, 163, 202–4, 208

Ibsen, Henrik, 39
Ickes, H. L., 191
Identification techniques, 149
Identity, 59, 108, 155, 180, 208
Ideologies, 5, 84, 87, 89, 95, 97, 112–43, 148, 157, 166, 181, 186
  dimensions of, 119
  multiplicity of, 116–17
  sociological, 122–38
  trap of, 113
  types of, 119
Immigrants, 64, 102, 178
Indeterminacy, principle of, 161
Indians (of India), 45, 208
Individualism, 99–100, 111
Individuals, 2, 28–52, 61, 103
Indochinese Undeclared War, 63, 70–71, 172, 177
Infeld, L., 14
Information explosion, 56, 65, 75–77
Innovation, 2, 12–14, 21, 25–26, 67, 71–72, 79, 94, 136
Innovators, 42, 101, 105, 107–10, 133, 166, 168, 198
Insanity, 57–59
Institute for Propaganda Analysis, 121
Institute for Social Research, 186
Instrumentalism, 2–3, 29
Insurgent Sociologist, The, 110
Intellectualism, 89, 114, 130, 132, 203
Intellectuals, 31, 35–36, 60, 69, 76, 87–89, 91, 95–96, 100, 113–15, 121, 132, 172, 197
  free, 75–76
Intelligence, 82, 162
Intrauterine device (IUD), 56, 73
Invasion, vertical, 95, 110, 138
Investigators, 55, 67, 115
Irish dissenters, 208
Irish Roman Catholics, 208
Italian-Americans, 171
Italians, 51

Jackson, H. H., 45
Jacobs, Glenn, xiv, 9, 183, 200
Jacobs, Jane, 73
Jaffe, Adrian, 12
Jahoda, Gerald, 76
James, William, x, 76, 108, 128
Jandy, E. C., 36
Janowitz, Morris, 121, 140, 156
Japanese, 85
Jaspan, Norman, 171
Jaspers, Karl, xi
Jay, John, 100
Jefferson, Thomas, x, 2, 99–100, 111, 154
Jennings, H. H., xiv
Jesus, 79, 147, 202
Jewish Defense League, 30
Jews, 80, 116, 208
John XXIII, 2
Jorgensen, B. B., xiv
Josephson, Eric, 61, 195
Josephson, Mary, 61, 195
Josephy, Alvin, 45
Journalists, 114, 126, 132, 143, 150, 171–72, 174, 199, 207
Junior League, 30

Kafka, Franz, xi
Kafka, Fritz, 33
Kahn, Herman, 80
Kahn, R. L., 33
Kallen, H. M., 17, 119, 208
Kalven, Harry, Jr., 66
Kardiner, Abram, 128
Katz, Daniel, 71, 140, 154, 156
Kellen, Konrad, 69, 115
Keller, A. G., 69, 81, 127, 130, 187, 198, 204
Keller, Suzanne, 73
Kelley, H. H., 48
Kelly, Walt, 5
Kemeny, J. G., 125
Kennedy, Daniel, xiv
Kennedy, J. F., 99
Kennedy, R. F., 56
Kent, D. P., 102
Kerensky, A. F., 88
Kierkegaard, Søren, xi
Kiernan, V. G., 15, 82
King, M. L., Jr., 2, 41, 71, 79
Kingsley, R. E., 100
Kinsey, A. C., 120
Klopper, Mary, 91, 132
Kluckhohn, Clyde, 162
Knebel, Fletcher, 51
Knudten, R. D., 194
Kolb, W. L., 114, 162
Konvitz, M. R., 87
Kosa, John, xiv, 36, 67, 102, 176, 195
Kreps, Juanita, 24
Kris, Ernst, 14
Kroeber, A. L., 11, 108–10, 128, 209
Kuhn, T. S., 122–23
Ku Klux Klan, 30

Labor, 65, 69, 73–74, 92, 95, 121, 131, 142
"Laboratory Confrontation," 48–52
Laboratory work, 31–33
La Feber, Walter, 130
Laing, R. D., 169
Landesco, John, 171
Lang, Daniel, 71
Lantz, H. R., 133
Larson, Arthur, 80
Larson, C. L., 74
Laslett, Peter, 63
Lasswell, H. D., 6, 140
Lawrence, C. R., xiv
Lawrence, E. A., 68
Lazarsfeld, P. F., 106, 126, 195
Lea, H. C., 114
Leadership, 42, 49–50, 96–98, 109, 127, 144–63, 206, 210
Least of evils, 157
Le Bon, Gustave, 140
Lecky, W. E. H., 10, 88, 108, 114
Lee, A. McC., 6, 15, 18, 20–21, 40, 43, 45–47, 54, 61–62, 64–65, 68, 103, 105, 107, 109, 115, 117, 120–21, 127, 135, 137, 141, 145, 147, 149, 154–56, 162, 168, 189, 201, 204, 205
Lee A. McC., III, xv
Lee, B. H., xv
Lee, E. B., xv, 120, 135, 137
Legitimacy, 20–21, 36, 69–70, 76, 166, 175–76
Leighton, A. H., 169
Leinwand, Gerald, 173
Leisure, 55, 64–68
Lenin, V. I., 140
Lenski, Gerhard, 15, 66
Lerner, Daniel, 6, 126, 140
Lerner, Jean, 69, 115
Lerner, Max, 205
Leviathan, 110
Levinson, D. J., 208
Lewis, H. G., xiv
Lewis, Sinclair, 39, 132
Li, Mew-Soong, 48
Lieberson, Stanley, 46
Lifton, R. J., 68
Lindzey, Gardner, 48, 68, 69, 147, 149, 154, 189, 193
Lippert, Julius, 161–62
Lippmann, Walter, 209
Lipset, S. M., 82, 105, 114, 152
Literacy, 79, 84, 94, 138
Literature, 39, 55, 69, 196–97, 200
Little, E. B., xiv
Lobbying, 131, 146, 158
Logical fallacies, 148–49
Loomba, J. K., 149, 189
Lowe, J. R., 73
Lowell, J. R., 83
Lubove, Roy, 195
Luce, H. R., 11, 189–91
Luckmann, Thomas, 116, 118
Lumley, F. E., 140

Lundberg, G. A., 75
Luttbeg, N. R., 156
Lynchings, 46
Lynd, H. M., 64, 127
Lynd, R. S., 127

McCall, G. J., 200
McCarthy, Joseph, 18, 149
McClelland, D. C., 82
McClintock, F. H., 82
MacDougall, C. D., 18, 115, 140, 191
McGinniss, Joe, 145
McGuigan, F. J., 32
McGuire, W. J., 68, 193
Machiavelli, Niccolò, 39, 108, 205
Machines, "idiot," 21–23
McIlwain, C. H., 87
MacIver, R. M., 10, 147, 152
Mack, John, 172
McKinney, D. W., Jr., xiv
McNeil, E. B., 172
MacRae, D. G., 114
Madison, James, 100
Mafia, 18, 42–44, 171
Maine, H. J. S., 59
Maley, Don, 50
Malone, Dumas, 100
Managerial-bureaucratic paradigm, 124–
    27, 129–30, 134, 184
Managers, 76, 94, 96, 181, 186, 188
Mangione, Jerre, xiv, 43
Mannheim, Karl, 108, 114–17
Manning, P. K., xiv
Marcel, Gabriel, xi
Marcson, Simon, xiv, 22, 58
Marcuse, Herbert, 59, 84
Marginality, 40–41, 64–65, 98, 109
Marijuana, 67, 74, 157
Maritain, Jacques, xi
Market economy, 63, 73, 91–92, 131
Market researchers, 75
Marotta, Michele, 70
Marrow, A. J., 50
Marston, W. G., 193
Martin, F. L., 191
Martineau, Harriet, 4, 8
Marx, Karl, xi, xii, 4, 57–59, 62, 91, 95,
    108, 114
Marxism, 58, 67, 91, 107, 118
Maslow, A. H., x, 62, 183
Mason, Philip, 16, 208
Masotti, L. H., 74, 208
Mass communications, 2, 37, 58, 67–68,
    73–74, 89, 118, 120–21, 140, 152,
    164, 167, 174, 183, 188–91, 198
Masses, 87–89, 91–92, 95–96, 110, 124,
    133, 138, 160, 197–98, 206
Mass media, 54–56, 67, 71, 73, 76, 114,
    118, 142, 144, 156–58, 184, 189,
    191, 205
Matson, F. W., xi, 9, 39
Matthew, 202
Maturation, 42, 64, 68–69, 71, 85, 113,
    129, 181, 203

Mayer, A. J., 193
Mayo, Bernard, 100
Mead, G. H., x, 76, 127
Mead, Margaret, 56, 128
Medicaid, 98
Medici, Lorenzo de', xii
Meerloo, A. M., 68
Mencken, H. L., 132
Mental deviants, 41, 72, 120, 166, 168–69,
    178, 200
Mental "illness," 59
Mental institutions, 92–93
Mental therapy, 30
Merchandising, 57, 62, 121, 184
Merrifield, C. W., 100
Merton, R. K., 6, 124, 126, 128, 154, 196
Methodology, 29, 125, 129, 134–35, 182–
    83
Metropolitan Applied Research Center, 47
Metzger, W. P., 152
Meyerson, Martin, 73
Michels, Robert, 100
Middle class, 17, 69, 83, 118, 131–32,
    172, 178, 196 (see Social class)
Milgram, Stanley, 147
Militarism, 1, 3, 77, 79–80, 113, 142–43,
    187
Military-industrial complex, 7, 9, 11, 14–
    15, 84, 95, 130, 133, 158
Military intelligence, 106
Miller, A. R., 67
Miller, D. R., 83
Miller, S. M., xiv, 11, 16, 54, 62, 105–6
Millis, Walter, 80
Mills, C. W., x, 9, 38, 60, 65, 76, 106–7,
    110, 128–29, 132, 175
Mills, T. M., 33
Milman, H. H., 110
Mind twisting, 65, 67–71
Mintz, Morton, 130, 206
Mitchell, Ewan, 171
Monarchies, 79, 117–18
Monovalence, personal, 88, 116, 204, 208
Moore, Barrington, Jr., xiv
Moore, Samuel, xi, 4
Morale, 145, 203–4
Morality, 68, 83, 117, 129, 154, 170, 191,
    196, 199, 203, 205
More, Thomas, xii
Morris, Norval, 171
Morse, A. D., 80
Mosbacher, E., 14
Motion pictures, 66, 150–51
Motivation, 96, 109, 154–55, 185, 198
Mott, Neville, 13
Moynihan, D. P., 72, 193
Mueller, M., 177
Muller, H. J., 20
Multivalence:
    personal, 68, 103, 119–20, 129, 141,
        144, 155, 199, 203, 208
    societal, 116, 129, 204, 208–9
    sociology's, 109–10
Munroe, R., 60

Murders, 78, 81, 113, 204
Murdock, G. P., 162, 208
Murphy, Frank, 210
Murphy, J. M., 169
Murphy, Robert, 80, 172
Muslim, 116
Mussolini, Benito, 85, 88
Myers, Gustavus, 162, 208
Myers, J. K., 169
My Lai, 158
Myrdal, Gunnar, 38, 46, 60, 110, 205
Myth, 3, 5, 10–15, 20–21, 81, 124, 131, 145, 163, 171, 209–10

Nader, Ralph, 71, 177
Name-calling terms, 143, 148, 160
Napalm, 78
National Association for the Advancement of Colored People, 192
National Commission on the Causes and Prevention of Violence, 77–78
National Council on Family Relations, 72
Nazis, 80–81, 97, 157
Negotiation, 47, 83
Neopositivism, 75, 184
Neufeld, A. M., xiv
News, 10, 18–19, 71, 74, 77, 149–52, 159, 184, 190, 206–7
New Society, 199
Newspapers, 71, 126, 150–51, 167, 171, 189, 190, 196
Newsweek, 198
Newton, Isaac, 123
Ng, Larry, 80
Nicolaus, Martin, 6
Niebuhr, Reinhold, xi
Nieburg, H. L., 14, 162, 173
Niederhoffer, Arthur, xiv, 67, 194
Niehoff, A. H., 40, 165
Nisbet, R. A., 11, 59–60
Nixon, R. B., 189
Nomadelfia, 41–42
Nonconformism, 99, 111, 134, 166
Nondirective social therapy, 45, 47–49, 52
Nonviolent methods, 41, 43, 45, 52, 79, 83, 85, 159, 173
"Normal," 59, 120, 168–69
North, R. C., 149, 189
Northern Ireland, 16, 18
Nottingham, Judith, 78

Observation, 53, 69, 75, 101
participant, 29–31, 33–35, 40–41
O'Casey, Sean, 39
Ogburn, W. F., 33, 126, 168, 198
Oliver, J. S., 70
Olmsted, M. S., 32
Olsen, M. E., 82, 162, 209
Omnibus words, 148, 165
Open University (English), 34
Operation Dragnet, 70

Operation Head Start, 63
Opinion surveys, 75, 91, 155–56, 184, 205
Opler, M. K., 169
Optimism, 44, 60–61
Oren, Paul, Jr., xiv
Organization man, 124–26
Organizations, 49, 61, 76, 94, 101, 109, 118, 134, 142–47, 150–51, 157–58, 174–75, 183
voluntary, 42, 72–73, 100, 127, 183, 200
Orientals, 74
Ortega y Gasset, José, 89
Orthodoxy, 10, 19–20, 36, 76, 89, 110, 151, 156, 160, 162, 181, 183, 191–92
Orwell, George, 14–15, 200
Ovshinsky, S. R., 13

Packard, V. O., 140, 200
Page, C. H., 147, 196
Pantaleone, Michele, 171
Paor, Liam de, 17
Paradigms, 102–4, 119, 122–30, 133–34, 138
Pareto, Vilfredo, 95, 108, 124, 186
Park, R. E., x, 64, 74, 76, 108–9, 123, 126–28, 204
Parkinson, C. N., 24
Parrington, V. L., 130, 133
Parsons, Talcott, 106–7, 124–25
Participants, 87–98, 135
Partinico, 44
Pascal, R., 114
Paul, C., 100
Paul, E., 100
Pauling, Linus, 80
Peace, 79, 84, 116, 172
conference, 80
Peace Corps, 63
Peaceniks, 158
Peasants, 3–4, 69–70, 74
Pecking order, 180
Periodicals, 71, 110, 126, 150–51, 184
Perry, R. B., 100
Personality, 50, 59, 64, 85, 97, 143, 148
Personnel, 143–45, 154, 157, 174
selection, 105, 184
Persons as documents, 29–31, 33–36
Person-to-person, 157, 160
Pessimism, 44, 60–61, 72
Peter, Laurence, 24
Peterson, Virgil, 171
Petrarca (Petrarch), Francesco, xii
Pettigrew, T. F., 208
Phelps, H. A., 128
Philosophy, 6, 70, 101, 128–29, 131, 182, 191, 196–97, 201
Pill, the, 56, 73
Plain-folks technique, 148–49
Plato, 6, 88, 110
Platt, Anthony, 47
Plessy v. *Ferguson*, 192
Plumb, J. H., 20, 210

Pluralism, cultural, 17, 115, 208
Plutocracy, 94, 97, 130–32, 187
Poles, 80, 157, 208
Police, 48, 51, 67, 77, 101, 145, 159, 170, 173, 177, 207
Policy sciences, 126, 134
Political scout technique, 155–56
Politicians, 47, 74, 100, 144, 156, 158
Politics, 65, 131, 158
Pollution, 3, 57, 63, 73, 96, 113, 156, 164, 166–67, 209
Popularization, 60–61, 198–99
Population, 73, 89
    diffusion, 74
    explosion, 9, 96
    pressures, 156
Pornography, 156
Porter, H. G., xiv, 33, 41, 45, 48–51
Potter, C. F., xii
Poverty, 51, 79, 83, 92, 95, 129, 135
President's Commission on Law Enforcement and Administration of Justice, 171
Pressure groups, 72, 112, 190
Presthus, Robert, 24
Prisoners, 92–93, 170
Privacy, 55, 64–67, 94
Privatization, 55, 65, 67
Problematic-technical paradigm, 124, 126–27, 129, 133–34
Professors, 28–39, 114, 183–84, 207
Program of deeds, 157, 160
"Progress," 4, 60
Project Camelot, 105–6
Proletariat, 63, 69, 87, 92
Promoters, 144–46
Propaganda, 68–71, 82, 112–15, 120–21, 132, 138–41, 145, 147–54, 156–58, 160, 162, 166–67, 174, 205–6
    analysis, 162–63
    analysis techniques, 149
Propagandists, 139–63
Property, 57, 59, 130, 133
Protestants, 16–18
Prototypes, 44–45, 120, 203
Proudhon, P.-J., 91
Psychological Abstracts, 76
Psychology, 105, 135, 169, 197, 208
Psychotherapy, 68–69, 169, 200
Ptolemaic paradigm, 123
Public Affairs Committee, 150, 199
Publicists, 112, 150, 154
Publicity, 44, 140
Public opinions, 92, 144, 150, 154–60, 174, 183
Public policy, 181–82, 187–95 (*see* Social policies)
Public relations, 95, 100, 143, 146, 205–6
Publics, 54, 115, 143, 155
Puerto Ricans, 95
Pugnacity, 81–82, 172–73

Quakers, 48

Quantification, 127
Quinney, Richard, 171

Race, 3, 15–17, 45–46, 57, 74, 82, 90, 97, 149, 170, 178, 200, 202–5, 209
Radicalism, 87, 110, 152, 154
Radio, 65, 71, 126, 150–51, 189–90
Rainwater, Lee, 72, 173
Raper, A. F., 46
Rapoport, Anatol, 125
Ravitz, Mel, 193
Raymond, Jack, 14
Reality, conceptions of, 45, 62, 70–71, 75, 82, 86, 93, 116–17, 130–31, 133, 135, 161–62, 167, 200
Reckless, W. C., 194
Regier, C. C., 132
Regin, Deric, 59, 64
Reich, Charles, 207
Reid, Ed, 171
Relativity:
    cognitive, 161–62
    cultural, 161–62, 199
    personal, 199
    social, 199
    societal, 161–62
Religion, 3, 10, 62, 65–67, 71, 148, 196
Religious Society of Friends, 48
Resource persons, 43, 47, 92–93
Reston, James, 192
Retirement, 23–26
Reynolds, J. M., 6
Reynolds, L. T., 6
Rhetoric, 118, 143, 159, 166
Ricci, Luigi, 205
Riddell, Patrick, 17
Rienow, L. T., 209
Rienow, Robert, 209
Riots, 77–78, 81, 84, 135, 145, 150–51, 159, 173
    race, 46, 50–51
Ripsaw, 110
Roach, J. L., 167
Roby, P. A., 16
Rolfe, A. F., 45
Roman Catholics, 16–18, 42, 139–40, 145
Rootes, T. P., Jr., xiv
Rose, A. M., 136–37
Rose, Thomas, 80, 172
Rosenberg, Bernard, 69, 197, 206
Ross, E. A., 35
Rosten, L. C., 191
Roszak, Theodore, 23
Roth, J., 60
Roucek, J. S., 8, 70
Rovere, Richard, 132
Ruchames, Louis, 46
Rudwick, E. M., 46
Rumor, 150, 159
Rural Sociological Society (RSS), 136
Rutledge, W. B., 210

Saberwal, Satish, 179

Sacred Congregation for Propagating the
  Faith, 139–40
Salerno, Ralph, 171
Sapir, Edward, 128
Sargent, S. S., 115
Sartre, J.-P., xi
Saturday Review, The, 198
Scapegoating, 157–58
Scheff, T. J., 169
Schein, E. H., 50, 121
Schettler, Clarence, 115
Schiller, F. C. S., xii
Schlesinger, A. M., Jr., 56
Schmidt, E. P., 127
Schofield, Michael, 194
Schon, D. A., 168
Schramm, Wilbur, 189
Schultze-Pfaelzer, Gerhard, 140
Schumpeter, J. A., 173
Schwartz, B. N., 15
Science, 7–10, 12–14, 22–23, 27, 31–33,
  53–57, 70, 79, 104, 148, 152, 159,
  162, 168, 173, 198, 209
  normal, 122–23
  social impact of, 9–10, 112, 197
Scientism, 8–10, 22–23, 135, 196
Scientists, 75–76, 94, 96, 101, 104–5, 109,
  123–24, 129, 135, 166, 184
Scots, 71, 208
Scott, J. F., 125
Seaver, Edwin, xiv
Seeman, Melvin, 58–60
Segregation, 26, 74, 95, 203
Seldes, George, 11, 146, 191
Seligman, B. B., 22
Senior citizens, 51
Sensationalization, 55
Sensitivity, 36–37, 40–41, 50, 55, 63, 179
Sentiments, 68–69, 144, 154–57
Sevareid, Eric, 14
Sewell, W. H., 106, 195
Sex, 3, 25–26, 57, 65, 120, 149, 156, 158,
  200, 202–5, 209
Sexual perversion, 92–93
Sharp, Gene, 195
Shatzky, Jacob, 59
Shaw, C. R., 127
Shaw, G. B., 39
Shenker, Israel, 44
Sheppard, Harold, 24
Sheridan, P. H., 45
Sherif, C. W., 32
Sherif, Muzafer, 32
Shift of scene, 157–58
Shils, E. B., 22, 106, 114
Sicilians, 42–44, 171, 208
Silverman, A. R., 46
Simmel, Georg, 5–6, 128, 167
Simmons, J. L., 200
Simon, Joan, xiv
Simon, Kenneth, xiv
Simon, William, 194
Simpson, G. E., 17
Simpson, George, 8, 33, 60, 137

Sinclair, Norman, 51
Sinclair, Upton, 132
Skolnick, J. H., 93
Slater, P. E., 90
Slavery, 46
Slums, 51, 72–73, 164, 167, 173
Small, A. W., 126
Smelser, N. J., 105
Smith, A. W., 63
Smith, B. L., 140
Smith, D. L., 6
Snell, J. L., 125
Social action, 6, 29–31, 40–41, 43, 58,
  61–62, 68, 84, 112–13, 136, 145, 152,
  173–74, 205–6
Social actionists, 41, 63, 83, 139–63
Social adaptation, 2, 67, 85, 101, 109,
  133, 209
Social agitation, 101, 112, 150, 159
Social change, 5, 41–52, 64, 74, 82–85,
  96, 157, 191–92, 209–10
Social class, 40–41, 74, 81–83, 90, 95,
  105, 108, 117, 154, 156, 178–79, 188,
  204–5, 209–10 (*see* Middle class)
Social cohesion, 132, 147
Social competition, 72, 101, 120–21, 140–
  41, 156, 166
Social conflict, 45, 48, 72, 74, 77, 79, 101,
  117, 120–21, 129, 132, 140–41, 157,
  159, 166, 204–6, 209
Social context, 47, 140, 162, 165, 169,
  173–77
Social control, 22–23, 36–37, 54–55, 79,
  82, 87, 89–90, 94–95, 118, 129–30,
  134, 145, 147, 157, 166, 174–76, 188,
  204, 206, 209–10
Social Darwinism, 107, 118
Social decision making, 42, 48, 87–91, 98,
  115, 138
Social diagnosis, 53–54, 59–60, 140
Social distance, 199, 204, 207
Social engineering, 54, 135, 152, 185–89,
  191–92
Social expediency, 97–98
Social experimentation, 2, 31–32, 42, 75,
  136
Social facilitators, 47, 49, 52, 92
Social ferment, 101, 111, 136
Social functionaries, 71–72, 75–76, 90–92,
  112, 150
Social games, 125, 180–82
Social inequality, 82–83, 207
Social instrument, 1–6, 101, 109, 138, 140,
  158, 166, 174, 179, 191–92
Social investigation, 42, 47, 63, 69, 93,
  129, 157, 164–79 (*see* Social re-
  search)
Social irrationality, 120–21, 131
Socialism, 97, 132
Socialization, 69, 71–72, 82, 85, 103, 109,
  120, 172, 181, 203
Social knowledge, 41, 53–86, 105, 126,
  134, 161, 167–68, 177, 196–97, 201,
  205–6

Social leverage, 43, 52, 57, 96, 114, 136, 207
Social manipulation, 37, 54, 58, 76, 91–93, 112, 118, 125, 127, 130, 139–63, 166, 174, 181, 183–87, 206
Social mobility, 64, 104, 156
Social models, 101, 110, 125, 136
Social movements, 144, 150, 159
Social networks, 176–77
Social nostrums, 53, 72
Social panaceas, 138, 207
Social participation, 7, 30–31, 43–45, 89–92, 94–95, 110, 162, 198, 206–7
Social perception, 55, 63, 140, 164–79, 181
Social planning, 25–27, 49, 138, 200
Social policies, 11–12, 126, 134, 200, 207 (*see* Public policy)
Social power, 3, 11, 21, 36–37, 52, 55, 58–59, 79, 81–82, 89, 94–95, 98, 118, 125–26, 128, 132–33, 143–45, 151, 166, 173–76, 184, 206
structures, 73, 85, 180–81
Social practitioners, 53–86
Social problems, 29–31, 50, 57–58, 62, 118, 127, 130, 134–35, 164–65, 176–77, 179, 199–201, 207
Social Problems, 137
Social process, 59, 64, 71, 83–84, 96, 118, 132, 148, 172
Social reform, 87, 119, 133, 135, 138, 143, 184, 196
Social reorganization, 64, 87, 138, 209
Social research, 11–12, 40, 43, 47, 53–86, 91, 123–29, 134, 153, 167, 178, 183, 185, 187, 209 (*see* Observation, Social investigation)
Social revolts, 46, 81, 84, 89, 130, 134–36, 138, 202, 208–9
Social revolution, 51, 83–84, 87, 113, 119, 206, 210
Social rituals, 151, 182
Social roles, 48, 90, 104, 106, 115, 120, 132–33, 144–45, 152, 155, 188
Social science, 69, 90, 95–96, 104, 110, 123, 130, 132–36, 164–79, 210
societies, 134–36
Social Science Research Council, 125
Social scientists, 53, 60, 62, 76–77, 104–11, 120, 138, 142–43, 164–79
Social Security, 66
Social setting, 40, 166, 176, 179
Social situation, 62, 144, 156
Social status, 56–57, 64, 82, 104, 114, 115, 117, 127, 175
Social stereotypes, 47, 155, 162, 168–72, 184
Social strategies, 41, 44, 47, 51–52, 75, 112, 114, 117, 142–63, 174
Social structures, 58, 82, 124, 137–38, 145–47, 152, 156, 174, 198
Social struggles, 77, 112–20, 141
Social "system," 1–6, 10, 20–21, 30, 36,

Social "system" (*Cont.*)
51, 63, 82, 116, 124–25, 129, 147, 202, 209
Social techniques, 42, 57, 75, 117, 140, 157, 184
Social theory, 29, 53, 75, 117, 122–23, 127–28, 134–35, 167, 182–83, 186–87, 197 (*see* Sociological theory)
Social therapy, 53–86, 184
Social wisdom, 6, 56, 62, 89, 141, 161, 196–97
Social work, 152, 173, 183, 200
Society, 199
Society for Applied Anthropology (SAA), 135–36
Society for the Psychological Study of Social Issues (SPSSI), 135–37
Society for the Study of Social Problems (SSSP), 134, 136–37, 138
Sociological Abstracts, 33, 76, 200
Sociological approachers, 182–83
Sociological biases, 105–8
Sociological materials, nature of, 199
Sociological societies, 134–38
Sociological theory, 29, 41, 106, 183–84, 200 (*see* Social theory)
Sociologist-actionist, 41, 44
Sociologists, 69–70, 75–76, 124, 128–29
clinical, 43–52
Sociologists for Women in Society Newsletter, 110
Sociology, 8–9, 28–52, 77, 95, 104–5, 122–35, *et passim*
as a social problem, 38–39
"cow," 185–87
for everyman, 181, 197–201
humanist, 112, 122, 181, *et passim*
industrial, 183
managerial, 60, 124–26
"normal," 123–24
organismic analogy in, 70
potentialities of, 36–37
"pure," 182
radical, 135
Solomon, E. T., xiv
Solomon, H., 125
Sondern, Frederic, Jr., 171
Sons of the American Revolution, 30
Sorel, Georges, 4, 60
Sorokin, P. A., 8–9, 70, 79–80, 108, 110, 128, 168, 204, 210
Sowle, C. R., 67
Spanish-Americans, 46, 93, 95
Spanish civil war, 88
Spaulding, J. A., 60
Special interests, 76, 128, 185 (*see* Vested interests)
Special Operations Research Organization, 106
Spencer, Herbert, 4, 108, 128, 161–62
Spender, Stephen, 173
Spindler, G. D., 179
Spiro, M. E., 195
Sponsor pandering, 153

Stalin, Joseph, 85, 97
Stalling, 157
Stanford, E. H., xiv
Starr, H. E., 35
Statistics, 101, 127, 172, 186, 189
Staude, J. R., 64, 166
Steffens, Lincoln, 30, 128, 174
Stein, Maurice, 105, 125
Steinbeck, John, 39
Steiner, G. A., 68
Steiner, Stan, 45
Stern, B. J., 187
Stern-Rubarth, Edgar, 140
Stetler, Russell, 17, 78
Stone, H. F., 210
Stonequist, E. V., 109, 127
Stoodley, B. H., 169
Stouffer, S. A., 115, 124, 126
Strachey, John, 14
Streeten, Paul, 38, 60, 110, 205
Street traffic safety, 176–77
Strikes, 43, 46, 151, 159
Stroup, H. H., 109
Students, 62–63, 93, 111, 178, 184–85,
    197–98, 206–7
  protests, 63, 78, 156, 172
  revolts, 1, 20, 113, 151
Subcultures, 105, 117–18 (*see* Culture,
    group)
Subsidies, 76, 124, 152–53, 185
Suburbs, 24–26, 72–73, 113, 164
Suicides, 74, 78
Sumner, W. G., x, 35, 69, 76, 81, 107,
    114, 128, 130–32, 147, 162, 187, 204
Sutherland, E. H., 76, 93, 171–72
Suttles, Gerald, 173
Swanson, G. E., 83
Swiss Guards, 130–31, 138
Sykes, Gerald, 59, 61, 194
Sykes, John, 48
Symbolic-interactionism, 127
Symbols, 101, 114, 117–18, 144, 147–49,
    160, 210
Szasz, T. S., 169

Taeuber, K. E., 193–94
Taft, D. R., 172
Tarbell, I. M., 132
Taylor, Harold, 10, 23
Taylor, Telford, 80–81
Tax, Sol, 23
Technicians, 36, 69, 74–76, 94, 96, 101,
    104, 107–9, 114, 124, 126–30, 133,
    152, 181, 183–84, 187
Technology, 73, 173, 181–88
Teleology, 205
Television, 65–66, 71, 77, 126, 143, 150–
    51, 158, 160, 167, 185, 189–90, 196,
    206
Terborgh, George, 22
Testimonial techniques, 148–49
T-grouping, 50
Therapists, 62, 91–93

Thibaut, J. W., 48
Thimme, Hans, 140
Thomas, E. J., 32
Thomas, W. I., 76, 108, 128
Thoreau, H. D., 5, 99–100, 111
Thrasher, Frederick, 127
Tillich, Paul, xi
Time, Inc., 190, 198
Toch, Hans, 147
Tompkins, J. S., 171
Torrance, E. P., 198
Trade unions, 43–44, 146, 151, 153, 206
Transfer technique, 148–49
Tribalism, 10, 15–17, 74, 204, 208
Trivia, sociological, 181–84, 196
Tyler, Gus, 171

Understanding, 55, 57, 70, 75, 138, 172,
    178–79, 184, 198, 201, 207
United Press International, 190
Universities, 76–77, 146, 152–53, 178,
    183–85, 201
Untermann, Ernest, xi, 4
Urban decay, 113
Urban redevelopment, 188
Urban tensions, 156, 200
U. S. Army, 125
U. S. Bureau of Labor Statistics, 65
U. S. Commission on Civil Rights, 100
U. S. Department of the Army, 106
U. S. Department of Defense, 78
U. S. National Advisory Commission on
    Civil Disorders, 16, 100
U. S. National Highway Safety Bureau,
    177
U. S. Public Health Service, 78
U. S. Supreme Court, 47, 190, 192

Valla, Lorenzo, xii
"Value free," 106–7, 125
Values, 1–6, 60, 68, 71, 85, 104, 107,
    113, 115, 117, 122, 127–30, 140,
    142, 162, 203–6
van Gelder, Robert, 102
van Nieuwenhuijze, C. A. O., xiv
Van Riper, P. P., 94
Veblen, Thorstein, 35, 76, 108
Vested interests, 108, 130, 152, 165, 181
    (*see* Special interests)
Vidich, Arthur, 105, 125
Viet Cong, 70
Viet Nam, 70, 78
Vietnamese, 4
Vietnamization, 84
Vincent, E. R. P., 205
Vinogradoff, Paul, 57
Violence, 43, 47, 52, 56, 65, 77–85, 166,
    172–73, 204
Virtue by association, 149
Virtue by heredity, 149
Virtue words, 148
Voltaire, F. M. A. de, 39

"Vulgarization," 88, 198–99

Wagenfeld, Jeanne, xiv
Wagenfeld, M. O., xiv, 62
Wald, George, 9
Walker, Daniel, 19, 173
Walker, J. L., 88–90
Wallace, Michael, 45
Wallace, P. A., xiv
Wallace, W. L., 33, 125
Waller, Willard, x, xiii, 23, 35, 76, 80–81,
    108, 121, 128–29, 141, 147
War, 9, 14–15, 18–19, 78–85, 91, 113,
    121, 156, 158–59, 164, 166, 172–73,
    206–7
  criminals, 81
  gaming, 188
  guilt, 81–82
  on poverty, 98
  psychological, 154
  theory of, 80–81
Ward, C. H., 14, 79
Ward, Jean, 189
Ward, L. F., 35, 187
Warner, S. B., Jr., 73, 195
Warner, W. L., 127–28
Warren, Earl, 192
Warren, H. C., 141
Washburn, W. E., 45
WASP, 15, 48
Watnick, Morris, 58
Watson, Goodwin, 84, 101
Waugh, Coulton, 206
Waxman, C. I., 113
Weber, Max, 60, 106–8, 117, 124, 175
Weiers, R. M., 177
Weiss, Walter, 69, 154, 189
Welfare roles, 51, 92, 183
Welsh, 71, 208
Wenglinski, Martin, 173, 195
Wertham, Frederic, 206
White, A. D., x, 116
White, D. M., 69, 197, 206

Whites, 46, 83, 95, 178, 202–3
Whiting, J. W. M., 128
Whitman, Walt, ix, x, 99, 111
Whittemore, L. H., 194
Whyte, W. F., 36, 40, 128, 165
Whyte, W. H., Jr., 73, 82, 185, 187, 200
Wiatr, J. J., 133
Wicker, Tom, 100
Wilensky, H. L., 106, 195
Wilhelm, S. M., 6
Wilkinson, John, 209
Williams, W. A., 130
Williamson, E. E., 84
Williamson, R. C., 115
Wilson, Woodrow, 99
Winance, Eleutherius, 68
Wirth, Louis, 62, 114, 126–27, 155
Wohl, Martin, 177
Wolf, E. R., 4
Wolff, K. H., 6, 167
Wolfgang, M. E., 82, 93
Wolin, S. S., 152
Women's organizations, 71
Women's revolts, 21, 93, 113, 130, 138,
    151, 156, 202, 209
Woods, F. A., 79
World War I, 78, 80, 177
World War II, 78, 80, 125, 150
Wren-Lewis, John, 167
Wright, Quincy, 80

Yablonsky, Lewis, 195
Yancey, W. L., 72
Yinger, J. M., 17
Youth, 51, 56, 71, 91, 130, 136, 138, 202,
    207, 209

Zander, A. F., 32
Zeno, 110
Znaniecki, Florian, 108, 128
Zoll, L. S., xiv
Zorbaugh, Harvey, 127